IBM® ASSEMBLY LANGUAGE SIMPLIFIED

IBM® ASSEMBLY LANGUAGE SIMPLIFIED

DR. RUTH WESSLER

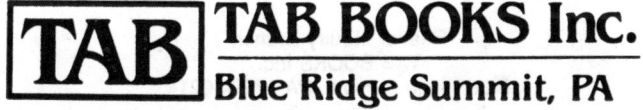

TAB BOOKS Inc.
Blue Ridge Summit, PA

TRADEMARKS

CP/M is a registered trademark of Digital Research Company.

IBM is a registered trademark of International Business Machines Corporation.

MS-DOS and Microsoft are registered trademarks of Microsoft Corporation.

Sidekick is a registered trademark of Borland International.

FIRST EDITION
SECOND PRINTING

Printed in the United States of America

Reproduction or publication of the content in any manner, without express permission of the publisher, is prohibited. The publisher takes no responsibility for the use of any of the materials or methods described in this book, or for the products thereof.

Copyright © 1988 by TAB BOOKS Inc.

Library of Congress Cataloging in Publication Data

Wessler, Ruth, 1938-
IBM assembly language simplified.

Includes index.
1. IBM Personal Computer—Programming. 2. Assembler Language (Computer program language) 3. Intel 8088 (Microprocessor)—Programming. I. Title
QA76.8.1259W455 1988   005.265 88-2248
ISBN 0-8306-0439-1
ISBN 0-8306-2939-4 (pbk.)

TAB BOOKS Inc. offers software for
sale. For information and a catalog,
please contact TAB Software Department,
Blue Ridge Summit, PA 17294-0850.

Questions regarding the content of this book
should be addressed to:

Reader Inquiry Branch
TAB BOOKS Inc.
Blue Ridge Summit, PA 17294-0214

To My Mother

CONTENTS

	Exercises	**xi**
	Preface	**xiii**
	Introduction	**xvii**
1	**The Computer's Language: Numerical Code**	**1**

Binary and Hexadecimal Numbers 2
Number Conversion 5
Which Bit Is Which 7
The ASCII Code 8

2 Program Structure 10

Addressing Memory: Segments and Offsets 11
Program Segments 15
Tipe.com: Version 1 16
Creating the .Com File 20
Testing Your Program 24

3 The 8088 Registers and Instructions 25

The Registers 25
Numbers in Memory 30
The Instructions 31

4 Writing to the Screen 34

Displaying the Title: Version 1 35
Displaying the Title: Version 2 42

5 Getting the File Name — 46
Accessing the Program Segment Prefix   47
Flags and Conditional Transfers   52
Moving the String   57
More About Jumping   57

6 Opening and Reading the File — 61
Opening a File   61
Using the Stack   65
Meanwhile, Back at the Program   67
Defining Variables   68
Will It Fit in Memory?   72
Getting the File Size   74
Reading the File to Memory   79

7 Setting Up the Screen — 85
BIOS Display Services   85
Clearing the Screen   89
Moving the Cursor   91

8 Displaying the File — 99
Keyboard Input   100
Showing a Page   104
Reversing the Display   113

9 Creating .Exe Files — 119
The Structure of .Exe Files   119
The Old Version   123
The Modern Version   126

10 Enhancements to Tipe.com — 130
Determining and Saving the Display Characteristics   130
Adding Color   134
Restoring the Screen   137
Adding an Extra Segment   141

11 Variations in Tipe.com — 149
Placement of the Data and the Stack   149
Neatness, Size, or Speed   152
Include Files   158

12 Writing a File to Disk — 163
Retrieving Two File Names from the Command Line   164

Buffered Keyboard Input 167
Writing a File to Disk 172

Appendix A
Complete Program Listings 177
The Complete Tipe.asm for Tipe.com 178
The Complete Upcase.asm for Upcase.com 185
The Include Files 188

Appendix B Character Attributes 194
Appendix C ASCII Codes 196
Bibliography 206
Index 205

EXERCISES

1-1 Converting Numbers from Hexadecimal to Decimal	6
1-2 Converting Numbers from Decimal to Hexadecimal	7
2-1 Finding Any Address in Memory with Debug	12
2-2 Using Debug to View the Program	22
3-1 Reading What Is in Memory	30
4-1 Changing What Is in Memory with Debug	41
5-1 Viewing the PSP	47
6-1 Looking at the Stack	65
6-2 Using Debug to Simulate Conditions	79
7-1 Viewing the Video Display Pages and Changing Attributes	87
7-2 Creating Windows	90
8-1 Examining the Key Codes	101
8-2 Changing Your Program with Debug	108
10-1 Changing the Screen's Attribute	131
10-2 Switching the Active Display Page	136

PREFACE

The fact that you are reading this indicates that you have an interest in assembly language programming. People are usually interested in assembly language for one of several reasons. First, by learning assembly language, you can more easily learn how your computer works—because it works by understanding assembly language (or its version of assembly language). Second, there are some tasks that can be done only in assembly language or certainly more easily. Third, assembly language is fast and compact in computer speed and disk size, although not necessarily in the time it takes you to write a program. And last, it is fun.

If you like to solve problems, then you will enjoy assembly language programs. With assembly language, there are two types of problems. The first is how to do a task in the first place, and there are many solutions. The second problem is to figure out why your solution did not work; this activity is known as *debugging*. By using assembly language, you can command your computer and make it do exactly what you want. But for many of us, until we are initiated into it, assembly language seems like a mystery—a series of strange letters and numbers.

The intent of this book is to take the mystery out of assembly language programming. Several years ago I became interested in learning how to program in assembly language. I wanted to learn more about how a computer functions, and I wanted to be able to tell it how I wanted it to function, in its own language. Even with some programming knowledge, I found the descriptions of assembly language mysterious and baffling. I discovered later that the books I had acquired describing the instructions and format of assembly language were quite useful resources—once I had developed a frame of reference in which to use them. I developed that frame of reference from a book by Ken Barbier, called *CP/M Assembly Language Programming*. (CP/M was the operating system of my first computer, an ancestor of DOS.) The concept of that book is to take the reader from scratch through the development of a simple program. Although I had much to learn when I finished the book, the language was no longer mysterious, but fascinating. I hope this book will serve the same purpose for you.

In this book, you will learn a subset of assembly language instructions that are part of the 8086, 8088, 80186, and 80286 sets of instructions. My intent is for you not just to learn a few assembly language instructions, but to learn how to do assembly language programming. *Instructions* are things; *programming* is a process—a process of program development. As important as writing the instructions is testing how they work (and whether they work) in the context of your programs. As you develop a program in this book, you also learn how to use an invaluable tool in program development, **Debug.com**.

I hope you find the experience of learning assembly language an enjoyable one.

IBM ASSEMBLY LANGUAGE
SIMPLIFIED

INTRODUCTION

The language of the IBM PC and its compatibles is called *8088 assembly language*, named after the Intel 8088 microprocessor, the "brains" of the computer. Some IBM compatibles have an 8086 microprocessor. The instruction set for the 8086 and 8088 are identical, so I will use "8088" in this book to avoid the clumsy "8086 or 8088." The instruction sets for the 80286 and 80386 microprocessors include the complete 8088 set, so the programs developed in this book will run on any of these microprocessors.

In this book, I take you through the development of a simple 8088 program called *tipe.com*. Like the "type" command of *DOS* (the disk operating system), it displays a text file to the screen. Like DOS's **more** command it pauses at the end of a screen display, but it also allows the user to go back to previous screen displays. After tipe.com is developed, I will also show you how to produce .exe programs, and add some enhancements and variations to tipe.com. Finally, the instructions you have developed are used to create a program that writes a file back to the disk. Besides learning about assembly language instructions and program structure, you also learn something about using the resources of DOS and *BIOS* (basic input output system) to manipulate files and the screen display.

Although most people who become interested in assembly language have had experience writing programs in other languages such as Pascal or BASIC, that background is not necessary. This book includes everything you need to know to write the program, including three appendices: the complete program listings for tipe.com and a second program you can write using most of the instructions for tipe.com, the ASCII code for characters, and the code for character attributes (e.g., color). It does not include the complete 8088 instruction set, nor does it include the complete descriptions of DOS and ROM-BIOS subroutines (interrupts). You will want to build your library with books that have this information and describe it in detail. The references listed in the bibliography are those that I have found useful and relied upon in developing this book.

SOFTWARE THAT YOU WILL NEED

As you learn the 8088 language in this book, you create the program piece by piece, assembling, linking, transforming the result to a .com file and then testing it with a *debugger*. You need a version of PC-DOS or MS-DOS that is 2.0 or higher. As standard software included with DOS, you have most of what is needed: LINK, the linker, EXE2BIN, which transforms .exe files produced by LINK to .com files, and DEBUG.

You also need to obtain an assembler. There are assemblers in the public domain as well as assemblers that are commercially available. The two assemblers that dominate the commercial market are the Microsoft Macro Assembler and the IBM Macro Assembler, both called *MASM*. Both come with a number of other useful programs, which you will use if you continue assembly language programming.

You also need to create your programs using an editor or word processor that produces text files in pure ASCII format. The assemblers mentioned above treat special formatting characters as errors.

I suggest you create a working program disk to receive your program files. Place the programs DEBUG and EXE2BIN on this disk. On a second disk, place your assembler and linker. Your word processor or editor could go on either disk or on a third disk if it is extremely large. You will not need or want fancy formatting, so if your word processor can be trimmed down to its basics, so much the better.

CHAPTER 1

The Computer's Language: Numerical Code

Information is stored in a computer very simply—by the presence or absence of an electrical signal. Some of these signals are built into the computer in what is called *ROM* (read-only memory), which is activated when the power is turned on. Much of the computer consists of RAM (random-access memory, really read-and-write memory). Some of RAM is used by the *system*, which is read into memory when you turn on or reboot (as with CTRL-ALT-D) the computer. The rest of RAM awaits signals from a variety of sources, such as the keyboard, the disk drives, and whatever other devices may allow for communication with the computer.

Coordinating the communication within the computer is a *central processing unit* (CPU), an amazing little chip, and one of the least expensive parts of your computer. You use the services of the CPU to communicate with the rest of the computer when you send it a program, be it in BASIC, Pascal, or any programming language. The language the CPU understands is called *machine language*. Machine language is akin to turning on and off electrical signals. It consists of patterns of 0s and 1s that have special meaning to the CPU. One pattern, for instance, could mean fetch the data at a particular address in RAM.

The CPU in IBM and compatible computers is the 8088 microprocessor (or one of its relatives). The language, or pattern of 0s and 1s, that it understands is thus 8088 machine language.

Fortunately, you do not have to learn machine language. Instead, you learn a code using *mnemonics*, like MOV for move, called 8088 assembly language. Once you write your program assembly language, it is converted into machine language for you by an assembler and a linker.

BINARY AND HEXADECIMAL NUMBERS

Years ago, I was surprised to learn that decimals numbers are not the only ones around. It took a bit of getting used to. Decimals, it turns out, are very handy for people, but not so handy for a machine that "knows" only that a signal is present or absent. Perhaps someday a computer will be invented that can detect one tenth, two tenths, and so on, of the intensity of a signal. In the meantime, to use our present (and, I think, future) machines to the fullest, you will find it helpful to be conversant with its language—binary numbers. Learning assembly language is like learning another human language, such as Russian; you can be conversant without being fluent. My goal is to help you become conversant with binary and hexadecimal numbers. You could choose to become fluent, but fluency is not necessary.

A number system that has only zero and one as its members is called a *binary number system*. Although you do not need to know the patterns of binary numbers that make up machine language, you will find it difficult to do any advanced programming in one of the high-level languages, and even fairly simple programming in assembly language, without a working knowledge of binary numbers and how they fit into the scheme of computer data manipulation and storage.

The program you write using this book does no *number crunching*, except for an occasional add or subtract. Its purpose is to display a text file to the screen. Even so, you will be using very many numbers—numbers to count, numbers to represent the position of the cursor on the screen, numbers to designate the address of alphabetic characters in memory, numbers to represent these characters themselves, and much more. It is best to forget the use of numbers in the mathematical sense for now (although computers are known for their mathematical feats), and bring to mind all the other ways in which you use numbers in your life: addresses, phone numbers, identification numbers like your VISA number or social security number, code numbers like 1 for Freshman, 2 for Sophomore, and so on. It is this kind of use of numbers that takes up the bulk of most programs, even those designed to carry out mathematical functions. Keep these kinds of number usage in mind as you explore binary, then hexadecimal numbers.

The Need for Hexadecimal Numbers

The binary numbers of zero and one do not code much information. They can only represent two distinct things, true or false, up or down, animal or vegetable (but not mineral). Knowing whether something is true or false or up or down can be useful (and in fact you will make use of this knowledge to make decisions in your programs), but for other uses, zero and one are obviously quite limited. In the case of street addresses, single binary numbers would suffice for only a very small hamlet or an extremely tiny computer. Thus, to encode more information, it is necessary to put them together in sets.

If you consider not one but two binary digits in tandem, you go from two to four distinct possibilities: 00, 01, 10, 11. You can build two new houses on your street. You get the idea—the more binary digits in a pattern, the more the possible combinations, and the possibilities increase rapidly. With a package of four binary numbers there are 16 possible combinations. Table 1-1 displays these combinations along with their decimal and *hexadecimal* (*hex*, for short) equivalents. I will discuss hexadecimals shortly. First, here's some more terminology.

The on-off components of the computer are referred to as *bits*: *b* for Binary and *it* for digIT. Thus, a pattern of four binary digits corresponds to four bits in the computer. In tipe.com, you are seldom manipulating bits, but most often *bytes* (pattern of eight bits) and *words* (pattern of 16 bits). For the moment I will stay with four bits, a pattern of four binary numbers.

Look now at the hexadecimal equivalents in Table 1-1. Hexadecimals are numbers in the base of 16. Because numerals only go up to nine, the inventors of the hexadecimal system added alphabetic letters, so that decimal 10 equals hexadecimal A, decimal 11 equals hexadecimal B, and so on. As you move from patterns of four to patterns of eight binary numbers, you will see how neatly hex numbers fit the patterns, and how poorly decimal numbers do so. Although it is important to become conversant with hexadecimals in order to develop proficiency in writing assembly-language programs, it is also not too hard. You do not have to recite hex numbers from one to 0FFFFFFFFH to be familiar with them. You do not have to be able to do math in hex; the computer can do that for you. As a start, all you really have to know is the page number of Table 1-1. It is helpful to be able to convert from decimals to hex and back again. The techniques for doing so are presented later in this chapter. But first, a return to bits and bytes.

A byte is composed of eight bits. Therefore, a byte can be represented by two hexadecimal digits. Now put Table 1-1 to work.

Table 1-1. Binary, Hexadecimal, and Decimal Equivalents.

Hexadecimal Digit	Binary Digit	Decimal Digit
0	0000	0
1	0001	1
2	0010	2
3	0011	3
4	0100	4
5	0101	5
6	0110	6
7	0111	7
8	1000	8
9	1001	9
A	1010	10
B	1011	11
C	1100	12
D	1101	13
E	1110	14
F	1111	15

What would be the two digit hex number for this eight-bit pattern: 0010 0100? Look up each one in the table. Yes, it is 24H (typically, the H is put after a hexadecimal number to distinguish it from decimal). The number 24H, you will find out later, is equivalent to 36 decimal. Here is a big one: 1111 1101. Table 1-1 tells you that it is 0FDH. (Because the assembler will want to be able to distinguish between a number and a variable, it requires you to use at least a zero to start the number. I will follow that practice in this book.) 0FDH is equivalent to 253. The maximum eight-bit number is 1111 1111 or 0FFH, or 255. Eight bits can provide a lot of information—enough to accommodate addresses for a small town; enough to encode all the usual printing characters of a typewriter with plenty of room to spare.

Early computers were built, and many are built today, to accommodate information one byte at a time. Using bytes in combination made it possible to manipulate very large numbers. The 8088 was developed as a 16-bit microprocessor, enabling 16-bit words to be manipulated very easily, accommodating even 32-bit double words. Let's convert a few words. First: 0111 0001 1101 0000. Find each pattern in turn in Table 1-1, and you have 71D0H. The largest word is 1111 1111 1111 1111, which is 0FFFFH, equivalent to 65535. The double word of 0FFFFFFFFH is equal to 4,294,967,295. Now, that will provide addresses for most of the world's population. When you start stringing words together, the amount of different information that can be coded is vast indeed.

NUMBER CONVERSION

First, let me assure you that your career as an assembly language programmer will not be spent converting numbers from one base to another. If it were to be spent that way, hardly anyone would pursue the task. As a preview, if you want to instruct the computer to compare a value in AX (a register you will soon know) to 12, you can say either CMP AX,12 or CMP AX,0CH. With no letter following the 12, the assembler knows you mean a decimal number and does the work of conversion for you. This is the usual case, but there will be times when you will want to be able to do it yourself. One time will be when you are using Debug in the development of your program, because Debug only speaks hex.

Hexadecimal to Decimal Conversion

I will start with how to convert from hex to decimal, because going in that direction is easier than going from decimal to hex. (Perhaps the easiest way of all is to get a program that will do this for you. I don't have one.) The one and only thing you have to know (or look up on Table 1-1) are the decimal equivalents for A through F in hex. Here is a two digit number: 32H. It is the same as 30H plus 2H. If you can find the two decimal equivalents and add them together, you have the decimal number. The number 2H, of course, is 2. Now, because hex has a base of 16, 10H is 16, 20H is 32, 30H is 48, and so on. With a two-digit number, multiply the most significant hex digit by 16 and then add the decimal equivalent of the least significant digit. In the case of 32H, the decimal equivalent is 50: 3*16 is 48, plus 2 equals 50.

Here are three more two-digit hex numbers for you to convert. Try to get the decimal equivalents before you look at the answers.

Convert: 6FH, D3H, and AAH.

    6*16 is 96 plus 15 equals 111.
    13*16 is 208 plus 3 is 211.
    10*16 is 160 plus 10 is 170.

Before continuing, try a simple problem. What is the decimal equivalent of 153? Yes, it is 153, but now compute it. The number 153 is the sum of *100* times 1, plus *10* times 5, plus *1* times 3. (I put the numbers

6 IBM Assembly Language Simplified

in italics so they would stand out.) Decimals have a base of 10, so 100 is 10^2, 10 is 10^1, and 1 is 10^0. Following this procedure, but using the base 16, you can readily convert any hex number to decimal. Here are the powers of 16 starting with 16^3 and going down:

4096   256   16   1

Exercise 1-1: Converting from Hexadecimal to Decimal

Here are some hex numbers and their decimal equivalents. See if you can arrive at the same answers. I will do the first one for you:

	Hex	Decimal	
1	13C7H	5063	1*4096 + 3*256 + 12*16 + 7 = 5063.
2	2222H	8738	
3	D5A9H	54697	
4	7CCBH	31947	
5	FF00H	65280	
6	47E93H	294547	

I have included number 6 to make you think. See if you can solve it before reading the explanation.

The pattern of the powers of 16 can be expanded to encompass the number of digits in any hex number. With five digits you need to start with 16^4, which is 65536, so start the conversion with 4*65536.

Decimal to Hexadecimal Conversion

Converting from hex to decimal, you see, is not difficult, particularly using a hand calculator in which you can store and accumulate the sums in memory. Going the other way, from decimal to hex, is a bit more tedious, but follows the same logic. Given a decimal number, the first step is to find the most significant hex digit. Take the decimal number 573. The question is, what is the largest power of 16 that you can use to divide into 573 and obtain a nonzero result? The answer is 256. Do the division and see that the result is 2.2382, so the most significant hex digit is 2. Now subtract 2*256 from 573 to obtain 61. Next, move down a power, so the question is, how many times does 16 go into 61? The answer is 3.8125, so the next hex digit is 3. Subtracting 3*16 from 61 leaves 13, or D in hex. The final result is 573 = 23DH.

Follow the same procedure using 2816. The highest power would be 256. 2816 divided by 256 is an even 11. Thus, the most significant digit is B. Because 11 times 256 is 2816, you are done. B is the third digit, and the number is 0B00H.

Exercise 1-2: Converting from Decimal to Hexadecimal

Following the procedure described above, convert the decimals to hex numbers. You should obtain the answers listed in the Hex column.

	Decimal	Hex
1	4900	1324H
2	357	165H
3	55002	0D6DAH
4	9050	235AH
5	33	21H

I concluded the exercise with a two-digit hex number because probably the majority of conversions you will be doing in programming will be converting byte-sized numbers; however you can see that you can convert any number, going either way, by keeping in mind a few simple things. First, remember that decimal 10 equals 0AH, on up to 15 which equals 0FH. Second, remember that the least significant hex digit is that digit times 16^0, or 1. The power is raised by one for each subsequent digit. Half the time when I am converting numbers, I don't remember that 16^3 is 4096, but I can calculate it easily.

WHICH BIT IS WHICH

You will read in the computer literature statements like "bit 0 will indicate if any disk drives are connected to the computer," or, "with ASCII code numbers the most significant bit holds a 0." That may be nice to know, but only if you know which bit they are talking about. Bytes are composed of eight bits. To reference each one, they are given numbers, and a particular convention is always followed. The least significant bit is 0, the next is 1, and so on, with the most significant bit labeled 7. Here is an illustration:

```
        Bits
7 6 5 4 3 2 1 0
0 0 0 0 0 0 0 1    equals 1
1 0 0 0 0 0 0 0    equals 80H
0 0 0 1 0 0 0 0    equals 10H
```

There are various statements that can be made about these numbers. For instance, the byte that represents the number 1 has all bits cleared but the least significant bit; that is all its bits are zero but bit 0. On the other hand, the number 80H is represented by a byte with only the most significant bit set; that is, only bit 7 is 1; the rest are zero. Finally, the number 10H is represented by a byte that has only one bit set, bit 4.

Keep in mind two things. First, the least significant bit is zero. Second *clear* means zero, and *set* means one. The bits of a word are referred to in the same way, except that now the most significant bit is 15 or 0FH, rather than 7, reflecting the total of 16 bits. In tipe.com, you will not be manipulating individual bits defined by number, but you will be setting and clearing particular bits and checking their status in a different way. That comes later.

THE ASCII CODE

Here is one last set of numbers, the *ASCII* (pronounced "askkey") for representing characters. ASCII stands for *American Standard Code for Information Interchange* and is a standard code used by many computers, not just the IBM and its compatibles. The code numbers are 7-bit numbers ranging from 000 0000 to 111 1111, or from 0 to 7FH, resulting in 128 code numbers. This leaves the 8th bit (bit 7) clear; it then can be used for other purposes. IBM provides a second set of characters, the extended set, with code numbers going from 80H to 0FFH.

The ASCII code is used for two purposes, one to represent the standard printing characters, and two, to represent various control functions. The first 31 code numbers, 0 to 1FH, correspond to these

The Computer's Language: Numerical Code 9

control functions. You will find the ASCII code in Appendix C. Pressing the CTRL key plus the character shown in column four of the table will send a control code (1 to 1FH) to the computer. There is one ASCII code which corresponds to no key, the null (nothing) code of 0.

In your programs you can define the meaning of the control codes, even the character codes, to be anything that you want. For instance, you might define CTRL-P (ASCII code 10H) to mean send the data to a printer. There are some control codes that are almost universally used in certain ways, the meaning of which you may not want to change. These meanings are listed in column five in Appendix C, along with the description of some printing characters that could be confusing (is it a comma or an apostrophe?). Column 1 shows the printing characters associated with each code. Those associated with the control codes and for 7FH, delete, are NOT part of the ASCII set; these are provided by IBM to use if you want to print these characters to the screen. Don't try to send them to your printer.

In the case of the ASCII code, you can see the value of using the computer's numbers, hex rather than decimal. Take, for instance, the decimal equivalent of the letters A and a. They are 65 and 97. Look also at the decimal equivalents for H and h. They are 72 and 104. Now look at the hex codes: A = 41H, a = 61H, and H = 48H, h = 68H. The letter A, upper- or lowercase, is the first letter of the alphabet; H is the eighth. You can convert a letter from upper- to lowercase by adding 20H, or go the other way by subtracting 20H. Note the codes for numbers. In hex, 0 is 30H, 1 is 31H and 9 is 39H, which is easy to remember. Try remembering that 0 is 48, 1 is 49, and 9 is 57. The ASCII code in hex is a masterpiece of simple hexadecimal patterns.

In this book I use the terms *text file* and *ASCII file* synonymously, because a text file is composed of ASCII coded characters. (Some text files may include certain control codes as formatting commands. These will be ignored in tipe.com.) Typically the file ends with 1AH, the traditional end-of-file marker in ASCII files. It is composed of the printing characters as well as carriage returns (0DH) and line feeds (0AH) at the end of each line. Some ASCII files may also include 09H, the horizontal tab.

To help you to learn to "think" in hex, I will try not to use a decimal number in this book if it is appropriate to represent the number in hex. Now let's put these numbers to use and begin to create tipe.com.

CHAPTER 2

Program Structure

Whenever DOS is presenting its prompt (e.g., A>), you know it is awaiting your command. There are only four kinds of commands that DOS expects:

- its own built-in commands, actually assembly language programs read into memory when the computer is booted
- files with the extension .com
- files with the extension .exe
- files with the extension .bat, batch files which are convenient ways to group the first three kinds of commands

With the 8088 assembly language you can create either .exe or .com files. The .com extension means *command*, because you can enter its name from the command line just as you can with a DOS command such as ERASE or RENAME. .Com files have been around for a long time as computers go, coming from the days when 64K was the limit on user memory. With the expansion of RAM memory upward from 64K to 640K, it became possible to write executable programs in a different way, making possible larger and larger program files. 64K was no longer the limit. Programs capable of using that much memory take on a somewhat different structure than .com files and have the extension .exe, for execute.

When a command is given DOS, like TIPE MYFILE, it first seeks to match the name of the command with one of its built-in commands. Failing that, it searches the disk directory for a file named tipe.com. If found, it reads the file into memory and sets the CPU to execute the program. If no .com file is found, it once again searches the directory for a file named tipe.exe. If it is found, DOS reads that file into memory and prepares the CPU in a different way for that type of file. If the .exe file is not found, DOS finally looks for a batch file. If a batch file is not found, you see the familiar, "Bad command or file name."

The 8088 programs can be written either as .com files or .exe files. The structure of .com files is simpler, so there is less to learn to be able to write a working assembly language program as a .com file. For that reason, tipe will be a .com file. Once tipe.com is complete, Chapter 9 describes how to restructure it as an .exe file so you have some familiarity with .exe as well as .com files. The main difference between .com and .exe files is how the segments of the program are structured. *Segment* has a very specific meaning; it means *part of the program*, and more specifically, *part of memory used by a part of the program*. To understand segments, it is necessary to understand how to represent addresses in the computer's memory.

ADDRESSING MEMORY: SEGMENTS AND OFFSETS

Probably the most important task of all in any assembly language program is keeping track of addresses. By *address*, I mean simply a number that designates a particular location in memory. The CPU, which runs your program, has to know at all times where the next instruction is located so that it can be retrieved and executed. It has to know where the variables that you define for it are stored. It has to know where to find values that have been temporarily stored so they can be retrieved. It has to know where to locate procedures that are called by other instructions in the program.

Perhaps the most important difference between writing a program in a high-level language like BASIC and writing a program in assembly language is using and referencing addresses. In BASIC if you wanted to print "HI" to the screen, you could say simply PRINT "HI". In assembly language, you first have the task of writing a set of instructions that will accomplish the PRINT function, and then tell the CPU exactly where to find the letters "HI". In programming in BASIC, you let the interpreter or compiler do all of that for you.

In continuing this discussion I will use the term *register*. The registers of the CPU are discussed in detail in the next chapter. Most assembly language instructions are about moving numbers in and out of these registers, which are particular places for numbers to be held, manipulated, and transferred.

Each byte in memory is given a unique numerical address. The 8088 registers can hold 16-bit words. That means the numbers that a single register can hold can range from zero to 0FFFFH. So if you want to put a number in a register to represent an address, the highest address that can be referenced is 65535. That is 64K worth of addresses. If you have only 64K of memory, a single register can hold the absolute address of any spot in memory, starting with zero and going up to 0FFFFH. But an IBM computer can have up to 640K of RAM; in addition, addresses for ROM starting at the top of RAM and go up to 1024K, the highest address being 0FFFFFH, or 1,048,575. The magnitude of these addresses brings up the concept of *segments*, the breaking up of memory into different pieces or blocks.

Just as two houses in a town might have the same numerical address, you know their location by the street they are on. Perhaps a better analogy is two people who have the same phone number, but different area codes. A segment is defined with a number, which represents a large block of memory, 64K to be exact. The location of any byte, therefore, can be pinpointed by two numbers: the number of the segment (the street or area code) and the specific location within that segment called an *offset* (the house number or phone number). All addresses within a segment start at zero. The first byte has an offset of zero, the second has an offset of one, the last an offset of 0FFFFH.

Exercise 2-1: Finding Any Address in Memory with Debug

Debug, you will find, can serve more purposes than its name implies. It certainly is very useful in debugging programs, but it can also be a very useful tool in helping you learn more about your computer and how it operates. Here you will use it to see what is in your computer's memory, or at least Debug's representation of what is in memory. This is the first of a number of exercises using Debug. If you are using a different debugging tool, the commands may be different. Try following the instructions in the exercises. If the command does not work, then find the appropriate one in your manual. It is likely to work, however, because I believe that most debugging tools incorporate Debug's commands and then add more of their own.

To review the discussion of memory addressing, an offset is an address, but not an absolute address in memory. An offset is a place in memory compared to a specified starting point—a segment address.

With computers that use only 64K (zero to 0FFFFH) bytes of memory, any point in memory can be referred to by one 16-bit register, but with more than 64K of memory, there is a problem that occurs for instance, when you want to refer to the memory address at the absolute location of 114K. The address in hexadecimal is 1C800H. Now an additional register is needed to hold this number. As you might imagine, keeping track of absolute addresses in two registers would be cumbersome if not confusing. The clever solution of the inventors of the 8088 was to devise a way to refer to relative addresses rather than absolute ones. Two registers are still required to do this, but you can set and forget one of them until you want to change it, so usually you only need to keep track of the other—the one with the offset.

The first part of the relative address is called a *segment*. A segment is simply the starting address of 64K of memory, which can be any place in memory, as long as that address ends in a zero (using hexadecimal numbers). Any address ending with a zero is known as the beginning of a *paragraph*. Remember, a byte is eight bits, a word is two bytes. A paragraph is 16 bytes. 16 bytes is 10H bytes. Thus, in absolute memory, the first paragraph starts at 0H, the second at 10H, the third at 20H, and so on. Because a segment always starts at the beginning of a paragraph and thus always ends with a zero, you can drop the zero. It is always assumed. So if you wanted to refer to the segment starting at 20H, it would be simply 2. If you wanted to refer to the address 27H, it would look like this: 2:7, meaning the segment is 20H, and the offset is 7. By using segments and offsets from them, there are any number of ways to refer to the same address; the higher the location is in memory, the more ways there are to address it. Let's run through some examples (all numbers will be in hexadecimal). 27 is 2:7, and also 1:17 and 0:27. 1C800 is 1C80:0, 1C70:10, and 1000:C800. A good way to get used to this system of relative referencing is with Debug. Debug requires this form of addressing.

Using your program disk (or any disk with Debug on it), enter debug at the DOS prompt. No program name is necessary. Debug uses the hyphen prompt (-) to say it is waiting for your command. Take the time to look at the manual for Debug's possible commands. In this exercise you will be using D, H, U, and Q. Also remember, you talk to Debug in hexadecimal, not decimal numbers. I will drop the H to denote hexadecimal numbers in exercises using Debug. At the dash prompt type: D40:0. D is Debug's dump command, so you have asked to see (to have dumped) 80H worth of bytes stored starting at 400. When I did so the first two lines looked like this:

```
-d40:0
0040:0000  F8 02 00 00 00 00 00 00-78 03 00 00 00 00 00 00
0040:0010  1D 53 00 00 02 00 02 00-00 00 22 00 22 00 30 0B
```

    You will see to the right of the screen these numbers shown as if they were ASCII printing codes, or as a period if they could not be translated to ASCII. To get just these two lines, enter D40:0 1F. This tells Debug to dump all bytes in memory from 40:0 up to and including 40:1F.

    Then at the prompt, enter D3E:20 3F. You should see the same two lines. You asked for the contents starting at the absolute address of 3E0 plus 20. (When I wrote the first draft of this book, I erroneously used the example 38:20. This mistake is easy to make for decimal-thinking people. The fact is that in hex, 380 plus 20 is not 400. If you are not sure what the answer is, at the - prompt, type in H380 20. H is Debug's Hex arithmetic command. You will see the sum and the difference of these hexadecimal numbers displayed for you.)

    Now use this technique to try different segments and offsets to display the same data. If you prefer, use the U (unassemble) command rather than D. If you use U, you will see the numbers in memory displayed as if they were assembly language instructions. They might or might not be. U simply treats these numbers as if they were. Mostly, it will look like gibberish (in fact, some is), but it might be easier to note down the letters and numbers than the numbers from a dump. As with Dump, you can shorten the display by specifying an ending offset. Try the difference between entering U40:0 and U40:0 10.

    Using either D or U play the game, "What are five ways I can get here?" Don't be easy on yourself. Suppose you start with 80:0B, meaning 80B. See the dump or listing. Now ask yourself, "What other segment and offset will get me here?" 7F:1B will do it. How can you get there if the segment is 52? Answer: 52:2EB. "How in the world am I supposed to figure that out?" you might ask. Answer, like me— with Debug's H command. I said to myself, the segment 52 means the address 520. The difference between 80B and 520 is the offset from segment 52. I let Debug figure it out for me. If you enter H80B 520, you will see as the second number displayed (the difference) 2EB, which is thus, the offset from the segment 52.

    Here is a harder one. Up in high, high memory in IBMs and some compatibles resides ROM-BIOS, which starts at segment F000. ROM-BIOS (BIOS for short—basic input/output system) contains the assembly language routines that do much of the input/output work of the computer. Look at what is at F0A1:04. (Normally, when viewing

BIOS, you would use the simpler F000:A14.) Jot down the beginning of what you see using either D or U. Now the question is, if the segment is F001, what is the offset to be at the same place? This is a bit harder because the absolute address I am speaking of is F0A14. How can Debug's hexadecimal arithmetic command, which accepts only up to four-digit numbers, help you? It can, once you write down the problem, such as:

```
  F0A14
- F0010    ;add the zero to the segment
   ()
  ────
   ()
   ?
```

Just as in decimal math, because F0 are the first two digits of both numbers, you can ignore them. In Debug enter HA14 10, and see the answer, A04. Try dumping F001:A04, and you shall see the same data as with F0A1:04.

It will be worth your while to play the "five-ways" game for a while. Although you will probably never use some of the strange combinations you come up with, understanding segments and offsets should seldom be a problem for you in writing assembly language programs. When done, tell Debug you want to quit with Q.

PROGRAM SEGMENTS

Understanding segments and offsets is important not only to be able to reference any byte in memory, but also to understand the structure of assembly language programs. When you call up a .com or .exe program by entering its name on the command line, DOS places it starting at a certain location in RAM. DOS and BIOS use low memory (starting at absolute zero), so DOS finds the paragraph in memory that is available to receive the program. This address is called the *program segment*. The program begins here at the offset zero. Because this position can vary from computer to computer or from time to time, depending upon config.sys or any resident programs like Sidekick, it is quite a service for us that DOS does this work. You do not have to know where DOS is placing the program. Wherever DOS places it is the start of your program segment. If you want to refer to any piece of information in the program, like the letters "HI", you can use the offset from the start of the program.

To complicate matters, although I have spoken of the program segment, 8088 programs are actually composed of four components; these are the *code*, which is the instructions to be executed; the *stack*, which is a place to store and retrieve numbers; the *data*, which are any variables you enter into the program; and an *extra* data area, which can be used for data manipulation and storage. These segments—code segment, stack segment, data segment, and extra segment—are conceptually different and are distinct entities to the 8088. Each has its distinct register (called, neatly enough, the CS, SS, DS, and ES registers), which holds its particular segment address. Programs can be written, given enough RAM, where there is no overlap among them, each using 64K of memory. Other possibilities are partial overlap or complete overlap. In the latter case, the analogy that comes to me is four people who have the same phone number because they live in the same house—same phone number, but four unique persons. This analogy describes the .com file, at least when it is loaded by DOS—all four segments are the same.

The program you will write takes less than 1K of memory for all of its components and has the capacity to use the rest of the common segment to store more data, specifically, the ASCII file that is displayed. Tipe is written as a .com program rather than an .exe program for two reasons. First, because it is quite small, it is appropriate to do so. Second, its simple structure makes learning assembly language easier.

TIPE.COM: VERSION 1

Now is the time to get ready to gear up your editor or word processor, because it is time to start to write tipe.asm. The .asm extension is expected by the assembler for the source programs you write. The complete listing of tipe.asm is found in Appendix A. As you build the program piece by piece, you will probably want to refer to that listing to see where you are in the scheme of things. First, you are going to enter a generic skeleton of a .com file program. You might save it with a name like generic.asm and then copy it to tipe.asm or vice versa. When writing new programs, it is handy to have the structure set and just fill in the new pieces.

Figure 2-1 shows the code to type in to your new file, be it generic.asm or tipe.asm. I use the term *code* here in the broad sense of the code to be interpreted by the assembler as well as the code to be eventually interpreted by the 8088. Actually, there are two types of code in an assembly language program: the 8088 instructions, which form the actual program, and instructions that inform the

```
;TIPE.ASM - PROGRAM TO DISPLAY ASCII FILES
;         ALLOWING THE DISPLAY TO BE REVERSED

CODE    SEGMENT
        ASSUME CS:CODE,DS:CODE
        ORG    100H
MAIN:
        int    20H        ;Quit
;end of MAIN

;Data for the program
CODE    ENDS
        END    MAIN
```

Fig. 2-1. The generic beginning of a .com program.

assembler how to translate that code into machine language for you. In the various program listings, I follow the format of using uppercase for instructions to the assembler and lowercase for 8088 instructions. (Case makes no difference to the assembler, so you may choose to type all the instructions in either upper- or lowercase to save the shifting back and forth.)

In this skeleton program, you see that practically all of the code is for the assembler. First note that there are comments here for the reader of the program. Any time the assembler encounters a ; , it ignores the rest of the line. Comments are particularly important in assembly language programming. Assembly language is so terse, taking the CPU step by step through each process, that it can be difficult, without painstakingly reading through each step, to figure out what should be going on, even for the author at a later date. As tipe.asm is developed in this book, I make liberal use of comments, many more than I usually make, but a good rule of thumb is "better too many than not enough."

Look at the one and only 8088 instruction in Fig. 2-1 and see what you have told the CPU to do. INT 20H means "call an interrupt." (Another convenience I use in the discussion is to put all instructions, assembler or 8088, in uppercase, simply so that they stand out in the text as instructions.) You will learn about interrupts in Chapter 4. For now, it is enough to know that this particular interrupt is a way to end a program. The effect of INT 20H is to say "quit."

All the rest of the code lines in Fig. 2-1 are instructions to the assembler telling it how to compile this instruction. The assembler I use is the Microsoft Macro Assembler (MASM) Version 4.0. Microsoft makes the IBM's MASM and the conventions are the same. If your assembler is different, you might need to check the manual if you find it gives you error messages when you have the code typed exactly as I have it here.

Look at the first line after the opening comment. It says simply CODE SEGMENT. (I like to make use of tabs to line up the code—the assembler doesn't care. It simply wants at least one space between the "words.") The term SEGMENT is a *directive* to the assembler (sometimes called a *pseudo-op* in which *op* stands for operation). The directive SEGMENT tells the assembler to define a segment. SEGMENT requires a name. The assembler nicely allows you to use names and labels that, when used later in the program, will be translated to the appropriate address. Doing the math to compute addresses for you is the chief function of the assembler. You do not need to keep track of the exact segments and offsets.

When a name or label is defined in the program, it should be placed first in the statement. Every word in the first column of Fig. 2-1 is a name or label of one sort or another. CODE becomes a name for a segment. When CODE is referred to in the next statement, the assembler replaces that name with the segment address of the beginning of the program. Why the beginning? Because CODE SEGMENT precedes any 8088 instructions in the source code. When you define the start of a segment, be sure you also tell the assembler where it ends. That is done with the ENDS (ENDS means end segment) directive and the statement CODE ENDS. The assembler now knows that all the instructions lie within CODE.

CODE is now a name for a segment, which has a beginning and an end. You can use almost any name or label you wish. The assembler reserves certain terms for itself, like SEGMENT. Check your manual for reserved names. How about GEORGE SEGMENT . . . GEORGE ENDS? Quite OK. All that has been accomplished so far is to define a name to stand for a segment. Later you will use many more labels in the program for the assembler to convert into addresses of instructions or of data variables.

When looking for labels that are required for execution, like JMP DONE (jump to the instruction labeled DONE), the assembler needs to know where to find DONE. It first needs to know which segment to use to find DONE; then it can compute the offset. Now there is only one segment, CODE. But .exe programs, as you shall see in Chapter 9, typically have at least three segments defined. The segment is indicated with the ASSUME directive: ASSUME CS:CODE. (Remember, CS holds the code segment, the segment with assembly language instructions.) Without this statement, when you start using labels with your instructions, the assembler will give the error, "No or unreachable

CS," meaning it has no idea where the code starts.

Likewise, when you refer to variables (data) in your statements, the assembler needs to know where to find them. Variables are expected to be in the Data Segment. In tipe.com, the Code and Data Segments will be the same. Thus the statement can be written as **ASSUME DS:CODE**. This can be written as a separate statement or combined as in Fig. 2-1. The ASSUME directive provides necessary information to the assembler and does not affect the contents of the CS or DS registers. Remember ASSUME is an instruction to the assembler, not the CPU. In tipe.com, no labels will be associated with the stack or extra segments, so there is no need for ASSUME directives for these segments.

If the ASSUME directive simply informs the assembler where to find the addresses of labels, how are values put in the segment registers to begin the program? The answer is that DOS does that for you when it sets up the execution of a .com file. For a .com file, the segment registers, CS, DS, ES, and SS, will all be initialized with the segment address of the beginning of the program segment when the program is placed in memory. Then DOS will load the program in sequence, beginning with the first instruction, starting at the offset of 100H. ORG 100H relates to this fact, and I will return to it after discussing MAIN.

MAIN: is another assembler directive. It is the label you will use to denote the start of the program instructions. The colon following is necessary for this label as it is for all labels that are associated with actual 8088 instructions in this program. Note the last statement in the program is **END MAIN**. It is the END directive that is particularly important. It not only tells the assembler that this is the end of the source code in this .asm file, but also, by the label, indicates where the address of the first instruction is found. If you were writing a longer program and combining several .asm files, all should finish with an END, but only one should have a label.

Now to return to the directive ORG (for organize) 100H. As I mentioned, although the .com program starts at offset zero of the specified segment, the program instructions themselves are placed starting at offset 100H. The reason for this is that in setting up any program, .com or .exe, DOS fills in the first 256 bytes or 100H of the program with useful information. So to preserve that information for the programmer, (and some of it will be used by tipe.com), .com programs start at 100H—each and every time. DOS will always put the first instruction there, whether you have an ORG 100H directive or not. (Other uses of the ORG directive are discussed in Chapter 11.)

The purpose of placing ORG 100H before your first instructions for a .com program is that it guides the assembler in doing its math in determining offsets of the labels you will use. Because the first instruction will be at offset 100H, not zero, without the ORG 100H directive, all offsets would be computed 265 bytes off target. The purpose of ORG 100H is not, as you might read elsewhere, to let the code start in its proper position. DOS does that, and if you used no names or labels, your program will run just fine. In fact if you use no names or labels, you do not even have to define a segment. A segment is defined to enable the assembler to compute offsets. Tipe.asm will use many labels, as will almost any program you write.

Finally you see the comment ;data. This is where you will place the variables that you will define. Because the data segment and code segment are the same, you can place data almost anywhere within CODE. Some programmers like the data at the start. I like the data at the end, primarily because when I edit the program, I can get right to the code. Also, tipe.com is going to read in the text file immediately following the defined variables.

CREATING THE .COM FILE

It is time to create the first version of tipe.com, which will do nothing but quit. Actually, this is the way any assembly language program is developed. Assembly language programs are built piece by piece. Code that does a task is written, assembled, compiled, made in to a .com file if that is your desire (which it is in this case), then tested and debugged. When you are assured that it works properly, the next piece is added. Unless, the program were very, very simple, it would be a folly to write it as a whole before testing it. So much could be wrong that it would be very difficult to track down the bugs, and bugs you will have. Usually, you would want a bigger piece than INT 20H, but this is a good time to test out the assembler and linker and the use of DOS's EXE2BIN.

The first step is to assemble the code to produce what is called an *object file*. It will have the extension .obj and is the translation of your assembly code into machine language. The linker does the final compilation and sets up the code in the .obj file as an .exe file.

Those of you who have the SYMDEB symbolic debugger that comes with the Microsoft's MASM might want to read the manual on how to assemble a program so that you can make use of SYMDEB. The procedures described here simply produce an object file ready for linking and subsequent debugging with DOS's Debug.

When I write programs, I have MASM and LINK on drive B, and my program, DEBUG, and EXE2BIN on drive A, which is why I suggested you create a program disk including the latter two files. I have the default drive as A. Given that setup, the entry to assemble is this:

B:MASM TIPE TIPE ;

or

B:MASM TIPE, ;

   MASM looks for tipe.asm and creates tipe.obj. It could create some other files, too, which are unnecessary for our purposes. The semicolon means you only want the object file, no more. In the second version, the comma following TIPE means create an .obj file with the same name as the .asm file.
   MASM either creates the .obj file or displays one or more error messages. If you get any, you need to check the manual. There is one error message you might get that is hard to figure out. It is, "End of file, no END directive." You look at your program and see that you did indeed put in the END directive. What you did not do, and MASM will not tell you, is that you did not put a blank line after that statement. MASM secretly insists on one last blank line.
   Assuming a successful assembly the next step is to enter this:

B:LINK TIPE,TIPE ;

or this;

B:LINK TIPE, ;

   The format is the same. In this case LINK expects the first named file to be an .obj file, and from it LINK will create tipe.exe.
   With a .com file, you will always get one warning: "Warning no stack segment." Because .com programs do not define stack segments, this warning appears. It tells you that tipe.exe will not be a good .exe program. In this case, it makes no difference because you will quickly convert tipe.exe to tipe.com with EXE2BIN. Enter the following:

EXE2BIN TIPE TIPE

   EXE2BIN expects the first name to have an .exe extension. It creates the .com file from this file. When this is completed you have two files on the disk, tipe.exe and tipe.com. The first is worthless as an .exe file, so if you do not want it taking up disk space, erase it.
   Once the .asm file has been successfully assembled into an .obj

file, there is little chance for error in the link. To accomplish the task of linking, converting to .com, and erasing the .exe, I use a batch file that I call Lk.bat, which you might want to add to your program disk:

B:LINK %1,%1 ;
EXE2BIN %1.EXE %1.COM
ERASE %1.EXE

Then after a successful assembly, you can enter the following:

LK TIPE

If there was an error in the link process, you could capture this error with a more sophisticated .bat file; however, these errors seldom occur, and if they do, EXE2BIN and ERASE in turn just say they cannot find the .exe file for the good reason that LINK did not create it.

Now create the .com file; then take a look at it with Debug. You can see how it looks in the computer's memory and get previews of the registers of the CPU that you will be using in developing the program.

Exercise 2-2: Using Debug to View the Program

Assuming Debug is on the same disk with tipe.com, enter Debug tipe.com. Debug, like DOS itself needs to know whether to set up for a .com file or .exe file, so the extension is necessary after the file name. In this exercise you shall use these Debug commands: U, R, and G.

First, look at a listing of your program. Enter U, for "unassemble". You see a list of the first 10 or so instructions starting at offset 100. Actually, despite what is listed, there is only one instruction, INT 20. The rest, starting at 102, are numbers stored in that location of memory and treated by Debug as if they were instructions. When you press U again, you will see Debug continue to list the "instructions." Now enter U100, and you will see the original listing. You know the first (and only) instruction is INT 20. Before you execute it, take a look at how the registers are set up.

Enter R (for register), and Debug will display the instruction that would be executed next. Because no instructions have been executed, you see the condition of all of the 8088 registers at the beginning of the program. You know about a few registers, and you will learn the rest in the next chapter. When I enter R, this is what I see:

```
AX = 0000   BX = 0000   CX = 0002   DX = 0000   SP = FFFE   BP = 0000   SI = 0000   DI = 0000
DS = 35AD   ES = 35AD   SS = 35AD   CS = 35AD   IP = 0100   NV UP DI PL NZ NA PO NC
```

On the second line find the values of CS, DS, ES, and SS, the code, data, extra, and stack segment registers discussed above. The segment in your registers will probably be different than the 35AD in mine. No matter what the value, note that they all have the same value; this is always true at the beginning of a .com program. Because Debug itself is the working program and sits under yours, these are not the values DOS would give your program—Debug has gotten those.

The absolute values in the segment registers are seldom ones to worry about. You can refer to their contents by referring to the registers themselves. The point here is to look at how DOS sets up the registers, emulated for you by Debug. The segment registers are all the same, the *instruction pointer* (IP) is set to 100, and all other registers, except the *stack pointer* (SP) and CX are set to zero. (DOS sets CX to zero, too. Debug puts the length of the program file in the CX register.) You are looking at the beginning of any .com file. The instruction you see on the third line is printed out in "assembly" by Debug: INT 20. At the beginning of the line is the address of that instruction in the form segment: offset followed by some hexadecimal numbers. When I did this exercise I saw:

35AD:0100 CD20 INT 20

Your code segment is probably not 35AD, but the rest of the line will be the same. The instruction awaiting its execution is located at the offset of 100H from the beginning of the code segment. The machine language instruction is in fact 1100 1101 0010 0000 or 0CD20H. 0CDH means "call the interrupt." The one you want called is 20H. Again, the nice thing about assembly language is that you do not have to learn what 0CD20H means to the CPU. But for the curious, it is nice to know that Debug displays instructions not only in assembly language, but also in the hexadecimal equivalent of the machine language understood by the CPU.

Looking back at the right of the second line, you can see a series of two-letter codes that look like this:

NV UP DI PL NZ NA PO NC

These represent the condition of eight bits in a special register, called the *flag register*. Don't worry about what they mean at this point; they are all clear (zero) at the beginning of the program. You will be keeping your eye on at least a couple of these bits as tipe.com is developed.

To finish the exercise, at Debug's dash prompt, enter G (for go). The program will now execute. After it has executed the one instruction, you see "Program terminated normally." Finish by entering Q for quit, and you are out of Debug.

TESTING YOUR PROGRAM

Another way to test your program is to send it to the screen, although for "virgin" code, running it through Debug first is highly recommended. If you continue with assembly language programming, you should learn to live with the "agony of defeat" because when you are working in the way the computer works, byte by byte or word by word, it is so easy to make the wrong move. With one simple typo, you can ask the computer to do all sorts of things you can regret, and probably will. Mostly, the errors will put you in some endless loop, or somewhere so that the computer sits there and does nothing—"locks up," as they say, or "goes to never-never land." No big deal, just reboot or restart the computer, then use Debug.

I am, however, a bit sensitive about my rule—Debug First—because about two weeks ago, the unwanted results of code I was writing was not a lock up, but the eradication of all data on the disk I was using that held the program files. Although I had backups of the files, the most recent work was gone. When running assembly language programs for the first time, errors, or *bugs*, are the rule, not the exception (usually they are of a lesser nature than the one I just mentioned). Achieving proficiency in assembly-language programming is evidenced not so much in avoiding errors (although you will get better at that, the more experience you have) as in being able to detect and correct them.

Naturally, you want to get the program to do more than quit. Most of your instructions to the CPU will be to move numbers in and out of its registers. The next chapter gives you an understanding of the fourteen 8088 registers, which you have seen displayed in the last exercise.

CHAPTER 3

The 8088 Registers and Instructions

For the uninitiated, looking at an assembly language program might be similar to looking at a bowl of alphabet soup—lots of little letters thrown together—with some numbers thrown in for good measure. The intent of this chapter is to give those letters meaning for you.

THE REGISTERS

The registers of the 8088 are part of the CPU. They are special places where numbers are stored, manipulated, and changed. These registers are usually what you "talk" to when creating assembly language programs, and they do the bulk of the work of any program, no matter what the language. The 8088 has fourteen 16-bit, or word-sized, registers. With a computer that has, say, 256K of working memory storing 128K worth of 16-bit words, the capacity of the 8088 registers—14 words—is tiny indeed. But it is here where the work of the computer is done.

When you refer to a datum in memory, you use its numerical address; that is, its segment and offset. The registers, however, are referred to by letters, mnemonic codes suggesting their function. You have encountered four of the 14 registers in the last chapter: the four segment registers, CS, DS, ES, and SS, which stand for the code segment, data segment, extra segment, and stack segment. DOS initializes them at the beginning of a .com program to the beginning of the program segment. In your programs you can change any of the segment registers, and you will do so when you create tipe.exe in Chapter 9 and in an enhancement of tipe.com in Chapter 10. For your first program there will be no need to change their initial values, so you will write no instructions to change those registers. This is one more reason I have chosen to write tipe as a .com program. There is less to keep track of.

Three of the remaining nine registers are called *pointer* registers. All of the registers hold numbers. The special purpose of pointers is to keep track of locations in memory. The numbers in pointers (and pointer variables that you might define) are always addresses in memory. A pointer, then, points to a particular address. When you want to know what is stored at that address, the contents of that address, you have only to refer to the pointer.

In our daily lives we use a variety of numbers that serve as pointers—for instance, a checking account number. Let's say your checking account number is 678351. Now you can do all sorts of things with that number—take its square root, divide it by six, and so on. But it does not make much sense to do these things, however, because the purpose of this number is to point to the balance in the checking account.

A better example is your address, which points to where you live. Like the values in pointer registers or variables, it can change. You might move, but your address always points to where you currently live. Thus, a pointer is a special variable. The number it currently holds is considered an address, actually an offset, and it points to the contents stored in the designated offset in memory.

One pointer register, the *instruction pointer* (IP), always points to the current instruction to be executed. It holds the offset of that instruction relative to the segment in the CS register. Indeed, the CPU will always execute that instruction, even if, thanks to a mistake, you wish it had not. After the instruction is executed, the pointer is updated to the next instruction, which is executed, and so on.

It is this register that DOS sets to 100H when it gives control to a .com program. You will never change the IP (instruction pointer) directly in your programs by moving values in or out of it. You will, however, learn several instructions to change its value indirectly. The CPU watches over this register, running the instructions in the sequence you have given it.

The two other pointer registers are used to point to a place in memory called the *stack*. I had mentioned that the stack is a special area in memory where numbers can be temporarily stored (stacked one on the other) and retrieved. You will learn more about the stack as you continue to write the program, but for now the *stack pointer*

The 8088 Registers and Instructions 27

SP

(SP) points to the offset in the stack that holds the last number on the stack. In other words, the number in the SP corresponds to that offset. The segment used by the 8088 to compute the address pointed to by the SP is, as you might have guessed, in the SS register, which in a .com program is the same as the CS.

A second register, the *base pointer* (BP) can also be used to point to offsets in the stack. It, too, uses the SS for the segment. One way to use the BP is to first place some data (a number) on the stack and then set the BP to its offset so it can be referenced later. You will not use BP in the program and will not use the SP in any direct way, although you will learn how your instructions affect the SP. Until you move into advanced programming, the rule is to never directly change the SP within your program. Thus, for your purpose right now, the SP and BP can be ignored. That leaves seven registers.

BP

One register, the *flag register*, has a very special purpose. It lets you know the state of certain conditions to allow you to make decisions or change certain conditions that affect the CPU. Unlike any of the other 8088 registers, it does not hold numbers in the usual sense of the word. You cannot move numbers into it or out of it. In fact, there is not much you can do directly to it, except save and retrieve it from the stack and change the status of some of its bits. Yet it is an extremely useful and much-used register.

FR

In writing programs, it is important to provide for all (hopefully all, but at least most) options and conditions that can occur. The programs you write ultimately sit inside the computer and run, making many decisions. <u>Has a valid file name been entered?</u> Has the end of the file been displayed? These are just some of the questions that can be answered with the help of the flag register. You test for certain conditions, and this register *flags* these conditions for use by your program. Different conditions are signified by whether a particular bit is on or off, set or cleared, true or false, 1 or 0. The flag register is also sometimes referred to as the *status flags*. No initials are used for the flag register. <u>Of the 16 bits in the flag register, nine are used as flags. The other bits are simply ignored</u>. In the program you use three of the nine flags: the zero flag and the carry flag to help make decisions, and the direction flag to help move data into memory. You will learn instructions to change these bits as well as ways to check their status.

Six registers are left. Data can be moved into and out of them. Winston Churchill once said, "Never was so much, owed by so many, to so few." He was not speaking of the registers of a CPU, but the statement is certainly apt. It is really rather amazing that the bulk of the work is carried out by six word-sized registers. Before looking at these six, it is important to know that they all can be used interchangeably for most purposes. You can move numbers in and out of them, add and subtract them, compare them, and do a whole variety of other things. In fact, BP can be added to these six, because you are not required to use BP just to point to the stack.

It was helpful to me when I first began to learn assembly language programming to know I was not required to use each register in one specific way. Actually, because assembly language programs essentially start from scratch, there is probably more flexibility for the programmer in writing in assembly language than in writing in any of the high level languages.

There are some 8088 instructions that require that certain kinds of data be in a particular register. For instance, when you want to move or compare blocks of data (as small as a byte or as large as 0FFFFH bytes), two index registers are required. These are called the *source index* (SI) and *destination index* (DI). Suppose that you want to move the letter X, which is located at one spot in memory (the *source*), to another location (the *destination*). The offset of the source goes into SI and the offset of the destination goes into DI. These registers then function like pointers. You can instruct the 8088 to place the data found at the offset pointed to by SI into the offset pointed to by DI. It is a requirement of the 8088 that, when such a move is made, the segment for SI be in the DS register, and the segment for DI be in the ES register. Because all the segment registers have the same value in tipe.com, you do not have to concern yourself with that requirement until much later in this book.

Now there are four registers remaining—the *data registers*—which are AX, BX, CX, and DX. These are your workhorses. Actually, these four 16-bit registers can be treated as eight registers, for they can be used to manipulate bytes as well as words. You could, for instance, put one byte in the low eight-bits of AX, and another in the high eight-bits of AX. When AX is treated as two eight-bit registers, they are referred to as AH (high byte), and AL (low byte). Likewise, there are BH and BL, CH and CL, and DH and DL. As you might imagine, like SI and DI, there are times when these X registers must be used in a certain way. The letters do serve as mnemonic reminders of their special use.

AX is the *accumulator*. It is the register of choice for holding the results of mathematical operations. Although you can carry out addition and subtraction using any of the seven other working registers (the other X registers: SI, DI, and BP), the multiply and divide instructions require the number to be multiplied or divided to be in AX or AL. It also takes fewer machine-language instructions to move constants or variables in and out of AX or AL.

BX is the *base* register. Actually, the mnemonic is not quite right, because the special purpose of BX is to point to offsets in the DS segment. Using BX as a pointer allows you to easily retrieve data from memory or to store data into memory. When used as a pointer, the segment in the DS register is actually the base, and BX holds the offset from that segment. BX is really the data pointer or data index, and it is the only one of the four data registers that can be used to retrieve or store data in memory.

CX is the *count* register. Its special purpose is to hold the count for various repeatable instructions, like the count of the number of bytes or words to be moved using SI and DI, or the number of times a loop is to be performed.

DX is the *data* register. It is the most general of the four data registers, but it does have some special uses in multiplication and division and in some input/output operations. Specifically, when your program asks for DOS's help, DOS typically wants the data in DX or DL.

An assembly-language program can be written ignoring all of the special purposes of the data registers, except perhaps that of BX, if you want to access data in memory. Even when you want to access data, you could use SI, DI, or even BP. Nevertheless, keeping each register's special purpose in mind as you choose which register to use in a statement makes for much more efficient code. Table 3-1 summarizes the 14 registers of the 8088.

NUMBERS IN MEMORY

Before looking at the 8088 instructions, you should understand how numbers are stored in memory. Why? First, because you use Debug frequently to look at your program and numbers, and second, because you need to understand number storage if you continue with assembly language.

There is a very simple answer to how numbers are stored in memory. The answer is: backwards (unless you are a computer, in which case we are backwards). Remember that for a byte, the low bit is 0 and the high bit is 7, or the *least significant* bit is 0 and the *most significant* bit is 7. This same logic (unfortunately for us) holds when storing bytes in memory. The low byte goes into the first address or lowest address, the high byte follows. Thus, if you wanted to store the word 9467H, you would see it in memory as 67,94.

Table 3-1. The Registers of the 8088.

Segment Registers:
    CS Code Segment   (8088 instructions)
    DS Data Segment   (Data variables and storage)
    ES Extra Segment   (Extra data storage)
    SS Stack Segment   (Temporary number storage)

Pointer and Index Registers:
    *CS: IP Instruction Pointer
    * SS: SP Stack Pointer
    **SS: BP Base Pointer
    **DS: SI Source Index
    **ES: DI Destination Index

Data Registers:

Word	High Byte	Low Byte
AX	AH	AL
BX	BH	BL
CX	CH	CL
DX	DH	DL

Flag Register:
(16 bits, 6 used to indicate status, 3 to control the program)

---

  *Segment is always assumed to be in these registers.
**Segment is sometimes required to be in these registers.

Exercise 3-1: Reading What Is In Memory

There is a wealth of information starting at 0:0 in your computer. You can use Debug to look at what is there with its D (dump) command. At the absolute location 0 (thus segment 0) where the very beginning of memory starts, there are a number of addresses for interrupts. These interrupts are special assembly-language routines that carry out a task. Their addresses are stored here, with both their offsets and their segments, and serve as pointers to the specific routines located at those addresses.

Enter Debug and give the command D0:0. You are looking at a number of pointers stored at 0:0 to 0:7F.

Take a close look at one pointer. My choice is INT 20H because it has already been used in the program. Its address is located starting at offset 80, so press D again. Look at the first four numbers starting at 80. The first two bytes at 80 and 81 are the offset, the second two bytes at 82 and 83 are the segment. When I do this I see 07 0B E3 00. The segment is 00E3, and the offset 0B07; thus the address is E3:B07. Notice that not only are the bytes stored with the least significant byte first, but the offset is stored before the segment, unlike our convention of referring to the segment first. To the computer, least significant comes first. This takes a bit of getting used to, but it is important to remember when you want to use Dump to read what is in memory.

Continue this exercise by looking at the routine that is INT 20H. Use U, the Unassemble command. Enter UE3:B07 (or your segment and offset, if different). You can see the instructions that some assembly-language programmer wrote to terminate a program.

Go back to the stored addresses for the interrupts with D0:80. The four bytes starting at offset 84 contain the address for INT 21H, one you will use a lot. Convert these bytes into the segment and offset, and use U to see the beginning of this routine. If you have done this properly those of you with IBMs should see these instructions:

```
CMP    AH,4B
JZ     018A
CS:
JMP    FAR [0BAB]
PUSH   ES
PUSH   DS
PUSH   BP
PUSH   DI
```

and more PUSHes.

Whatever you see are your computer's instructions for this interrupt.

THE INSTRUCTIONS

The 8088 has a set of instructions that it understands. You have seen some of them doing the last exercise. My intent here is for you to understand the general nature of these instructions, not to develop the complete instruction code, nor even the portion of that code you will use in the program. The specific examples I use are intended to give you a general overview of the instruction set, not to teach you that particular instruction. You begin to learn specific instructions by using them in the next chapter.

Think of the 8088 instructions as very terse sentences. A sentence needs at least a verb. The verbs of the language are written as short mnemonic codes of two to five letters, like MOV for move, which are translated by the assembler into the machine-language instructions, which in turn, tell the CPU what to do. In machine language they are called *opcodes* (operation codes). Often, "opcode" is also used to refer to the assembly-language mnemonic. I will do so in this discussion, and use "instruction" to mean the whole "sentence."

Just as we can communicate quite well at times in English with one-word sentences ("Stop!"), some 8088 opcodes stand alone, like STD (Set the Direction flag). Most of these "verbs" require an object, many times two objects. The opcode DEC means decrease the value of a register or variable by one. The CPU needs to know the object—which register or variable is to be decreased. The "object" is called an *operand*. Thus, the instruction DEC CX contains the opcode DEC and the operand CX. An opcode like MOV (for "move") requires two operands—move what to where. The 8088 instructions, then, consist of an opcode, with perhaps one or more operands.

In most cases with instructions that require two operands, one will be changed, and the other unaffected. If, for instance, you move the value in the AX register to the BX register, BX will be changed to have the same value as AX. The CPU always expects the one to be changed to be placed first following the opcode. You would write the instruction that means move the value in AX into BX this way:

MOV BX,AX.

The form is important:

OPCODE DESTINATION,SOURCE

The comma is necessary, but the spacing is not. The assembler will accept tabs and spaces between the "words." For instance, **MOV   BX,   AX** is quite acceptable because it fits the form.

Putting the destination first might take a bit of getting used to. Once again it is the reverse of what we usually do. We are more likely to say in English, "Move AX into BX." Think of an instruction with two operands as saying it this way: "Take the first operand and change it using the second." **MOV BX,AX** means take the BX register and place into it the value that is in the AX register. **ADD DX,CX** means take the value in DX and add to it the value in CX. **MOV COUNT,CX** means take the previously defined variable COUNT and move into it the value in CX.

With the exception of some special instructions using SI and DI, when you want to use a register to function as a pointer to access data in memory, you indicate this by the use of brackets. A reference to BX refers to the actual number in BX, whereas a reference to [BX] treats the number in BX as an offset and refers to the contents at that offset in memory. Let's say that BX holds the number 5623H. Look at the difference between these two instructions: **MOV AX,BX** and **MOV AX,[BX]**. The first instruction places 5623H in the AX register. Now let's assume that starting at offset 5623H in the data segment is the word 1000H (00H at 5623H and 10H at 5624H). The second instruction places 1000H in the AX register.

With this background, you are ready to begin to develop tipe.asm. You now can add to its one and only instruction, INT 20H, and make it do more than quit. It will go out in a big way—it will have written its title to the screen.

CHAPTER 4

Writing to the Screen

As you develop tipe.asm, you do several things. You define constants and variables for use by the program, and you write assembly-language instructions. The instructions are primarily written as subroutines or procedures. A *procedure* is typically a set of assembly-language instructions that carries out a specified task. By defining procedures with names, you can use them again and again in your program.

You also add instructions to MAIN to guide the execution of the program. MAIN prepares for and uses the procedures you write to carry out the task of obtaining and then displaying the text file. MAIN is not written as a procedure (although it could be), but it serves as a procedure. Its task is to orchestrate the program.

You begin by adding instructions to MAIN that accomplish the task of writing the title of the program to the screen. You will make some modifications at the end of this chapter—version 2 of the program—but the difference is in structure, not in result.

So far, you have in your program the solitary instruction, INT 20H. You know the result—terminate the program. Here is what it literally means to the CPU: INT is the mnemonic for the opcode that means "call an interrupt." 20H is the operand that designates which interrupt to call. An *interrupt* literally can interrupt what the CPU is doing. Hardware can interrupt by sending a signal to the CPU. For instance, the keyboard sends a signal that signifies that a key has been pressed. The CPU can pause in what it is doing (say, writing a string to the screen), carry out the routine to retrieve the code for the key pressed, store it, and then return to its task. There are many interrupts built into the system, with space for programmers to write their own.

An interrupt is essentially an assembly-language routine. Some are simple and others quite complex. When you call a particular interrupt, such as interrupt 20H, you ask the 8088 to fetch its address (each stored in a unique location in low memory, which you examined in the last chapter) and carry out the instructions found at that address. Some of the interrupt addresses point to routines in BIOS and some to routines read in with DOS when you boot the computer. You can call any interrupt with INT (number).

INT 20H is one of DOS's interrupts. Just as DOS takes the program entered on the command line, sets up the program in memory, and then passes control to that program, the instruction INT 20H calls a routine that gives the instructions to reset DOS for the next command.

DISPLAYING THE TITLE: VERSION 1

If you have learned to program in a high-level language, you probably remember starting with printing some words to the screen like "hello, world." Assembly language is more complex because you first have to write the instructions that serve to print strings of characters to the screen. Then you can use the procedure to print the title line of the program: "Tipe—Displays ASCII files."

A string is simply a series of bytes; 6,7,3,8 is a string that is four bytes long. Typically, but not necessarily, *string* means a series of printable characters. This sentence is a short string. The letter *a* is even shorter.

Assembly language offers a number of ways to print any string to the screen. That is one of the beauties of the language—you can do it your way, and you may choose different ways depending on the task and how it fits into the program. You can move data directly to the screen byte by byte or even bit by bit (probably best when doing graphics), or you can use the built-in services of BIOS or the functions of DOS.

To write strings to the screen, you will call upon the services of the DOS interrupt 21H. Interrupt 21H is extremely complex, composed of a large number of subroutines called functions. These functions carry out tasks related to disk and file management, keyboard and screen management, and more. In tipe.com, you use interrupt 21H for a variety of purposes. First, you use it to print the title line by calling upon a particular function. You will later learn two other ways of print-

36 IBM Assembly Language Simplified   INT 21H = DOS FUNCTION

ing strings to the screen using different DOS functions. Whenever you see the term *DOS function*, it refers to one of the many tasks done by interrupt 21H.

To print the title line, you use DOS function 9. When interrupt 21H is called, it first checks to see which of its many functions is wanted. It always expects the number of the function to be in the AH register. The instructions that call function 9 are the following. Type them into tipe.asm right before INT 20H:

```
mov     ah,9
int     21H
```

Using INT 21H is simple even for a beginner. You don't have to be skilled or even knowledgeable in using the registers. You just have to be careful to follow DOS's instructions. It wants the function number in AH, so you put it in AH. The instruction MOV AH,9 accomplishes that task.

MOV is an instruction you will use quite often. Its purpose is to move data from one place to another. You can move data from a register to memory or to a variable or vice versa. You can move data from one register to another or, as in this case move a constant into a register. Here you move the value 9 into the register AH.

One way, and perhaps the most common way, to alter the value of a register is to move data into it. Whatever was there before is now gone, replaced by the new value. The format of MOV is as follows:

MOV DESTINATION,SOURCE

Remember that in writing assembly-language programs, if an instruction has two operands, the one that is changed is always placed first. That is clear with MOV AH,9 because 9 is a constant and can't be changed. But later you will use instructions like MOV BX,AX. Which one is changed? Keep the above rule in mind. After a while, you will get used to it.

Most DOS functions need more information than just the function number. In this case, function 9 expects to find in the DX register the offset of the beginning of the string to be printed. DX, then, points to the beginning of the string. Function 9 uses the value in the DS register to be the segment of that offset. A short way of saying this is that DOS expects the address of the beginning of the string to be in DS:DX. Furthermore, DOS expects to find a dollar sign at the end of the string. This is a very useful function if you do not want to print the $ in the string itself. In the case of the title, and several other strings

Writing to the Screen 37

within the program, you do not want to print a dollar sign, so you will use this function.

Here is the title line. Type it under the comment ;Data for the program:

TITL   DB   'Tipe - Displays ASCII files$'

DB is an assembler directive that defines a variable. The assembler reserves the number of bytes required by the variable.

When you define a variable, you have the option of giving it a label. Most often you will want to do so because you may then use that label in your instruction code to refer to the variable. I have chosen the label TITL. I would have chosen TITLE to be the label, except for the good reason that TITLE is one of the names reserved by my assembler.

You also need to tell the assembler what type of variable TITL is. It is a string of characters. Characters are stored as ASCII code numbers that each take one byte. So the type is *byte*, as opposed to word (16 bits), *doubleword* (32 bits), and more. DB means define byte. The only other type you will use in this program is DW, define word. The assembler allows you to enclose strings in single (as above) or double quotes, so you do not have to laboriously enter each ASCII code number.

Now, you have defined for the assembler the string that will be the title line and have given it the label TITL. To satisfy the requirements of function 9, you place, right before MOV AH,9, the following statement:

MOV   DX,OFFSET TITL

Actually, this statement could come after MOV AH,9. It makes no difference. The important thing is that the AH register has 9, and the DX register the offset before calling INT 21H.

Once again you use MOV. In this case, you move into DX the offset of the variable called TITL. The ASSUME DS:CODE directive enables the assembler to compute the offset for any variable in your program from the beginning of CODE. The term OFFSET tells the assembler that you want the address of the beginning of the string. Remember that DOS also wants the segment of that offset in DS. Conveniently, DS also has the segment of CODE, so you are all set. Although function 9 of interrupt 21H is expecting the offset of a string in DX, some of you might be thinking that, if TITL is defined as DB, a byte variable, why use a 16-bit register, DX? Why not put it in DH or DL? Good question: yes, TITL is composed of bytes, but its offset is a 16-bit number and requires a word register.

Here are some variations that will do something other than that which is wanted—putting the offset in DX:

    MOV   DL,TITL

If you use just the variable name, without the offset, this means to the assembler that you want the contents of the variable. So here you are asking for the present value held by the variable. Whatever value is stored at the address of TITL will be placed in DL. DL can hold one byte, so it gets one byte—54H, the ASCII code for T. This is a perfectly valid instruction, just not what you want to do.

    MOV   DX,TITL

Let's use DX, which holds a word, rather than DL. Here two things can happen. First, despite defining TITL as a byte, the word at that location ("Ti" or 5469H) will be placed in DX with DH getting 69H and DL getting 54H. In the more recent versions of MASM, it simply won't assemble. You will get an error message saying "Type mismatch," which usually means you are trying to move a byte into a word register or a word into a byte register. As usual, there is a way around this if you want to move a byte in a word register or vice versa. In this case, however, you do not want to do that.

    MOV   DL,OFFSET TITL

This will always get you the type-mismatch error, because DL expects a byte, and an offset is always a word.

Next, you are going to add two control codes to TITL—a carriage return and a line feed. Without these codes, when TITL is displayed to the screen, the cursor would remain after the last character displayed, the "s" in "files." You want to put the cursor on the next line awaiting another message, so TITL should look like this:

    TITL   DB   'Tipe - Displays ASCII files'
            DB   CR,LF,'$'

First, I want to point out that the reason I have used two lines for the data has nothing to do with assembly language programming, but with the constraint of this book. Given 80 columns to work with, TITL can be written on one line: put a comma after the last quote and then the CR,LF,'$'. No matter how our data looks on a page or a screen, they are stored in a continuous sequence in the computer.

Writing to the Screen   39

In higher-level programming languages, you might have to define separate string variables, character variables, and numeric variables. In assembly language, all variables are numbers: bytes, words, and doublewords. It is how you use the numbers that make them what they are. TITL as written here combines both alphabetic and numeric variables, once you define CR and LF. CR means the carriage-return character (0DH), and LF means the line-feed character (0AH). I could have written TITL as a string, two numbers, and another string:

```
TITL    DB    'Tipe - Displays ASCII files'
        DB    0DH,0AH,'$'
```

Actually, TITL, no matter how it is entered, is a series of numeric bytes. When you use ' ', the assembler converts the symbols enclosed to the ASCII code number equivalents. Another variation follows:

```
TITL    DB    'Tipe - Displays ASCII files'
        DB    0DH,0AH,24H
```

The 24H is the ASCII code for the dollar sign; however, it is usually easier to enter the code as its string equivalent because it is hard to remember all the ASCII codes and a pain to constantly look them up. Here is one more equivalent:

```
TITL    DB    54H,69H,70H,65H
        DB    ' - Displays ASCII files'
        DB    0DH,0AH,24H
```

Just as it is easier to enclose strings of printing characters in quotes than to write out the ASCII codes, it is also easier to use mnemonic labels like CR and LF than the ASCII codes.

The assembler allows you to define constants with labels, so that when these labels are encountered in the program, they are replaced with the appropriate number. You define constants with the term EQU. Thus you can tell the assembler from the outset:

```
CR      EQU    0DH
LF      EQU    0AH
```

Whenever the assembler encounters CR, it replaces it with 0DH; similarly, LF is replaced with 0AH. Place these two equates at the top of the program. Now your program should look like Fig. 4-1.

By now you are probably ready to find out the results of your

```
;TIPE.ASM - PROGRAM TO DISPLAY ASCII FILES
;       ALLOWING THE DISPLAY TO BE REVERSED

CR      EQU     0DH             ;Carriage return character
LF      EQU     0AH             ;Line feed character

CODE    SEGMENT
        ASSUME CS:CODE,DS:CODE
        ORG     100H

MAIN:   mov     dx,OFFSET TITL  ;DS:DX holds string
        mov     ah,9            ;print $ terminated string
        int     21H             ;Call the interrupt
        int     20H             ;Quit
;End of MAIN

;Data for the program

TITL    DB      'Tipe - Displays ASCII files'
        DB      CR,LF,'$'
CODE    ENDS
        END     MAIN
```

Fig. 4-1. Ready to show the title—Version 1.

programming. Create the .com file; then see if you can resist the urge to run it directly at the command line and send it through Debug first. If you run it directly from the command line, you might see the title—but then again, you might not. Better Debug than be sorry.

Enter Debug and, at its dash prompt, enter U to see the listing of your program starting at 100H. If this were an .exe file, you would want to note down your code segment number in CS, which also precedes the display of each line. The reason to keep a record of it is that if you accidentally trace into interrupt 21H, which is in a different segment, you can return. With a .com file you can find your way out.

The first instruction is displayed as MOV DX,#### with the pound signs standing for a hex number. That should be the offset of TITL. Check it with the dump command. Enter D (the number). If your program is exactly like Fig. 4-1, you would enter D109. Dump will display 80H worth of the hex numbers starting with that address. You do not need to enter a segment number for this dump because Debug uses the segment in DS as a default.

On the right of the screen are the ASCII equivalents. With dump, you can visually check that the number in DX is indeed the beginning of TITL. Assuming that it is, enter T to trace to the next instruction, which is MOV AH,9. Trace executes the current instruction; then it shows the state of the registers and the next instruction to be executed. The next T will put you at INT 21. Pause to see if the registers are set as DOS wants them, in this case, 9 in AH and the offset of the $-terminated string in DX. (Did you see the $ in the dump you made? If you did not, quit with Q and be sure to put it in the .asm file.)

If you want to go exploring into INT 21, continue tracing. For the moment, however, let's not be explorers and continue following the program. Some debuggers have a command that will skip over the display of calls and interrupts. Debug does not have such a command, so you have to go around the interrupt. To go to the next instruction (INT 20), you need to give Debug its offset. Use the U command to find it. Enter U and Debug will show the present instruction of the trace and those following it. You can see on the left of the screen that INT 20 has the offset of 107. Now enter G107; Debug executes the interrupt, you see the title line displayed to the screen, and the next instruction is ready for execution. Success! Now enter either Q for quit or G to complete the program; then enter Q.

If you accidentally or intentionally trace into INT 21 and want to get back to your program, here is what to do. The CS may no longer hold the code segment of tipe.com, but instead the code segment of the interrupt. U and G assume the segment in the CS register. However, like with dump, Debug allows you to specify any segment you wish. All you have to do is know what the original CS was. If you cannot retrieve the original CS, there is probably no way back and it is time to quit—using a plain G to finish the program or Q to quit Debug.

One way to retrieve the original CS is to have remembered it (hard) or to have written it down (easier).

These hints are good with .exe files, but with .com files you know the segment registers were all the same before you called the interrupt. The one segment register that will be unchanged by DOS or BIOS is the SS. Therefore, whatever number is in SS will be the same as the original CS. Go ahead and trace into INT 21. Trace far enough until you see the CS change. Now look at the SS register, and then use that number as a segment for the U command. Let's say SS has 3000. Enter 3000:100 to see a listing from the start of your program. You will see that INT 20 has the offset of 107. Enter G3000:107, and you shall have returned to your program.

Exercise 4-1: Changing What Is in Memory with Debug

Here is a quick lesson on using Debug's E (enter) command, one

I have not discussed yet. Let's say you forgot to put in the dollar sign (24H) following the string for TITL. Let's also say that you had several other procedures to test subsequent to your attempt to get the title on the screen. As far as you can tell there is nothing wrong with your call to INT 21, except for the missing dollar sign. Now you could go back to the .asm file and put the $ in—you will have to do it at some point. However, for the test, you can enter the $, or 24H, into an appropriate spot in memory, correcting the mistake, and continue to test the rest of the code. Here's how you can use E to do that.

Enter debug tipe.com. TITL starts at 109 of the Data Segment. Let's put a $ at the end of the phrase "Tipe -" so that the $ will immediately follow the dash. When you run the program, you will not get the whole string, but no matter. The test is to see if the call to INT 21H works. Use D109 to dump what is there. Then find the address immediately following the dash. You find that the address after the dash is 10F. Now enter E10F. Debug will show you its present contents, in this case 20, and the space, followed by a period. On my screen it looks like this:

35AD:010F 20.

When you use D or E without specifying a segment (as in D40:0 or E40:0) Debug assumes the offset currently in the DS register because that is what you usually want, as in this case. 35AD was in my DS register. It will probably be different for you. Enter 24 and press ENTER. To check that you have indeed placed a dollar sign at 10F, use D109 and see what is there. Now enter G and run the program. You should see "Tipe-" displayed on the screen. Debug's Enter command can serve a number of purposes. In this case, it can save you from reassembling and compiling a program to correct one error, only to find that there is another error further down in the code.

Running the Program

Now that you know the program works, go ahead and run it to the screen. Enter tipe at the command line, and there you have the title line.

DISPLAYING THE TITLE: VERSION 2

In this version, the one you will keep and expand, you write the call to function 9 as a procedure named WRITEM (my choice of name for "write message"). You write WRITEM as a procedure so that it may be called by MAIN or by other procedures you write, and you use it several times in the program. You could repeat these instructions each time you need them, but it is a neater as well as more efficient use of program space to write a *procedure*. An exception to this rule is if you are looking for speed of execution, because calling and returning take time. Speed, however, is not a problem for tipe.com, as you noted when you ran the program. Delete the following instructions:

    mov   ah,9
    int   21H

Replace them with CALL WRITEM. The procedure WRITEM is shown in Fig. 4-2.

    WRITEM is the first of many procedures you shall write. The instruction WRITEM PROC NEAR is for the assembler. It gives a procedure the name WRITEM and the attribute NEAR. You will learn about NEAR and FAR attributes later. Basically, NEAR means that the procedure is in the same segment from which it is called. That is true of all procedures in tipe.com; in fact it is true in all .com programs. If no attribute (NEAR or FAR) follows PROC, the assembler assumes NEAR; therefore the NEAR could be omitted. I leave it in as a matter of habit.

    Like the SEGMENT directive, procedures have a beginning and an end—PROC and ENDP. The two instructions PUSH AX and POP AX are ways of saving the value in the AX register, which is changed in this procedure. At this point you do not care if AX is changed. Perhaps later, when you use WRITEM again, you will care. You will learn more about PUSHing and POPping in the next chapter. Finally, the procedure ends with RET—return.

    Two of the new instructions added—CALL and RET—affect the flow of program execution. When the program is set to begin, the IP (instruction pointer) is given the value of the offset of the first instruction to be executed. The instruction there is executed, then the IP is set

```
WRITEM PROC NEAR
;entry DS:DX address of $ terminated string
        push    ax      ;Save AX
        mov     ah,9    ;print $ terminated string
        int     21H     ;Call the interrupt
        pop     ax      ;Get it back
        ret
WRITEM ENDP
```

Fig. 4-2. Procedure to display $-terminated string.

```
;TIPE.ASM - PROGRAM TO DISPLAY ASCII FILES
;         ALLOWING THE DISPLAY TO BE REVERSED

        CR      EQU     0DH     ;Carriage return character
        LF      EQU     0AH     ;Line feed character

        PUBLIC  WRITEM

        CODE    SEGMENT
                ASSUME  CS:CODE,DS:CODE
                ORG     100H

        MAIN:   mov     dx,OFFSET TITL
                call    writem   ;Show title of program
                int     20H      ;Quit
        ;End of MAIN

        ;**** DOS SCREEN HANDLING ROUTINES ****

        WRITEM PROC NEAR
        ;entry DS:DX address of $ terminated string
                push    ax       ;Save AX
                mov     ah,9     ;print $ terminated string
                int     21H      ;Call the interrupt
                pop     ax       ;Get it back
                ret
        WRITEM ENDP

        ;Data for the program
        PUBLIC  TITL

        TITL    DB      'Tipe - Displays ASCII files'
                DB      CR,LF,'$'
        CODE    ENDS
                END     MAIN
```

Fig. 4-3. Ready to show the title—working version.

to the offset of the next, it is executed, then the IP is set to the next, it is executed, and so on.

This sequence can be changed in several ways. One is by the instruction JMP (jump), which you have not yet used. The effect of JMP is to change the IP to the offset designated by the JMP instruction. Thus, the program "jumps" to the new instruction, and the usual sequence continues from that point.

Another way to alter the sequence is with the CALL instruction, which you shall use to execute WRITEM. When a procedure is called, the offset of the instruction following the call is saved (how this is done will be described when you learn more about PUSH and POP), and the offset of the called procedure is placed in the IP. Now the sequence begins again until changed in some way.

One important way to change the sequence is to get back to where you started by using the RET (return) instruction. When a RET is encountered, the effect is to place the saved offset back in the IP, so the sequence picks up with the instruction immediately following the call. The instruction INT is a special case of CALL. All interrupts have a return instruction to return to the calling routine.

Figure 4-3 shows tipe.asm as it now looks. Note that near the top of the program, is the statement **PUBLIC WRITEM**. This is an assembler directive that says this procedure name is *public*, it can be referenced in other files that might compose the program. Because the source code for tipe.com resides entirely in one file, the PUBLIC directive is not necessary for this purpose. A second reason for declaring names and labels public is if you have a symbolic debugger. Typically, only those symbols declared public are known to the debugger.

You should type **WRITEM** in tipe.asm after **MAIN** and before the comment line *data for the program*. Include the ;*** comment line. Later you will add more character-handling routines. Because this change in the code is slight, a matter of reorganization, you might prefer not to test the code at this time, but to move to the next step—finding the name of the text file. You might, however, find it instructive to follow what happens to the IP and SP by tracing through the call to WRITEM.

CHAPTER 5

Getting the File Name

Now you can begin to get into the meat of the program: getting the file name, reading the ASCII file into memory, and displaying it. Before you can have the file read into memory, you have to know which file to read. Thus the first decision to make is how to obtain the file name from the user. One possibility is to have the user enter the name of the file to be displayed in response to a prompt you could create (such as, "Enter file name:$"), which would be displayed using WRITEM.

My choice is to have the user include the file name on the command line, just as is done in DOS commands, such as the following:

A>tipe myfile

Before you can do anything else, you need to find out if a file name, or anything in fact, has been entered on the command line after tipe. If nothing is there, there is nothing to do, and the program can exit. If something is there you, move the string to a variable to be defined as FNAME in preparation for finding out if it is an existing file.

For this particular program, moving the string is not really necessary, primarily because tipe.com accesses the file name only once, and it remains in its location in memory for access again if needed. But you will write a procedure, GET_FILE, which you can use in other programs where these conditions might not be true. Before developing GET_FILE, let's see where you can find the file name entered on the command line.

ACCESSING THE PROGRAM SEGMENT PREFIX

Remember that when DOS sets up either a .com file or .exe file for execution, it places 256 bytes worth of information starting at the very beginning of the program segment, at CS:0 for .com files. DOS assures that .com files start at offset 100H in order to preserve this information. These 100H bytes are called the *program segment prefix* (PSP).

The PSP contains a mixture of information, including the instruction INT 20H right at the very beginning at offset zero. For some of its file-handling functions, DOS formats any file name entered with the program command in what is called a *file control block* (FCB) at offset 5CH. It also places any text entered on the command line after the program command at offset 80H.

Programmers can have access to any location in the PSP to obtain information for their programs. For the kind of file processing you will use in tipe.com, your interest will be in the text at 80H. Let's actually look at the PSP while you learn more about it.

Exercise 5-1: Viewing the PSP

Enter Debug with the command line tipe.com myfile. Debug sets up the PSP for tipe.com just as DOS would do if you ran the program directly from the command line. Let's find myfile in the PSP. At the dash prompt, enter D0, which tells Debug to dump 80H worth of contents starting at DS:0. Remember, when no segment is given to the dump command, Debug assumes the segment indicated in the DS register. In this case, DS (and the other segment registers) all point to the beginning of the PSP.

Starting at the offset of 5C, you will see the number 0, and then the file name that you entered on the command line after tipe.com. The file name is in uppercase letters, whether you entered it that way or not. DOS nicely makes the translation. The first byte, zero, refers to the disk drive referenced, in this case none, so zero means the default drive. A one means drive A, a two means drive B, and so on.

You then see *myfile* translated to capital letters, and you can see it is followed by five spaces or blanks (20H). You might try this exercise again when you are finished, with a file name like b:yourfile.doc, the maximum length of a file name with an extension (ignoring the period before the extension). At 5C you would see the number two (for drive B) and then YOURFILEDOC. If that file exists on the disk, that is exactly how it is stored in the disk's directory, making for easy matching.

The offset at 5C begins what is called the *file control block* (FCB). There are a number of DOS INT 21H functions that use the FCB for file management. These are referred to as the traditional file management functions. With DOS version 2.0 or higher, a number of extended file management functions have been added. You will use these, for they are much simpler and are more versatile. With these functions, DOS does much of the work that programmers had to do using the traditional functions.

The extended functions start with the file name as typed in by the user, and accommodate directories and path names for which there is no room in an FCB. The extended functions also allow for *piping*, or redirection of input and output. Although you will not use that feature, it is this capability that makes the extended functions more versatile.

Assuming you have entered D0 and have been looking at the screen, enter D once again to see the PSP starting at offset 80. Right at the top of this dump you see the file name exactly as you entered it on the command line. DOS does not change the case of the letters. The very first byte at 80 contains a special number. This is the number of characters entered on the command line following tipe.com.

If nothing were entered after the program name, it would be zero. In the case of myfile, you see seven. There were seven characters entered after the program name: space, m, y, f, i, l, and e. DOS puts in the final carriage return (0D) marking the end of the string. It is this information stored for you by DOS at offset 80 of your program that you will use in for file management. Try running through this exercise once again; enter this line:

A> **debug tipe.com Now is the time to look at the PSP**

Your dump shows you that there are now two FCBs. At 5C, there is an FCB for the file NOW, which is expected to be on the default drive. At 6C, there is a second FCB for the file IS, also on the default disk. At 80H, there is the number of characters typed in starting with the space after .com. Because anything typed after the program name (up 127 characters) is stored here, you can use the information typed in for purposes other than just retrieving file names. For instance, you might write a program called *wipe*, which might take a command line like this: **wipe jan 85**. It then would search for and erase all files with

Getting the File Name 49

dates before January 1985. For tipe.com, you will simply use the information starting at 80H to find a file name.

Updating the Data Section

Put FNAME in the data section right after TITL.

FNAME   DB   50 DUP (0)

FNAME holds the file name as well as any path name that might be entered with it, so you need to reserve plenty of room for it—room for 50 characters.

MASM's DUP (duplicate) operator allows you to easily reserve all the room you want for any variable. Because FNAME is defined as Byte, the number in the parentheses represents the byte 0, which will be duplicated 50 times. (If you wanted 50 capital A's, you could say 50 DUP ('A')). The other way to enter 50 zeros would be like this:

FNAME   DB   0,0,0,0,0,0,0,0,0,0,

and so on until 50 were entered.

The Get_File Procedure

GET_FILE is shown in Fig. 5-1. The purpose of GET_FILE is to determine if any text has been entered after the program name, and if so move it to the location of FNAME. The first task is to check to find out whether or not the number stored at 80H is zero, for if it is zero, nothing was entered and that's that. To determine if this number is zero or greater, the first step is to move the number stored at 80H into a register so that it can be examined. There is more than one way to do this (practically always the case with assembly-language programming). Here is an alternative:

MOV   CL,[80H]

This is an alternative that does not work, but I present it because it clearly shows what will happen. The statement says move the contents of the offset 80H into CL. Where is 80H? In the PSP. Remember that all segment registers in a .com program start with the segment of the PSP.

The effect of MOV CL,[80H] is different from MOV CL,80H. The latter instruction simply says move a particular number into CL. This number

```
GET_FILE PROC NEAR
        mov     si,80h          ;Command line chars
        mov     cl,[SI]         ;Number of characters
        cmp     cl,0            ; which is moved into CL
        jz      GT_EX           ;If CL is zero, exit
        dec     cl              ;First char is a space
        sub     ch,ch           ;Make sure CH is zero
        inc     si              ;Move to space
        inc     si              ;Now to first char
        mov     di,OFFSET FNAME ;Place for name
        cld                     ;Go forward
        rep     movsb           ;CX has count for move
        mov     al,0            ;Make it 0 and stow it
        stosb                   ; after the last char
GT_EX:  ret                     ;If zero set, not found
GET_FILE ENDP
```

Fig. 5-1. Procedure to obtain text from the command line.

could represent many things depending on the context. It could be an address in memory, a constant in a formula, the length of a string, or many other things. On the other hand, MOV CL,[80H] is much more specific.

Remember from Chapter 3 that the brackets mean that the number is being used as a pointer. Thus 80H is an offset in memory, and you want to retrieve the contents of that location in memory. So 80H is not just any old number, but a pointer to an offset in memory. You are interested in this particular location because it contains the number of characters entered after the program name on the command line.

The reason this particular example does not work is that the assembler assembles the instruction MOV CL,[80H] as MOV CL,80H, which is not what you want. The assembler does this because it does not know which segment to use to compute the offset of 80H (despite the fact that we know that all segments are the same in a .com program). The way to do it properly is to use a segment override (you will learn about this later, in Chapter 10), or to use the indirect means of moving 80H into a register and then moving its contents into CL. This is the tack taken in GET_FILE, not just to make the assembler happy, but because it is easier to use registers when you also want the contents of 82H, 83H, 84H, and so on—the complete file name.

If you use registers rather than absolute numbers, the assembler assumes the segment register. Typically, it is DS, the data segment register. So whenever you use [SI], [DI], or [BX] in an instruction as a pointer, the segment is assumed to be DS. For the remainder of this book, I will point out those occasions when some segment register other than DS is the one used to determine the offset. Before moving on, following the rationale just given, note once again the difference between the instructions MOV CL,[SI] and MOV CL,SI. The first says move the contents of the offset in SI into CL; the second says move the value in SI into CL (which would produce an assembler error, "Type mismatch").

There are only four registers that can be used to access the contents of memory: BX, BP, SI, and DI. (You cannot say MOV CL,[DX]). My choice of SI over the other three is based on the fact the 8088 provides some easy to use and powerful statements to move and manipulate strings and blocks of data. They require the use of two registers, SI (source index) and DI (destination index). The mnemonics make it easy to remember which is which. Because you hope to be moving a string from its source at 82H to some destination, SI is used from the outset, by moving into it 80H.

Now which register should receive the contents of 80H? You could put the bye in [SI] into any of the 8-bit registers, AH, AL, BH, BL, CH, CL, DH, DL. Why CL? The choice once again is based on that impending string move coming up. How many characters will be moved? You need a count. The instruction you will use requires that the count be in CX. In fact, any 8088 instruction that requires a count expects the count in CX. So into CL it goes. (It could also go to CX. In the case of CL, because it is a byte register it will get just the byte. In the case of CX, because it is a word register, CL gets the byte at 80H, CH the byte at 81H. Because you are going to zero CH later, it makes no difference.)

Thus the number stored at offset 80H is moved into CL. Is the number zero? Because you can never see the content of a register, unless you write a routine to display it to the screen or trace a program with a debugger, you have to find some other way of determining a register's contents. The flag register provides this means.

The third instruction is CMP CL,0—compare the value in CL with zero. Let's first look at an alternative instruction: SUB CL,0—subtract zero from the value in CL and put the result into CL. When you add, subtract, and change values in some other ways, the flag register is affected. I will discuss this register in more detail, but if, for instance, the number in CL were zero, and you subtracted zero, the result would be zero, and the zero flag would be set. If the result were anything else, the zero flag would not be set.

CMP (compare) is more useful because its effect on the flags is exactly the same as SUB, but the register is not changed. Obviously

CL will not be changed by subtracting zero, but perhaps you want to know if CL holds the number 6. CMP is a better choice if you want to preserve the value in the register, which you usually want to do. Here again are the first four instructions:

```
mov      si,80h           ;Command line chars
mov      cl,[SI]          ;Number of characters
cmp      cl,0             ; which is moved into CL
jz       GT_EX            ;If CL is zero, exit
```

JZ is one of a number of conditional jump instructions. As pointed out in Chapter 4, JMP has the effect of changing the IP to the offset of the instruction indicated by the label. JZ GT_EX means "jump to the offset of the instruction with the label GT_EX, if, and only if, the zero flag is set."

FLAGS AND CONDITIONAL TRANSFERS

The 8088 has six flags to help you make decisions, and three others to help it make decisions. One of the latter, the direction flag, tells the 8088 which direction, up or down in memory, you want to go with string operations. So, typically you set or clear the direction flag to tell the computer something. On the other hand, the first six flags are typically set by the computer to tell you something. Each flag is one of the 16 bits of the flag register, so each can have only one of two values: 0 or 1. If the value is 0 (false), we say the flag is *clear*. If the value is 1 (true), we say the flag is *set*.

In this program, you are concerned with three flags: the direction flag that you shall set, the zero flag to test for results of zero or not zero, and the carry flag to test if a remainder of a subtraction is less than zero. The carry flag is also set by DOS in many of its functions to indicate an error. You will want to become familiar with using and setting flags for your own purposes as you pursue assembly-language programming. When the flags are used along with the conditional instructions available to you, they are powerful friends. Using conditional instructions such as if . . . then . . . else, allow you to structure your programs to make decisions. In GET_FILE, if the zero flag is set, go to RET, else continue.

I just looked at a reference book and found 31 conditional jump instructions. You will learn five. Four are used in the program—two to test the status of the zero flag and two to test the status of the carry flag. You will be introduced to another that is good to have in your repertoire.

The two conditional jumps dependent on the zero flag are JZ, jump if the flag is set, and JNZ, jump if the zero flag is clear. Thus, subtracting zero from zero produces zero and sets the flag. Comparing zero with zero also sets the flag. The choice of using JZ or JNZ depends primarily on the context. Which makes more efficient code? For instance, in GET_FILE you could have said JNZ (to a label given to DEC CL), but then you still have to exit, so you would then need a JMP GT_EX. JZ is more efficient here. This is not true in other parts of the program.

The other flag used is the carry flag. It is set (true) under certain mathematical conditions, like when a larger number is subtracted from a smaller number. It is also set if you try to add one or more to a byte register that holds the value 0FFH or to a word register that has the value 0FFFFH. If one is added, the result in the register in each of these last two cases is zero, so the zero flag as well as the carry flag is set.

One important reason for testing the carry flag is to check results of mathematical operations. As an example, let's say you have written a program in which the user can enter three options, 1, 2, or 3. You obtain the input, say in the AL register. Now you can use this sequence of instructions:

```
          CMP     AL,2
          JC      TASK1           ;less than 2
          JZ      TASK2
TASK3:    ...                     ;greater than 2
```

A very common use of testing the carry flag is to find out whether or not there is an error condition. It is a relatively standard practice to indicate an error or special condition by setting the carry flag to alert the calling routine. DOS typically does this, and you shall too, in creating upcase.com. The carry flag is not only set or cleared by mathematical operations, but it can be set manually by the programmer. The instruction STC says set the carry flag. The instruction CLC says clear the carry flag. You can set or clear the flag at will to provide information for later conditional instructions or calling routines.

You can also set or clear the zero flag, not with specific instructions, but by using a bit of knowledge. Because you know that any number minus itself is zero, you can take a register you do not wish to save and subtract the value in it from itself. Choose a register that has a current value not necessary to the program.

Let's say it makes no difference what is in DL. Set the zero flag with SUB DL,DL. Likewise, you can make sure the zero flag is clear by adding one to any register you do not wish to save—for instance, ADD DL,1. An instruction you have not encountered yet that increases the value of a register by one is a simpler way to do this: INC DL—increase DL by one. It works the same as adding one, and it takes less memory in the program. The only way in which increasing the value of DL by one will not work to clear the flag is if the value in DL is −1 or 0FFH.

The last conditional jump instruction to consider, one not found in tipe.com, is JCXZ. Look at the mnemonic closely, and you can see it means jump only if CX is zero. The condition tested is the state of the CX register, not the status of any flag. This is a useful instruction to know, even if you do not use it in tipe.com. Remember that CX is the counter to be used for several instructions. Typically, these instructions automatically reduce CX and then repeat until CX is zero.

I have often gotten myself in huge unwanted loops by starting the process when CX was zero. When zero is reduced in a word register, the result is 0FFFFH, and the loop will happily continue 65,535 times, sometimes doing things you would prefer it not do. If there is ever a possibility that a routine that needs CX as a counter will be given the value of zero, do test for it and jump to the exit if it is zero. A valid alternative in GET__FILE would be:

```
MOV      CL,[SI]
SUB      CH,CH            ;Make sure CH is zero
JCXZ     GT__EX
```

The routine returns with the zero flag set if no string was entered. The zero flag was set with SUB CH,CH. The jump, JCXZ GT__EX, is taken only if CL is also zero. JCXZ does not affect the flags.

In general, if you want to know whether or not CX is zero, and flags are not important, use JCXZ because it is more efficient. If, however, flags are important, then test the value of CX (or CL) in a way that will affect the flags, such as CMP CX,0.

MOVING THE STRING

Look again at the GET__FILE procedure in Fig. 5-1. If CL is zero, it exits with the zero flag set. Here is what is done if there is some text stored at 80H:

```
dec      cl               ;First char is a space
sub      ch,ch            ;Make sure CH is zero
inc      si               ;Move to space
```

```
        inc       si                  ;Now to first char
        mov       di,OFFSET FNAME     ;Place for name
        cld                           ;Go forward
        rep       movsb               ;CX has count for move
```

First, you know that the first character entered after the program name should be a space, so you need to skip the space by changing CL and SI. You reduce the count in CL by using the instruction DEC CL. INC will increase a value by one; DEC will decrease a value by one. You are going to use the whole CX register as a counter.

Assume that there are six characters in the file name, and therefore CL equals 6. It could be that CH is not zero but, thanks to some other instructions before this, it has some other value. (It doesn't in this program, but it may in some other program in which you decide to use the same procedure.) Let's say CH has the value 0FFH. The value of CL is 6, but the value of CX is 0FF06H. So, let's be safe and make sure CH is zero. No matter what is in CH, if CH is subtracted from itself it is zero. Now the space has been skipped in the count and the count is in CX. SI still has the offset 80H. As you know, the first character of the string resides in 82H. You could change SI directly with MOV SI,82H, or you could use ADD SI,2. These would work to set SI to 82H. Because SI is 80H, the simplest and quickest way to increase the value is with INC as I have done.

You now only need the address of the place for the string to be moved, its destination, which is FNAME. Its offset is put into DI. The move instruction that you use requires CX to have the count or length, SI to have the offset of the source string, and DI to have the offset of the destination. Further, DS will be the segment register used for SI, and ES will hold the segment for DI. Because both the string at 82H and its destination, FNAME, are in the same segment, and because both DS and ES have the segment address, you have no problem.

The move instruction also looks to the direction flag to know whether to go up or down in memory. If up, it moves the content pointed to by SI to the location indicated by DI and then increases both registers; if down, it takes the move and then decreases both registers. Because DI and SI are at the starting point for each location, you want to go up. When a program starts, all flags are cleared. A clear direction flag means up. You have not changed this, but when you write procedures that might be used in other programs, you want to be sure. To be sure, you can use CLD, clear the direction flag.

Now the move is made. MOVSB says MOVe a String of Bytes starting at the offset in SI to the offset in DI. The byte pointed to by SI is moved into the location pointed to by DI. After a byte is moved, both index registers are increased by one (decreased if the direction flag is set). The REP instruction says you want to do this more than once. In fact, you want to continue as long as CX is not zero. Thus, the function of REP (repeat) is to decrease CX, and repeat the process until CX is zero. When finished, CX will be zero; SI and DI will point to one place beyond the last byte moved, because they were increased after the move. Properly set up, REP MOVSB can certainly do a lot with a few simple instructions.

A close relative, which is not used in this program, is MOVSW, which says MOVe a String of Words. You use this if you want to move 16-bit words rather than 8-bit bytes. The only difference is that SI and DI are increased (or decreased) twice before the next move. You are almost done. You finish with the following:

```
            mov     al,0        ;Make it 0 and stow it
            stosb               ; after the last char
GT__EX:     ret                 ;If zero set, not found
```

The first two instructions serve the purpose of placing a zero right after the string in FNAME. Looking ahead, you will learn that DOS requires the string with the file name to be terminated with a zero. As you recall, FNAME was defined to have 50 zeros. So there is no doubt that there will be a zero immediately following the file name. Even though a zero is there, given the notion of writing procedures that can be used again and again, let's be sure there is one there every time the procedure is used.

STOSB is in the family of string instructions like MOVSB. STOSB takes the value in AL and places it in the address referenced by DI and then updates DI (increases or decreases). Again, as in all string moves, ES is assumed to hold the segment for DI. Thanks to MOVSB, DI holds the offset immediately following the file name. You put in the zero and finally return.

You might be wondering why the zero flag is clear, indicating that a string was found and moved, when the procedure will return with a zero in AL. The answer is that the last instruction to affect the zero flag was INC SI. Moving a value into a register does not affect the flags, so MOV AL,0 did not set the zero flag. If, on the other hand, the instruction were SUB AL,AL, AL would also contain zero, but then the zero flag would be set, something you do not want to happen here.

Soon you can see if GET_FILE works. Type in GET_FILE right after MAIN, and add FNAME to the data at the end of the program. Finally you call the procedure from MAIN, so MAIN looks like this:

```
MAIN:       mov     dx,OFFSET  TITL
            call    WRITEM              ;Show title of program
            call    GET_FILE            ;string from PSP at 80H
            jnz     MAIN1               ;Zero flag set = no text
            mov     dx,OFFSET NOFILE    ;Set up message
            call    WRITEM              ;  Show it
            jmp     SHORT DONE          ;  and exit
MAIN1:      nop                         ;do nothing
DONE:       int     20H                 ;Quit
;End of MAIN
```

You could have followed the call to GET_FILE with JZ DONE. There will, however, be several other reasons for terminating the program before displaying a file. It is always good practice to let the user know the reason for any deviation or error. So, using WRITEM, you state the reason, "No file entered." Define the variable:

```
NOFILE   DB     'No file entered$'
```

Place it in the data section. After sending it out with WRITEM, you jump to the exit. I will return to this in a minute. First, notice that if text was entered, you jump to MAIN1. Here you will place your next instructions. For the time being, you can fill this spot with an instruction that does nothing: NOP. When the program encounters NOP it simply moves on to the next instruction. Primarily, you can use it as a filler as you have done here.

Instead of JMP SHORT DONE, you could have used the instruction JMP DONE. Both will do the trick in this case.

MORE ABOUT JUMPING

There are three kinds of jumps you will use in this program: *conditional jumps*, *short jumps*, and *long jumps*. In machine language or object code, long jumps take three bytes of instructions, while both short jumps and conditional jumps take two bytes. In object code, all jumps start the same way—with a code number for the particular type of jump. JZ, JNC, and the rest of the conditional jumps each has its particular code. Each is then followed by the offset, or relative distance back or forward in the program to the address that is the destination of the jump. Fortunately, the assembler figures this out for us.

Conditional jumps are set up so that the offset is in one byte—0 to 0FFH. That means you cannot use them to jump very far, in fact no more than 128 bytes because bit 7 of the byte is used to indicate whether the jump should be forward or backward. If the conditional jump must be longer, you will see how to do that later in this discussion.

JMP is typically a three-byte instruction. First the code that means *jump* and then two bytes that hold the offset or distance. The two bytes allows for jumps anywhere in your program. (You can also jump out of the code segment if you say JMP FAR. You will not be doing that.) When the program is assembled, on the first pass through the code, if the assembler encounters the instruction JMP, it looks for the address of the label you are using.

If the label exists at that point (remember that the assembler starts at the beginning and assembles forward), the assembler computes the offset. If it can be held in one byte, it automatically sets it up as a short (one byte) jump. The label exists for the assembler only if the jump is backward, to previously defined labels. So if you use JMP to go back in the program, the assembler figures out for you whether to use one (SHORT) or two bytes. On the other hand, if the jump is forward, the assembler does not know whether the label is near or distant, so to be safe it saves two bytes for the offset.

If you follow the JMP instruction with SHORT, only one byte is reserved, just as with the conditional jumps. So, although JMP and JMP SHORT do exactly the same thing, the latter saves a byte of program space.

If you want to JMP to a forward address that is not too far away, save the extra byte with JMP SHORT. How far is too far? Again, you can let the assembler do the math for you. If the jump is out of range, needing two bytes, the assembler will inform you with the error message, "Relative jump out of range." Then you can go back and delete the SHORT.

Because all conditional jumps are *relative* jumps, using only one byte for the offset, what can you do if the assembler says "Relative jump out of range" to a JZ you have used? For example, assume MAIN1 is too far to reach with a one byte offset. Before you look at the code following this paragraph, try to write a different code that accomplishes the same end, getting to MAIN1 if the zero flag is not

```
;TIPE.ASM - PROGRAM TO DISPLAY ASCII FILES
;       ALLOWING THE DISPLAY TO BE REVERSED

CR      EQU     0DH     ;Carriage return character
LF      EQU     0AH     ;Line feed character

PUBLIC WRITEM,GET_FILE

CODE    SEGMENT
        ASSUME CS:CODE,DS:CODE
        ORG     100H

MAIN:   mov     dx,OFFSET TITL
        call    WRITEM      ;Show title of program
        call    GET_FILE    ;string from PSP at 80H
        jnz     MAIN1       ;Zero flag set = no text
        mov     dx,OFFSET NOFILE ;Set up message
        call    WRITEM      ;  Show it
        jmp     SHORT DONE  ;  and exit
MAIN1:  nop                 ;Do nothing
DONE:   int     20H         ;Quit
;End of MAIN

GET_FILE PROC NEAR
        mov     si,80H      ;Command line chars
        mov     cl,[SI]     ;Number of characters
        cmp     cl,0        ; which is moved into CL
        jz      GT_EX       ;If CL is zero, exit
        dec     cl          ;First char is a space
        sub     ch,ch       ;Make sure CH is zero
        inc     si          ;Move to space
        inc     si          ;Now to first char
        mov     di,OFFSET FNAME ;Place for name
        cld                 ;Go forward
        rep     movsb       ;CX has count for move
        mov     al,0        ;Make it 0 and stow it
        stosb               ;  after the last char
GT_EX:  ret                 ;If zero set, not found
GET_FILE ENDP

;**** DOS CHARACTER HANDLING ROUTINES ****
WRITEM PROC NEAR
;entry DS:DX address of $ terminated string
        push    ax          ;Save AX
        mov     ah,9        ;print $ terminated string
        int     21H         ;Call the interrupt
        pop     ax          ;Get it back
        ret
WRITEM ENDP
```

Fig. 5-2. Finding the file name entered on command line.

```
;Data for the program
PUBLIC TITL,FNAME,NOFILE

TITL    DB      'Tipe - Displays ASCII files'
        DB      CR,LF,'$'
FNAME   DB      50 DUP (0)
NOFILE  DB      'No file entered$'
CODE    ENDS
        END     MAIN
```

---

set, and sending out NOFILE and exiting if it is set. Here is one solution:

```
            call        GET_FILE
            jnz         MAINERR
            jmp         MAIN1
MAINERR:    MOV         dx,OFFSET NOFILE
            call        WRITEM
            jmp         DONE
MAIN1 :     nop
```

If you have not already done so, type in GET_FILE after MAIN, add NOFILE to the data, and make the changes in MAIN. Make the new labels public if you wish. Your program should now look like Fig. 5-2.

Go ahead and create the .com file. Trace it through Debug, first entering a file name and then doing it without a file name. Use Dump to view FNAME both before and after the move. Don't forget to Go around INT 21. Once you are sure the program is working, send it to the screen. If you run tipe.com with a file name, the result should be nothing (NOP). If you run it with no file name, the error message should appear on the screen.

The next step is to find out if that string is the name of a file that actually exists on the disk.

CHAPTER 6

Opening and Reading the File

The program now knows whether or not there is some text stored at DS:82H. If there is text, that text also resides in the variable FNAME. Assuming that the string is an existing file name, by the end of this chapter, you will have the file read into memory. To do so, you use several of DOS's extended file-handling functions. The very first question is whether or not the string in FNAME names a file that exists on the disk? DOS function 3DH will both answer the question and make the preparations to read the file if it exists. Function 3DH opens a file for reading or writing. Essentially the term *open a file* means to prepare a file for reading or writing. The only files that can be opened are those that already exist. There is also a function to create files that do not exist.

OPENING A FILE

Your first task is to write a procedure that calls the file opening function. I have called it OPENFL, and it appears in Fig. 6-1.

Type this procedure in the program following GET_FILE. Include the *** line, because you will have more disk handling routines to add to the program. You can place procedures anywhere after MAIN, but a little structure is neater.

Function 3DH is part of the set of extended disk-management functions, which are extremely easy to use compared to the old or

```
;**** DOS DISK FILE HANDLING ROUTINES

OPENFL  PROC NEAR
;Entry DX address of 0 terminated string in DS
        mov     ax,3D02H   ;3D = Open
        int     21h        ; 02 = read OR write
        ret
OPENFL  ENDP
```

Fig. 6-1. Procedure to open a file.

traditional functions. Like all DOS functions, the function number is put in AH. "Open a file," 3DH, has three options. The choice is placed in AL. Zero means open for reading, one means open for writing, and two means open for both reading and writing. Putting one in AL would do, because you are only going to read the file. You might choose that option. I have chosen to put two in AL in order to make OPENFL a more general procedure.

Like function 9 in WRITEM, this function expects a string address in DS:DX. Unlike function 9, which expects a question mark at the end of the string, function 3DH and other DOS extended disk functions wants a zero at the end of the string, which is why one was placed there in GET_FILE.

The file is either opened successfully or not. If the file is not opened successfully, the interrupt returns with the carry flag set to indicate an error. The AL register also contains a number indicating the kind of error. You can check these numbers in more advanced texts or the DOS manual. The most likely reason for an error is that the file was not on the disk (error 2). This is the error that will be assumed in the program, so you will simply check to see if the carry flag is set or not. If it is not set, the open was successful.

DOS has prepared the file for reading (or writing) and has given to the program an identification number to use to refer to the file from this point on. This number is called a *handle*; it is needed to read and close the file. Therefore it is important not to lose track of this number. The handle will be returned in the AX register.

OPENFL is then simple to use. Delete the NOP at MAIN1 and add the following:

```
MAIN1:  mov     dx,OFFSET FNAME ;Start of the file
        mov     si,dx           ; name Also to SI
                                ; for writing it later
        call    OPENFL          ;Open file for reading
        jnc     MAIN2           ;Carry = error
```

You satisfy the requirements of OPENFL by moving the offset of FNAME into DX. This offset is also moved into SI. You will understand more clearly why you do this later; it is preparation for writing the file name to the screen whether the open is successful or not.

Now you call OPENFL and await its results. If it returns a carry, then you quit. Before you do so, prepare to tell the user why. You could just say this:

```
    mov     dx,OFFSET NOTFND
    call    WRITEM
```

with NOTFIND being a string like, "File not found." The task will actually be done in a different way for two reasons. One is to show the user the name was properly retrieved, but the primary reason is for you to learn more character-handling techniques. What will be done is to give the user the message: "file name not found," using the actual file name.

Assume for the moment that you have a procedure that writes one character at a time to the screen, and this character is in AL. You shall soon have such a procedure, called DIROUT. You can build this procedure into another, which will take a zero-terminated string and send it out to the screen, character by character. STRINGO, shown in Fig. 6-2, does this.

The first instruction is LODSB (LOaD a String Byte). Remember STOSB used in GET_FILE. STOSB takes the byte in AL and stores it in the address referenced by ES:DI; then it updates DI (increases or decreases its value depending on the direction flag). LODSB takes the byte stored at the address referenced by DS:SI, loads it into AL,

---

```
        STRINGO PROC NEAR
        ;Entry SI has offset of 0 terminated string in DS
                lodsb           ;Put content in AL and inc SI
                cmp     al,0    ;Is it 0?
                jz      STREX   ;Yes, exit
                call    DIROUT  ;No, display it
                jmp     STRINGO ;Keep going
        STREX:  ret
        STRINGO ENDP
```

Fig. 6-2. Procedure to display a zero-terminated string.

and then updates SI. In your program, the direction flag is clear (up or forward), so LODSB has the effect of increasing SI. (Just as there is MOVSW and STOSW for word sized data, there is also the instruction LODSW.)

See what the STRING0 does. It is called with SI containing the offset of the string. It loads the character at this offset into AL and increases SI to the next address. If the character is not zero, it is sent to the screen, and the JMP returns to the top to loop again. When AL is zero, STRING0 returns.

DIROUT, shown in Fig. 6-3, uses one of several DOS functions to send characters to the screen. DOS almost always asks for its data in DX for words and in DL for bytes. Function 6 looks for one of two kinds of data in DL. The function is called "Direct console input/output," so it can be used to read input from the keyboard as well as to send characters to the screen. If DL had 0FFH in it, function 6 looks to read a character from the keyboard. Any other number is taken to be a character to be displayed.

Many times the characters you want displayed are in the AL register, obtained in ways like in STRING0. Thus DIROUT as written expects an ASCII code for a character in the AL register. The routine transfers it to DL, and it is sent out by the interrupt. Remember that when you wrote WRITEM, you pushed and then popped AX. That was because WRITEM altered AX, and you wanted to be sure to preserve the original value in AX. When DIROUT is called, it changes the value of two registers: AX, by moving 6 into AH, and DX, by moving whatever was in AL into DL. This makes no difference in your program, but, again, if you want DIROUT to be of general use, there might be times you want to preserve the values in those two registers. You do

```
DIROUT PROC NEAR   ;sends a char in al to the screen
       push    ax
       push    dx
       mov     dl,al
       mov     ah,6
       int     21h
       pop     dx
       pop     ax
       ret
DIROUT ENDP
```

Fig. 6-3. Procedure to send a character to the screen.

this by pushing their values on the stack and then popping them back at the end of the routine.

USING THE STACK

The stack is a place in memory for temporary storage and retrieval of numbers. These numbers can be offsets, segments, or any sort of number used in your programs. The programmer is not the only entity to make use of the stack. You have learned that when a procedure is called, the return address (the offset of the next instruction) is saved somewhere. The stack is the "somewhere." The 8088 PUSHes onto the stack the return addresses for CALL instructions, to be retrieved (POPped) into the IP with a RET. DOS and BIOS routines also use the stack when they are called.

When a .com program is entered, you know that the stack segment is the same as all other segments. Where in that area are the numbers stored and retrieved? A good place for the stack area would be at the top of the segment, because the PSP followed by your code and data start at the bottom. The authors of the 8088 language figured that out too. The area, actually the particular offset in the stack segment that is ready to receive a number, is pointed to by the SP (stack pointer). At the beginning of a .com program, the SP is set at the top of the stack segment, at offset 0FFFEH (given enough memory for a 64K segment). 0FFFEH and 0FFFFH are the addresses of the two highest bytes, the highest word in the segment.

Only words can be saved on the stack and retrieved—not bytes. If you were to instruct PUSH AL, you would get an error message from the assembler. When a number is saved (PUSHed) to the stack, the SP decreases and the high byte is stored; then it decreases and the low byte is stored. It is now pointing to that word. Sixteen-bit numbers are literally stacked, one under the other. As numbers are added to the stack, it grows downward in memory. When a retrieval instruction, like RET or POP, is given, the number retrieved is the last one placed on the stack, and the stack pointer increases by two.

Exercise 6-1: Looking at the Stack

In this exercise, I assume that you have enough memory for a 64K segment. Once again, enter Debug with tipe.com. Trace through the program, this time keeping an eye on SP. The SP starts at FFFE. Trace through the procedure WRITEM. When you enter WRITEM, you see the SP is now FFFC. FFFC and FFFD now hold the return address. See this by using dump, DFFFC FFFD. Note the word there, and check it with the address for the next instruction in MAIN, CALL GET__FILE. You will see it is the same, although stored backwards. Remember, the 8088 stores two-byte words backwards, low byte first, high byte next. The address ar FFFC and D appear as 06 01 for 0106.

See if you can follow the stack pointer all the way through the program. Look at the contents of the stack area from time to time using DFF80. Note that you are not the only one using this area. Debug has some numbers there. Particularly after a DOS function is called with INT 21H, you will see many numbers that were not there before. Because DOS and BIOS use your stack for their own calling, pushing, and popping, it is a good idea to reserve plenty of room for the stack, at least 80H of space, and more as your programs get more complicated and you learn to make more use of the stack. One way a program can crash is to have the stack grow downward over its data and instructions.

This exercise can give you a feel for how the stack works. The SP points to the word that is the next to be popped off the stack by a RET or by a POP instruction. The last on, first off sequence is used. The absolute values in the stack segment do not change with a POP or RET, the SP simply increases by two. A PUSH or CALL changes the SP, reducing it by two, and changes the actual values in the stack by placing the word at that offset.

Stack Management In .Com Files

In doing the exercise, you probably noted that the very highest word in the stack at 0FFFEH remained at zero. This quirk of the stack is only true for .com files. The program starts with the stack pointer at 0FFFEH and finishes at 0FFFEH when instruction INT 20H is executed. Let's review what you have learned to see why the 8088 folks keep a zero at the top of a .com file stack. First, what is stored at the offset zero in our program? Hint, remember the PSP. Second, what would happen if you ended the program with a RET rather than INT 20H? Here are the answers. At offset zero the two-byte instruction INT 20H is stored. If the stack pointer is at 0FFFEH, and the instruction RET is given, the zero there would be popped into the IP. The instruction at CS:0, INT 20H, would then be executed, and the program would be terminated. There truly is more than one way to skin a cat.

In using the stack, it is important to be compulsive about the order and matching of your pushes and pops. You can learn to do clever things with the stack, and there are some very useful tricks to learn. But for now, you will learn how to use it to save values and retrieve them in a very simple and efficient way—push them on the stack and pop them off. Because the only thing the CPU "knows" is the location of the SP, it does exactly what you ask. Here is an example:

```
PUSH      AX
PUSH      DX
—
—
POP       AX
POP       DX
```

See what will happen. Although there are the same number of POPs as PUSHes, the values in AX and DX would be switched. That would be fine if you wanted them switched, but not so fine if you did not, as is usually the case. You will be in trouble later in the program. Here's another example:

```
PUSH      AX
PUSH      DX
—
—
POP       DX
RET
```

What will happen here? When the RET is reached, whatever number was in AX is treated as the return address and is placed in the IP. I can assure you that you can end up in many interesting places in this way. The example clearly indicates the problem, but in long procedures, it is possible to lose track of what was pushed, even with careful scrutiny. This is one of the many reasons it is a good idea to run your programs through Debug before trying them at the DOS prompt.

A special case of PUSH and POP to be aware of is PUSHF and POPF. These instructions say "push the flag register" and "pop the flag register." Sometimes you will want to save the current status of one or more flags for later decision-making. If there is a possibility that some operation will change the flags, just push the contents of the register on the stack, to be retrieved when needed.

MEANWHILE, BACK AT THE PROGRAM

Take a look at DIROUT again. The procedure is written so that

68   IBM Assembly Language Simplified

the registers will be exactly the same as they were before the procedure was called. Type DIROUT and STRING0 after WRITEM in the program.

Here are additions to MAIN. The portion starting at MAIN1 looks like this:

```
MAIN1:      mov         dx,OFFSET FNAME ;Start of the file
            mov         si,dx      ; name Also to SI
                                   ; for writing it later
            call        OPENFL     ;Open file for reading
            jnc         MAIN2      ;Carry = error
            call        STRING0    ;  Show file name
            mov         dx,OFFSET NOTFIND ;   and
            call        WRITEM     ; Say not found
            jmp         SHORT DONE ; And exit
MAIN2:      nop
DONE:       int         20H        ;Quit
```

You see that if the open was successful, a jump is taken to MAIN2, ready to continue. If there was a carry, you send out the file name with STRING0, say "not found," and jump to the exit. Add NOTFND to the data:

NOTFND DB   ' not found$'

You might want to assemble, compile, and test tipe.com as written to this point. Figure 6-4 shows the program as it looks now. Starting with this figure, I adopt a few conventions to save some redundancy. I do not repeat the code for the procedures you have already written and tested, but just show their place in the program. I use dashes in MAIN to indicate instructions already written, so only the new code will be shown. Variables already defined are shown in lowercase without their initial values. The new ones appear with their values and labels in uppercase.

DEFINING VARIABLES

Given that the file exists, you need to have a place in memory into which to read the file. You have defined a place in memory, FNAME, into which to move the file name, and you have reserved 50 bytes for it. If you used the same technique to reserve memory for the text file, you would have to define a very large variable, say 60K bytes, to be large enough to accommodate almost any ASCII file. Because the variable space you reserve is a part of the program,

Opening and Reading the File 69

```
        ;TIPE.ASM - PROGRAM TO DISPLAY ASCII FILES
        ;       ALLOWING THE DISPLAY TO BE REVERSED
CR      EQU     0DH         ;Carriage return character
LF      EQU     0AH         ;Line feed character

        PUBLIC WRITEM,GET_FILE,DIROUT,STRINGO,OPENFL
        CODE    SEGMENT
                ASSUME CS:CODE,DS:CODE
                ORG     100H

MAIN:   ----
        ----
MAIN1:  mov     dx,OFFSET FNAME ;Startof the file
        mov     si,dx       ; name Also to SI
                            ; for writing it later
        call    OPENFL      ;Open file for reading
        jnc     MAIN2       ;Carry = error
        call    STRINGO     ; Show file name
        mov     dx,OFFSET NOTFND ;      and
        call    WRITEM      ; Say not found
        jmp     SHORT DONE  ; And exit
MAIN2:  nop
DONE:   int     20H         ;Quit
;End of MAIN

GET_FILE PROC NEAR
        ----
GET_FILE ENDP

;**** DOS DISK FILE HANDLING ROUTINES

OPENFL  PROC NEAR
;Entry DX address of 0 terminated string in DS
        mov     ax,3D02H    ;3D = Open
        int     21H         ; 02 = read OR write
        ret
CLEARS  ENDP

;**** DOS CHARACTER HANDLING ROUTINES ****

WRITEM  PROC NEAR
        ----
WRITEM  ENDP

DIROUT  PROC NEAR   ;send a char in al to the screen
        push    ax
        push    dx
        mov     dl,al
        mov     ah,6
```

Fig. 6-4. Opening the file and exiting if there is error.

```
                int     21H
                pop     dx
                pop     ax
                ret
        DIROUT ENDP

        STRINGO PROC NEAR
        ;Entry SI has offset of 0 terminated string in DS
                lodsb       ;Put content in AL and inc SI
                cmp     al,0    ;Is it 0?
                jz      STREX   ;Yes, exit
                call    DIROUT  ;No, display it
                jmp     STRINGO ;Keep going
        STREX:  ret
        STRINGO ENDP
        ;Data for the program
        PUBLIC TITL,FNAME,NOFILE,NOTFND

                titl    DB
                fname   DB
                nofile  DB
                NOTFND  DB      ' not found$'

                CODE    ENDS
                        END     MAIN
```

---

tipe.com would be over 60K in length and not too handy to keep on a disk.

Fortunately, you do not have to reserve a variable; you only need to give DOS an offset to tell it where to start placing the file. You tell DOS to start the file immediately after the code and data. This is at the offset of BUFFR, which is defined this way:

BUFFR   DB   ?

BUFFR is defined as a byte. By using the ? instead of a number, the assembler does not initialize the variable, but reserves the space called for, in this case one byte.

Actually you could put any byte here, because once the ASCII file is read into memory, what will be at offset BUFFR will be the very first byte of the ASCII file, with the rest following. Placing BUFR at the very end of the data allows reference to its OFFSET as the beginning address for the file and means you do not have to define a variable large enough to hold the file. Put BUFFR as the very last entry in the data area, right above CODE ENDS. Also, make sure that when you add new data, BUFFR remains the last entry.

When you use DB or DW to define a variable like BUFFR, TITL, or FNAME, you are doing three things. First, you are giving the assembler a label to stand for an offset in memory, although the label is optional. The label is needed only if the program refers to it, which is often the case. For example, in my definition of FNAME the second line has no label (DB CR,LF,'$'), because there is no reference to these three bytes in the program. Second, you are telling the assembler what type of variable it is (byte or word). Finally, you are telling the assembler how many of these you need; that is, how much memory to reserve for it.

Most, although not all, of the variables you have so far defined have been strings to be used by WRITEM. Take TITL as an example. TITL refers to the offset. DB gives its type. The ASCII characters (including CR and LF) each take up one byte and together determine the memory needed to store it. The assembler directive TITL DB <string> gives the assembler the offset to use when TITL is referred to in the program, and thanks to the combination of DB and its length, lets it know where the offset of the next variable starts.

You have defined another variable, FNAME, as DB 50 DUP (0). You could have defined it as 50 DUP ('u'), or 50 DUP (163), or 50 DUP (?). In all four cases, FNAME is known to the assembler as the offset of a byte variable that includes 50 bytes. In all cases the assembler reserves the 50 bytes. The difference is this: in the first case, the assembler fills these bytes with zeros; in the second case with u's; in the third case with 0A3Hs. The effect is to *initialize* the variables—the program starts with these values already in place. In the fourth case, the assembler simply reserves 50 bytes for the variable and keeps track of the next offset for the next variable.

If the initial value of the variable makes no difference, then if you can use ? in the declaration, as you have done with BUFFR, the assembler reserves the space called for, but does not put into the .obj file values to be placed in that space. Whatever is in memory at the time the program is loaded will remain there.

In order to show you some of the options you have in writing a program like tipe.com, I have defined Buffer with a question mark. My practice in writing programs is to give initial values to all variables, perhaps because it is easier to enter a zero, than a question mark, which requires pressing the SHIFT key.

Finish this lesson by pretending you are an assembler. The offset of variable DOG is 452H. The question is, what is the offset of variable CAT?

```
DOG        DB      5 DUP (0)
HORSE      DW      3 DUP (?)
CAT        DB      'C'
```

The answer is 45DH. Memory (in DS) would look like this, with the question marks standing for any byte currently in memory:

```
452 453 454 455 456 457 458 459 45A 45B 45C 45D
 0   0   0   0   0   ?   ?   ?   ?   ?   ?  43H
```

WILL IT FIT IN MEMORY?

Although you really want to get that file written into memory, there is some further checking to be done before doing so. As a preview, you are going to read the file into the data segment (which remains the same as the code segment), and you know that a segment cannot hold more than 64K of data. Most ASCII files are not that long, but it is a good idea to check the size just in case. In this case, what might happen when you move the characters of the file higher and higher in memory is that you could reach the top and run into the stack, with potentially disastrous results. You do not want your data to run into the stack any more than you want the stack to run into the data. The code at MAIN2 makes sure this does not happen.

As an aside, if the file would overwrite the stack, the program would crash. That can be a pain, but not necessarily a disaster. Some programs, like tipe.com, have not been developing valuable data, and so the only result is the bother of having to reboot. On the other hand, some programs have been developing valuable data, and it is at least a huge disappointment, if not a disaster, if they crash and the data is lost. That, of course, is why it is helpful to know sources of problems and have your programs handle them. Although you will learn about potential problems in tipe.com, you will discover new sources of trouble when you are writing other programs. That is what debugging is all about—making sure the expected works properly and catching the unexpected. Replace the NOP at MAIN2 with this code:

```
MAIN2:    mov     bx,ax           ;FSIZE needs handle in BX
          call    FSIZE           ;Returns AX = size of file
          jz      MAIN3           ;NZ means over 64K in size
MAINBG:   call    CLOSEFL         ;BX still has handle
          call    STRINGO         ;Show file name
          mov     dx,OFFSET BIGFILE ; say that
          call    WRITEM          ;Program can't take it
```

```
            jmp         SHORT DONE    ;And exit
MAIN3:      NOP
```

Look through the code. First the handle in AX is moved to BX, where it will be soon needed. Then the procedure FSIZE (file size) is called. If it returns NZ, then the file is over 64K in size and will not fit into the program segment. Add the following to the data section:

```
BIGFILE DB      ' is too large$'
```

If the file is over 64K, you close it and show the file name followed by the BIGFILE message. If it is less than 64K, you still need to check it against available memory. You do this at MAIN3.

First, write FSIZE. It is shown in Fig. 6-5. Put it after OPENFL. This procedure uses function 42H twice. This function moves a read or write file pointer. Remember, a pointer is a variable that holds an address; it points to an offset. Think of each byte in a file on a disk as having an offset starting with zero, the very first byte in the file. If the file pointer used by DOS in its read function has the value of 20H, it is pointing to the 33rd byte in the file. DOS nicely keeps track of this for you.

When you opened the file using function 3DH, DOS set the pointer

```
         FSIZE PROC NEAR ;Entry BX, handle of opened file
               push    dx
               push    cx
               sub     cx,cx     ;CX:DX offset for
               sub     dx,dx     ;  start of move both 0
               mov     ax,4202h  ;Move pointer, 2 = to EOF
               int     21h       ; New pointer in DX:AX
               cmp     dx,0      ;If DX > 0, more than 64K
               jnz     FSZEX     ;  exit zero flag clear
               push    ax        ;save on the stack and
               mov     FILESZ,ax ;in FILESZ for later
               mov     ax,4200h  ;CX and DX still 0
               int     21h       ;AL = 0 go back to start.
               pop     ax        ;Has file size
         FSZEX: pop    cx        ;Retrieve the pushed values
               pop     dx
               ret               ;Ret zero if 64K or less
         FSIZE ENDP             ;   and size in AX
```

Fig. 6-5. Procedure to obtain the size of a file.

74 IBM Assembly Language Simplified

to zero. In FSIZE you use function 42H twice, once to find the end of the file and thus its length, and a second time to move the pointer back to zero so it is again set properly for the read.

Like all DOS functions, 42H has its requirements. I will just cover those that are appropriate for use in tipe.com. First, I will present a brief lesson about double words, which are used in this function.

You are now familiar with expressions like DS:82H, ES:SI, meaning segment address and offset. There are other expressions you encounter in the literature (and in this chapter), like CX:DX or DX:AX, that mean something else. These are references to *double words*, which are four bytes, or two 16-bit words. Files, for instance, can be longer than 64K. In order to reference their length, two words, and thus two registers, are needed. The first register of the pair holds the most significant word; the second holds the least significant word. Whenever you see expressions showing pairs of registers joined by a colon, look at the first register. If it is a segment register, the expression represents an address—the segment and the offset. If it is not a segment register, the expression represents a double word.

GETTING THE FILE SIZE

Function 42H moves the file pointer to your specifications and returns the value of the pointer in DX:AX. Option 2, which was put in AL, enables you to determine the file size, because it moves the pointer to the end of the file (EOF) plus an offset. The offset must be in CX:DX.

If you set each of these registers to zero, the value returned in DX:AX (0 + EOF) will be the size of the file. If DX, the most significant word, is returned as anything but zero, the file is over 64K, and too big for the program. You test DX for zero, and jump to the exit if it is not zero. Note that you do not jump to the return because you must pop CX and DX or face the consequences.

If DX is zero, you can ignore it and consider the value in AX as the file size. You will want to take a look at that size immediately upon return from this procedure, but you will also use it later in the program for reading the file. For immediate use, you save AX by pushing it on the stack. For later use, you store it in a variable called FILESZ:

FILESZ   DW   ?

Put FILESZ right before BUFFR. It is given the type DW because you

Opening and Reading the File

```
CLOSEFL PROC    NEAR    ;BX has handle
        mov     ax,3E00H
        int     21h
        ret
CLOSEFL ENDP
```

Fig. 6-6. Procedure to close a file.

are interested in the 16-bit value in AX. Once a variable is defined, you can move data in and out of it. In FSIZE, you say **MOV FILESZ,AX**, and the data is stored with the low byte starting at the offset of FILESZ.

Consider the second use of function 42H, to reset the file pointer back to zero. Right now it is sitting at the end of the file. If you ask DOS to read the file, it starts with the byte pointed to; in this case it would be the end, and nothing would be read. To reset the pointer you put 0 in AL, (**MOV AX,4200H** does double duty: AH gets 42H, and AL gets 0). The pointer is moved to the beginning of the file plus the offset in DX:CX, both of which are still zero. You then exit with the POPs, and return with the zero flag set. It is still set from **CMP DX,0** because the move instructions do not affect the flags, and the interrupt preserved them for you.

Look at MAIN. After calling FSIZE, the first task is to check the zero flag. Zero means no error, and a **JZ MAIN3** jumps around an error exit. If the file is too big for the program, the first thing to do is close the file. CLOSEFL shown in Fig. 6-6 will do that for you.

Put **CLOSEFL** in with the DOS disk file handling routines. It is a simple little procedure using function 3EH—close a file handle. It asks for the handle in BX. The handle is still there because you have not touched BX in FSIZE. Closing a file releases the file's handle and updates the directory listing of files that have been written. Files opened to be read do not have to be closed. They have not been changed in any way. It is necessary to close files that have been altered, because otherwise the directory entry for that file will not be updated. Although unnecessary for your program, I think it is good practice to close files, even if you are only reading them, for some day you might be writing programs that end up trying to open more files than are allowed. Once a file is closed, its handle can be assigned to a different file.

If the file is more than 64K, the file is closed, the file name is sent out with STRING0 (SI was not changed in FSIZE and still has the offset of FNAME), followed by the message "is too large," and a jump is taken to the exit.

You are almost—yes, almost—ready to read the file. But, although you know the file is no more than 64K, what if it is 64K minus one byte? It is still too big, so you have one last check a fairly simple one that goes like this:

```
MAIN3:    mov     di,OFFSET BUFFR  ;Start of file
          mov     cx,0FEFFh        ;Leave 100H for Stack
          sub     cx,di            ;Memory left for our file
          cmp     cx,ax            ;Space minus file size
          jc      MAINBG           ;Carry means too big
```

Replace the NOP at MAIN3 with this code. It does a bit of simple math. The text file starts at the offset of BUFFR and extends upward in memory. The top of memory in the program segment is offset 0FFFFH. You need to let the stack have plenty of room to move downward, so make sure that you reserve 100H of space for the stack. 0FFFFH minus 100H is 0FEFFH. This means that the ASCII file can use the memory only up to FEFFH of the program segment. The available memory, then, is 0FEFFH minus the offset of BUFFR.

Finding the available memory is quite straightforward, as you can see. Put the wanted numbers in registers and use SUB to subtract them. A first choice of registers for math is AX, the accumulator, but AX right now is holding the file size, so you should pick some other registers. Any of the data registers will do, as would SI, DI, and BP, but SI has the offset of FNAME and BX has the file handle, both of which you want to keep. Therefore you need to choose from what is left. You see my arbitrary choices. SUB CX,DI puts the difference in CX. Remember that the first operand of the two is always the one affected. Then CMP CX,AX sets the carry flag if AX is larger than CX.

Remember that in subtraction (or comparison), if the carry flag is set, the second number was larger than the first, and the result would be negative. If the carry flag is not set, the result was positive. In this case, if the carry flag is set, it means the file is too big, so you jump back to MAINBG and use the same routine you used for files larger than 64K.

Figure 6-7 shows the code developed to this point. Create the .com file and check to make sure that it is working properly.

```
;TIPE.ASM - PROGRAM TO DISPLAY ASCII FILES
;        ALLOWING THE DISPLAY TO BE REVERSED

CR      EQU     0DH     ;Carriage return character
LF      EQU     0AH     ;Line feed character

PUBLIC WRITEM,GET_FILE,DIROUT,STRINGO,OPENFL,FSIZE
PUBLIC CLOSEFL
CODE    SEGMENT
        ASSUME CS:CODE,DS:CODE
        ORG     100H

MAIN:   ----
        ----
MAIN1:  ----
        ----
MAIN2:  mov     bx,ax           ;FSIZE needs handle in BX
        call    FSIZE           ;Returns AX = size of file
        jz      MAIN3           ;NZ means over 64k in size
MAINBG: call    CLOSEFL ;BX still has handle
        call    STRINGO         ;Show file name
        mov     dx,OFFSET BIGFILE ; say that
        call    WRITEM  ;Program can't take it
        jmp     SHORT DONE      ;And exit
MAIN3:  mov     di,OFFSET BUFFR ;Start of file
        mov     cx,0FEFFh       ;Leave 100H for Stack
        sub     cx,di   ;Memory left for our file
        cmp     cx,ax   ;Space minus file size
        JC      MAINBG  ;Carry means too big
        nop
DONE:   int     20H     ;Quit
;End of Main

GET_FILE PROC NEAR
        ----
GET_FILE ENDP


;**** DOS DISK FILE HANDLING ROUTINES

OPENFL  PROC NEAR
        ----
OPENFL ENDP
FSIZE PROC NEAR ;Entry BX, handle of opened file
        push    dx
        push    cx
        sub     cx,cx   ;CX:DX offset for
        sub     dx,dx   ;  start of move both 0
```

Fig. 6-7. Opening the file and exiting if there is an error or not enough memory.

```
                mov     ax,4202h ;Move pointer, 2 = to EOF
                int     21H      ; New pointer in DX:AX
                cmp     dx,0     ;If DX > 0, more than 64K
                jnz     FSZEX    ; exit zero flag clear
                push    ax       ;save on the stack and
                mov     FILESZ,ax ;in FILESZ for later
                mov     ax,4200H ;CX and DX still 0
                int     21H      ;AL = 0 go back to start.
                pop     ax       ;Has file size
        FSZEX:  pop     cx       ;Retrieve the pushed values
                pop     dx
                ret              ;Ret zero if 64K or less
        FSIZE ENDP               ; and size in AX


        CLOSEFL PROC    NEAR    ;BX has handle
                mov     ax,3E00H
                int     21H
                ret
        CLOSEFL ENDP


        ;**** DOS CHARACTER HANDLING ROUTINES ****


        WRITEM PROC NEAR
                ----
        WRITEM ENDP

        DIROUT  PROC NEAR
                ----
        DIROUT ENDP

        STRINGO PROC NEAR
                ----
        STRINGO ENDP


        ;Data for the program
        PUBLIC TITL,FNAME,NOFILE,NOTFND,FILESZ,BIGFILE
        PUBLIC BUFFR


        titl    DB
        fname   DB
        nofile  DB
        notfnd  DB
        FILESZ  DW      ?
        BIGFILE DB      ' is too large$'
        BUFFR   DB      ?       ;End of our data and
                                ; beginning of file

        CODE    ENDS
                END     MAIN
```

Exercise 6-2: Using Debug to Simulate Conditions

There are times when you want to test procedures and instructions but do not have the necessary conditions to do so. For instance, I do not have any ASCII files over 62K (about the size of the available memory), but I do have some .exe files of considerable length so I can use them to test the file size checking routines. They work, because all you are doing at this point is seeing if a file fits into the available memory.

Another more general way to check the code is by using Debug's R (Register) command. This is an extremely useful command to get to know. Just entering R displays the state of all the registers. Entering R with a register designation allows you to change the values of registers at will. For instance, entering RBX shows you the current state of the BX register and allows you to change that value. Start Debug with tipe.com and any existing file, even a tiny file of 30 bytes.

Find the procedure, FSIZE; then use G to go to the instruction immediately following the first INT 21H. This instruction says CMP DX,0. Then at the prompt, enter RDX. Debug gives you a colon prompt to enter any 16-bit hexadecimal number you wish (or press ENTER to skip). Enter any nonzero number you choose, changing DX from 0000 to your number. Proceed with your trace and check to see if it goes according to plan. FSIZE should return with the zero flag clear and should exit after showing the error.

Now test the second file size check. Enter Debug in the same way as last time, but this time go to the instruction following the call to FSIZE, which says JZ MAIN3. Enter RAX and then give AX the value of FFF0, which you know has to be too big. Then trace through the program to make sure it exits properly. Let me encourage you to test little used parts of your programs carefully. Often these are error-handling routines. Even though some errors might rarely be encountered, it is important to be sure the error handler is working properly.

READING THE FILE TO MEMORY

You have written quite a bit of assembly-language code to get to the point of reading the file. It is important in all programming to catch errors that could lead to problems for the user, to inform the user what the problems are, to allow for correction if possible, and if not, to exit politely and gracefully. High-level language like BASIC and Pascal either do the error catching or make it much easier for

```
READIN PROC NEAR
;Entry SI address of file name, BX has file handle
        mov     dx,OFFSET READMS    ;Show 'Reading'
        call    WRITEM
        call    STRINGO              ;File name
        mov     cx,FILESZ           ;# of bytes to read
        mov     dx,OFFSET BUFFR ;where to put them
        call    READFL
        jnc     REDA
        mov     dx,OFFSET READER ;Somethg is wrong
        call    WRITEM
        jmp     SHORT REDX
REDA:   call    CLOSEFL             ;BX still has handle
REDX:   ret
READIN ENDP
```

Fig. 6-8. Procedure to orchestrate the reading of a file.

the programmer to do so. With assembly language, you have to do most of it yourself. However, you will find that when you have written procedures and sequences of code to do various error-trapping jobs for you, you can use them over and over again in programs that could be affected by the same type of errors.

Now that you are finally ready to read the file, you should find it pretty straightforward. You will CALL READIN, which is shown in Fig. 6-8. Here are two messages to be put into the data:

```
READMS   DB      CR,LF,'Reading $'
READER   DB      ' Disk read error$'
```

Type READIN in the program after MAIN, and the data in before BUFFR. Scan the code. The first thing done is to say what is happening: the file is being read. READFL, which does the actual reading, is called to do the task. You then check that the read is OK. DOS sets the carry flag if there was an error. If the read was successful, you close the file and exit; if not, you send an error message and exit. If there was an error, the carry flag will still be set because WRITEM will not affect the flag register.

You are familiar with WRITEM and STRINGO by now, so let's go directly to READFL, the procedure to read the file that is shown in Fig. 6-9. Put this with the DOS disk file handling routines.

You can see what function 3FH expects. The address in DS:DX is the place where you want the results of the reading to start. The

```
READFL  PROC NEAR
;Handle in BX, address in DS:DX, num in CX
        mov     ax,3F00h
        int     21h        ;Carry set if error
        ret                ; else AX has bytes read
READFL  ENDP
```

Fig. 6-9. Procedure to read a file.

reason I use this language is that you do not have to read the total file in at one time. In this program you will read the entire file into memory at once and place it starting at the offset of BUFFR, but you could read the file in one byte at a time, 30 at a time, or any number at a time. If you chose any of these options, then each time you called READFL you would have to update DX. CX contains the number of bytes that you want read. For the moment, let's assume you want to read in one byte at a time. You start with CX holding one and with DX set to the offset of BUFFR. You call READFL; then you want to read another byte. If you do not change DX, the next byte will be read into exactly the same spot—the offset of BUFFR. The solution is to INC DX after every read, before looping back for the next.

Look back to READIN to see how you have set up to call READFL. First you know that the handle is still in BX. BX has not been changed by any instructions since the handle was moved into it. (If you were to have any doubt, you could have saved the handle in a variable, say HANDLE, like you have saved the file size in FILESZ.) Then you set up CX by moving FILESZ into CX. Finally you set DX to the offset of BUFFER. Now you are ready to call READFL to read the entire file.

If there was no error, the function returns the number of bytes read in the AX register. CX asks for a certain number; AX should have that number. A simple CMP could tell you if the two are the same. The zero flag should be set. READIN does not check the number of bytes read, because the whole file is to be read in one call to READFL, and you are assured there is plenty of room for it. If, however, you were to read a file in smaller chunks, say 100 bytes at a time, and AX is different from CX but there was no carry, you would know that the end of file was safely reached.

If there was an error in reading the file, DOS will set the carry flag and return a code number for the error in AL. Two kinds of errors DOS returns are "invalid handle" and the mysterious "access denied." You know the handle in BX is valid, because the open was successful. The other error suggests some sort of problem with the disk, and this is what is assumed with READER.

```
;TIPE.ASM - PROGRAM TO DISPLAY ASCII FILES
;        ALLOWING THE DISPLAY TO BE REVERSED
CR      EQU     0DH     ;Carriage return character
LF      EQU     0AH     ;Line feed character

PUBLIC WRITEM,GET_FILE,DIROUT,STRINGO,OPENFL,FSIZE
PUBLIC CLOSEFL,READIN,READFL
CODE    SEGMENT
        ASSUME CS:CODE,DS:CODE
        ORG     100H

MAIN:   ----
        ----
MAIN1:  ----
        ----
MAIN2:  ----
        ----
MAINBG: ----
        ----
MAIN3:  ----
        ----            ;JC MAINBG is last instruction here
        call    READIN  ;Reads the file into buffr
        JC      DONE    ;A read error was given
        nop
DONE:   int     20H     ;Quit
;End of MAIN

GET_FILE PROC NEAR
        ----
GET_FILE ENDP

READIN PROC NEAR
;Entry SI address of file name, BX has file handle
        mov     dx,OFFSET READMS  ;Show 'Reading'
        call    WRITEM
        call    STRINGO              ;File name
        mov     cx,FILESZ     ;# of bytes to read
        mov     dx,OFFSET BUFFR ;where to put them
        call    READFL
        jnc     REDA
        mov     dx,OFFSET READER ;Somethg is wrong
        call    WRITEM
        jmp     SHORT REDX
REDA:   call    CLOSEFL       ;BX still has handle
REDX:   ret
READIN ENDP

;**** DOS DISK FILE HANDLING ROUTINES
```

Fig. 6-10. Reading the file into memory.

```
OPENFL  PROC NEAR
        ----
OPENFL  ENDP


FSIZE PROC NEAR
        ----
FSIZE ENDP

CLOSEFL PROC    NEAR
        ----
CLOSEFL ENDP

READFL  PROC NEAR
;Handle in BX, address in DS:DX, num in CX
        mov     ax,3F00H
        int     21H       ;Carry set if error
        ret               ; else AX has bytes read
READFL  ENDP

;**** DOS CHARACTER HANDLING ROUTINES ****

WRITEM PROC NEAR
        ----
WRITEM ENDP

DIROUT  PROC NEAR
        ----
DIROUT  ENDP
STRINGO PROC NEAR
        ----
STRINGO ENDP

;Data for the program
PUBLIC TITL,FNAME,NOFILE,NOTFND,FILESZ,BIGFILE
PUBLIC READMS,READER,BUFFR

titl    DB
fname   DB
nofile  DB
notfnd  DB
filesz  DW
bigfile DB
READMS  DB      CR,LF,'Reading $'
READER  DB      ' Disk read error$'
buffr   DB      ?         ;End of our data and
                          ; beginning of file
CODE    ENDS
        END     MAIN
```

Check to see that your code corresponds to Fig. 6-10. Create the .com file and trace it carefully through Debug. Assuming the read was successful (and I will assume that for you), find your file in memory using the dump command. To do so, remember the last procedure in the code is STRING0. Use U to find that code; then use D to dump the data after it. Soon you will see BUFFR. Those of you with symbolic debuggers can easily dump the file to the screen using the symbol BUFFR.

The file is now in BUFFR. The next task is to get it to the screen.

CHAPTER 7

Setting Up the Screen

The contents of the file now reside in memory, ready to be displayed to the screen. The next task is preparing the screen for showing the file. In preparing and manipulating the screen, you will ask the help of BIOS. BIOS stands for basic input output system and is more basic than DOS. It really is ROM-BIOS, which is built into your computer's memory and is specific to the hardware quirks of your particular computer. You use the services of BIOS indirectly when you use DOS interrupts.

It is good practice to let DOS do the work, because then your programs can work on any computer run by DOS—there could be quirks in another computer's BIOS. There are times, however, when the only way you can accomplish a task is to call upon BIOS directly. Except for sending characters to the screen, DOS has no screen handling functions, so here you must use BIOS. You will find, in most cases, that BIOS is as easy to use as DOS.

BIOS DISPLAY SERVICES

The particular BIOS interrupt that handles display functions is INT 10H. I used the term *functions* because you are now familiar with DOS functions that go into the AH register for DOS's INT 21H. For INT 10H, the options also go into the AH register, but these are referred to as *services* rather than *functions*. DOS gives functions; BIOS gives services. You use INT 10H exactly like you used INT 21H. You find out what is required and put it into the proper registers. Your program uses two of the services of INT 10H, one to clear the screen and one to move the cursor. First, let's take a short tour of the video display and define some terms.

I have used the word *screen*. With a monochrome monitor *screen* and *display* are synonymous. There is an area in high memory (starting at 0B0000H, segment 0B000) that holds the characters that are displayed to the screen at any given time. With color capabilities *display* takes on a different meaning. Starting at 0B8000H (segment 0B800) there is enough memory reserved to hold characters for as many as eight different displays to the screen. These *displays* are called *pages* and are referred to in your programs by numbers starting with zero. The one you can see is called the *active display page*. There is a video service that can set the active display page that programmers can use to make visible any display page.

There are video services that allow you to write directly to the display. These require you to designate which display page is to receive the characters. The display page does not have to be the active one. While one page is being displayed to the screen, you can have your program write to another, and switch back and forth between the two (or more). For instance, among the very first things a word processing program I use does is to set the active page to zero and then write the help menu to page one. Whenever the menu is asked for, the display instantly changes to display it.

The display also has a certain *mode*. There are graphic modes and text modes. For our purposes, I will only discuss the text modes, of which there are four for machines with color capabilities. The mode determines the number of columns (40 or 80) and whether or not there is color. Mode 0 is 40 × 25 black and white. Mode 1 is 40 × 25 color. Mode 2 is 80 × 25 black and white. Mode 3 is 80 × 25 color. With monochrome monitors there is only one mode, 80 × 25 black and white, which has the mode number 7. As you might imagine, BIOS has services that allow you to check the current mode and to set the mode.

Characters are stored in their pages as two bytes. The first byte is the character to be displayed. The second byte is the *attribute*. The attribute determines how the character will appear on the screen. It may be one of many colors on many backgrounds. It may be solid or blinking. Appendix B explains and shows the codes used for the various combinations.

Exercise 7-1: Viewing the Video Display Pages and Changing Attributes

Once more enter Debug. First, make sure there is some text on the top several lines of your display. Pressing U several times will do it. Use the dump command to look at your screen display located at B0000H for monochrome monitors and B8000H otherwise. Enter DB000:0 or DB800:0. See how the characters are stored; each one is followed by a byte. That second byte is the code for the current attribute. Note, that each line of text is the same length 0A0H or 160 bytes if you are in an 80-column mode, or 50H or 80 bytes for a 40 column mode.

If you are in an 80-column color mode, try this to change the attribute at the beginning of the third row. First make sure there is a character at the beginning of the fourth row. If not, press ENTER until row four begins with some character. Then use the E (enter) command to change bytes in memory. (When you use the E command, the lines will scroll up so what was row four is now row three.) You used E in Chapter 4 to put a dollar sign in TITL. The offset of the first character in the third row is 140H and its attribute is stored at 141H. At the hyphen prompt, enter Eb800:141. Debug will display the current byte (the attribute) at that location followed by a period. Enter the number 2.

If you want to change the next byte, press the space bar and the next byte will be displayed for you. Press ENTER when you are finished. In this case, just enter the 2 and press ENTER. Watch the screen when you press ENTER. You have changed the attribute to green on black, and because the screen has scrolled up a line since it was displayed; the character at the beginning of row 2 has this attribute. Experiment if you like with other numbers and see what you get. You are doing what BIOS will do for you when a service asks for an attribute—placing it in the display memory.

For those of you with monochrome monitors, do the exercise by entering at EB000:141 the byte 70 (reverse video). Your choices are four: 0FH (white on black), 70H (black on gray), 07H (gray on black), or F0H (blinking black on gray).

Controlling the Cursor

The cursor is another display characteristic that you can control. There is a service to read the position of the cursor on any page, whether it is active or not, and a service to place the cursor on any page.

You use only the latter in the program because you always know where the cursor is, and so do not need to find its position. Being able to retrieve and then use the current cursor position is very handy in programs in which the user types in a response that could be of variable length and you want to send some characters to the screen right after that response.

The cursor position is designated by its row and column. It is important to know that the first row to BIOS is numbered zero, and the first column is also zero. Row numbers run from zero to 24 (18H), and column numbers from zero to 79 (4FH) or zero to 39 (27H), depending on the mode (80 column or 40 column).

The Active Display Page

One of the video services used in your program asks for the active display page. The default active page is zero when the computer is booted, and your program assumes that zero is the active page. One video service will also ask for the attribute. You could choose any you wish, with one exception—only combinations of black and white or black and gray can be used for a monochrome monitor. Your program makes two assumptions: the display is in an 80-column mode, and the active display page is zero. The attribute used is gray on black (07H), so it will be general to all displays, the code for monochrome or color.

Here is the code that will set up the screen for the display of the file:

```
mov     dh,24       ;Last row
call    CLEARS      ;Clr screen thru row in DH
call    LINEOUT     ;Dashes across row 23
call    BOTTOM      ;Cursor at start of row 24
mov     dx,OFFSET MES1  ;Prompt message
mov     cx,FNAME-MES1   ;Number of chars
call    WRITE       ;Write to the screen
sub     dx,dx       ;Set row and col to 0
call    CURSOR      ;Put the cursor there
```

Look over the code before reading the explanation. It calls several procedures you will need to write. In brief, you are going to clear the screen, put a line of dashes (- - -) across row 23, display a prompt message on the bottom line (row 24), and then set the cursor back to the top of the screen. (Remember to BIOS, the last row in a 80 x 25 display is 24, not 25.)

CLEARING THE SCREEN

First you will write a routine that will clear the screen. The procedure CLEARS is shown in Fig. 7-1. Type this procedure in, including the ** line, right before the data in the program.

As a useful generic procedure, the values in all registers that will be changed are saved by being pushed to the stack. AH has 6 to call BIOS service 6, which scrolls the active page up a specified number of lines. More literally, it scrolls a window of the active page because you must specify the row and column for the top left corner (in CH and CL) and the row and column of the bottom right hand corner (in DH and DL). You can make the window the whole screen or any portion of it by the values you place in CX and DX.

AL receives the number of lines you want blanked at the bottom of the window. If, for instance, AL had 2, the display in the window would move up two lines; then the last two lines would be blanked. The whole window will be blanked if AL has the value of zero, which is the case in CLEARS.

You use CLEARS for two purposes in the program. First you use it to blank or clear the entire screen. The entire screen is the window from row zero, column zero to row 24 (18H), column 79 (4FH). Second, you use it to blank from row zero through row 22, not removing the last two rows, which will have information for the user. You have two windows, the same in all respects except for the bottom two rows.

```
;**** BIOS SCREEN HANDLING ROUTINES

CLEARS  PROC    NEAR      ;Entry DH has row of bot
        push    ax
        push    bx
        push    cx
        sub     cx,cx     ;top row and col, both 0
        mov     dl,79     ;Col of bottom of window
        mov     ax,0600h  ;AL = 0 = blank window
        mov     bh,07H    ;Attribute, gray on white
        int     10H       ;BIOS video display interrupt
        pop     cx
        pop     bx
        pop     ax
        ret
CLEARS  ENDP
```

Fig. 7-1. Procedure to clear the screen.

Service 6 wants to find the top row in CH and the top column in CL. Because each shall be zero for both uses of CLEARS, you put a zero in CX by substituting it from itself or by using either MOV CX,0 or MOV CH,0 and MOV CL,0. The bottom row goes in DH, and the bottom column in DL. DH is different depending on whether you want it to be 24 or 22, but DL is the same—the last column—so you can put 79 in DL. DH is set in the program before CLEARS is called.

All that is left is to put the attribute in BH, right where BIOS wants it. Because 07H is the attribute for gray on black, you move it into BH. Now you can clear the entire screen in MAIN with the following:

```
mov     dh,24
call    CLEARS
```

Exercise 7-2: Creating Windows

Here is a simple exercise using the A (assemble command) of Debug to enter assembly code directly into Debug. The instructions make up a version of CLEARS, which allow you to experiment with changing its various parameters. Enter Debug and at the prompt enter A100 (Assemble starting at 100). Debug displays the current CS and then 100, as shown:

14F3:100

It awaits your entry. When the entry is complete and you press ENTER, the next offset is displayed, and so on. The assembly is complete when you press ENTER without entering any characters.

Here is a little program to create. I will list just the offsets that Debug gives you and put my comments in parentheses.

```
100   MOV CX,FFFF      (set up for a big loop 65535 times)
103   PUSH CX
104   MOV CX,510       (top row = 5 top col = 16)
107   MOV DX,1020      (bot row = 16 bot col = 32)
10A   MOV BH,20        (black on green)
10C   MOV AX,600       (clear the window)
10F   INT 10
111   POP CX
112   LOOP 103         (back for the loop)
114
```

Check your code carefully. If you see any mistakes, you can reassemble the instruction. Suppose you made a mistake in the instruction at 107. Just enter A107, and enter the corrected line. When you are ready, you can trace through this program just like one you entered from the command line.

Run through it once using G112. Use T to go back to 103 and then try it again. That might get boring 65533 times more, so experiment with changing CX at 104 and/or DX at 107. Use A104 to change CX and A107 for DX. Alternatively, you could use the register command to change the contents of these registers before INT 10 is executed. Remember that rows range from zero to 18 in hex and columns from zero to 4F. Make sure the top row and column are less than the bottom row and column; for example:

```
104    MOV CX,1630      (top row = 22 top col = 48)
107    MOV DX,1840      (bot row = 24 bot col = 64)
```

If the top row and column are greater than the bottom row and column, no harm will be done, except you will get a window bigger than the screen. You might want to try it and see what happens.

Here is a chance to check out the attribute codes in Appendix B, although you will see just the background colors. Change 10A to give BH a different attribute. Remember, you can quit at anytime with Q.

MOVING THE CURSOR

The next step is to put a message on the bottom line showing the user the options available (forward, reverse, quit), but before that you will add a simple cosmetic touch, placing a line of dashes across row 23 to separate the text of the file from the message. LINEOUT is the procedure to do that.

The first task of LINEOUT is to call CURSOR. Before you can display anything on line 23, you need to place the cursor there. CURSOR uses video service 2, to position the cursor. Put the CURSOR procedure, shown in Fig. 7-2, in the program after CLEARS.

Service 2 asks for three kinds of information. It wants the display page in BH. You want to move the cursor in the active page, which you presume to be zero. So the BH register is set to zero by SUBbing it. (Note that, I have used SUB REGISTER,REGISTER several times to put in a zero value. This is handy in that it takes one less byte than MOV REGISTER,0, but remember, it does affect the zero flag. Sometimes you might not want to change the zero flag.) Then Service 2 wants the cursor location, the row in DH and the column in DL. All that is

```
CURSOR  PROC    NEAR        ;Entry: DH = ROW, DL = COL
        push    ax
        push    bx
        sub     bh,bh       ;Screen Display page is 0
        mov     ax,0200h    ;set cursor
        int     10H         ;BIOS video display interrupt
        pop     bx
        pop     ax
        ret
CURSOR  ENDP
```

Fig. 7-2. Procedure to move the cursor.

needed in calling CURSOR is to set up DH and DL and call it. Again, this procedure has been written to preserve all of the registers it uses.

Now you can write LINEOUT, which sets the cursor at the beginning of row 23 and uses DIROUT to send out 80 dashes. Figure 7-3 holds LINEOUT. This procedure is probably clear to you except for the addition of a new instruction, LOOP. This is an instruction you will use quite a bit. In writing programs, you will find that you use many *loops*, or repeated instructions. A loop was used in STRING0, which looped back until AL had a zero. With STRING0, the number of characters in a string is unknown. On the other hand, with LINEOUT, the number of characters on a line is known. There are 80 (assuming, which LINEOUT does, an 80-column display).

Whenever you know the exact number of times you want a task to be done, you can put that count in a register, do the task, decrease the register, test for zero, and loop back if it is not zero. For instance,

```
LINEOUT PROC NEAR
        mov     dh,23       ;Row 23
        sub     dl,dl       ;Column 0
        call    CURSOR
        mov     cx,80       ;Set count to 80
        mov     al,'-'
LLOOP:  call    DIROUT      ;Send out the dash
        loop    LLOOP       ;Decrease CX and
        ret                 ;go again if not 0
LINEOUT ENDP
```

Fig. 7-3. Procedure to display a line of dashes.

you could put the following after CALL CURSOR in LINEOUT:

```
            mov     dx,80
            mov     al,'-'
LLOOP:      call    DIROUT
            dec     dx
            jnz     LLOOP
```

That will certainly do the job. It will do it because DEC affects the zero flag. If the result of decreasing a register is zero, the zero flag is set. The 8088, however, very nicely includes the special instruction LOOP, which automatically decreases the count as long as the count is in the CX register. LOOP decreases CX, and if CX is not zero, it jumps to the label you have provided. Remember that CX is designed to be used as a counter. If, by the way, the offset indicated by the label with LOOP is more than 128 bytes away, the assembler will give you the "Relative jump out of range" message. Then you would have to resort to another means of creating the loop.

Meanwhile, back in MAIN, the dashes have been sent to the screen and preparations are being made to show the prompt message. The first step is once again to move the cursor, this time to the beginning of the bottom line, which is where the message will go. BOTTOM, which will be used again, does the trick:

```
BOTTOM PROC NEAR
            mov     dx,1800h        ;ready for row 24 col 0
BOTTOM ENDP
```

"What is the trick?" you might be asking. Yes, there is a trick—and that's my main reason for showing you BOTTOM as a procedure. You have been carefully putting RETs at the end of all the procedures. The trick with bottom is that you place it right before CURSOR in the program. BOTTOM is a procedure that *falls through* to the next one. A RET is encountered at the end of CURSOR. By writing the two procedures back-to-back you save four bytes of code, three for a CALL and one for a RET.

Be sure that when you type BOTTOM you put it right before CURSOR, because when it is called, whatever code follows it will be executed. Assuming that BOTTOM immediately precedes CURSOR, the cursor will be placed at the beginning of row 24 by putting 1800H in DX. (Hex is convenient here, because you can put the row in DH and column in DL in one fell swoop.)

The cursor now sits at the beginning of the last row. Here is the message to be put on that line:

```
MES1       DB          ' Any key = forward  '
           DB          '<ESC> = reverse ^C = quit'
```

Place MES1 with the data right before FNAME. (Like TITL, it could fit on one 80 column line.) There is no reason not to put a ? at the end of MES1 and use WRITEM. Alternatively, you could add a comma and then a zero after the last quote and use STRING0—but then I would not be able to show you a third way to write characters to the screen. The method you will use is the procedure WRITE, which is in Fig. 7-4.

Here you are back to DOS. You have encountered a function that I have not yet introduced to you. Function 40H writes to a file or device. This is the same function you will use in Chapter 12 to write a file in memory back to the disk. Note its similarity to function 3FH, which you used in READFL to read the file into memory: the handle is in BX, the address of the beginning of data is in DS:DX, and number of bytes is in CX.

DOS reserves five handles for devices, handles 0 through 4. (You might have noticed in tracing through READFL that the handle given the file was always 5, the next available handle number after the reserved handles.) Here are the reserved handles:

```
0     Standard input device (keyboard)
1     Standard output device (screen)
2     Standard error output device (screen)
3     Standard auxiliary device (serial port)
4     Standard printer device
```

```
WRITE PROC NEAR
;Entry Address string in DS:DX, Length in CX
        push    ax
        push    bx
        mov     bx,0001 ; 1 handle for strd output
        mov     ax,4000h ;write to file or device
        int     21h     ; in this case the screen
        pop     bx
        pop     ax
        RET
WRITE ENDP
```

Fig. 7-4. Procedure to write a string to the standard output device.

The standard output device is the screen. The number of this handle is one, so by putting that number in BX, the data defined by DX and CX are sent to the screen. (If you put the number 4 in BX, the data will be sent to the printer—if you have turned it on.)

In order to use WRITE to send a string to the screen, you need to know its address and length. The address is easy; in this case, its offset is OFFSET MES1. You could count up the number of characters in the string and place them in CX, but that seems like a lot of work, so you can let the assembler do the work with this instruction:

    MOV   CX,FNAME-MES1

Given this structure, the assembler retrieves the offsets of both variables and subtracts the second offset from the first, placing the difference in CX. Because FNAME immediately follows MES1, the difference is the length of the string. Because the assembler is using offsets, not contents of variables, I do not know why the instruction is not written this way:

    MOV   CX,OFFSET FNAME-OFFSET MES1

because those are the actual numbers in the subtraction. The assembler, however, prefers the first structure.

The reason I asked you to place MES1 before FNAME is so that I would have a concrete example for this explanation. You could place MES1 anywhere in your data section before BUFFR and then substitute the label that immediately follows MES1 for FNAME in FNAME-MES1.

The last change to make is to insert a call to BOTTOM at DONE, right before INT 20H. The reason for this is to assure that the cursor will be on the bottom line, and not somewhere in the middle of the screen, when the program terminates and DOS's prompt reappears.

The preparation of the screen is completed. All that remains is to set the cursor back at the top of the screen to await the first line of text. You do this by putting zero in DX (both row zero and column zero) and calling CURSOR. The stage is set. Now is the time to test the code. There are five new procedures that should be in working order. Figure 7-5 gives a summary of tipe.asm to this point. Create tipe.com. Given a file of valid length, you should see the screen clear, a line of dashes across line 23, and the options displayed on line 24. Then it is finished. You don't see anything else, but the hard work is over. The file is there at offset BUFFR, just waiting.

Now the preparations are complete. You can finally write the code that makes the program do its task, display the file to the screen.

```
;TIPE.ASM - PROGRAM TO DISPLAY ASCII FILES
;       ALLOWING THE DISPLAY TO BE REVERSED

CR      EQU     0DH     ;Carriage return character
LF      EQU     0AH     ;Line feed character

PUBLIC WRITEM,GET_FILE,DIROUT,STRINGO,OPENFL,FSIZE
PUBLID CLOSEFL,READIN,READFL,CLEARS,LINEOUT,BOTTOM
PUBLIC WRITE,CURSOR

CODE    SEGMENT
        ASSUME CS:CODE,DS:CODE
        ORG     100H

MAIN:   ----
        ----
MAIN1:  ----
        ----
MAIN2:  -----
MAINBG: ----
        ----
MAIN3:  ----
        ----            ;JC DONE was last instruction here
        mov     dh,24           ;Last row
        call    CLEARS          ;Clr screen thru row in DH
        call    LINEOUT         ;Dashes across row 23
        call    BOTTOM          ;Cursor at start of row 24
        mov     dx,OFFSET MES1  ;Prompt message
        mov     cx,FNAME-MES1   ;Number of chars
        call    WRITE           ;Write to the screen
        sub     dx,dx           ;Set row and col to 0
        call    CURSOR          ;Put the cursor there
        nop
DONE:   call    BOTTOM          ;cursor at bot of screen
        int     20H             ;Quit
;End of MAIN

GET_FILE PROC NEAR
        ----
GET_FILE ENDP

LINEOUT PROC NEAR
        mov     dh,23           ;Row 23
        sub     dl,dl           ;Column 0
        call    CURSOR
        mov     cx,80           ;Set count to 80
        mov     al,'-'
LLOOP:  call    DIROUT          ;Send out the dash
```

Fig. 7-5. Preparing the screen for display.

Setting Up the Screen   97

```
                loop    LLOOP           ;Decrease CX and
                ret                     ;go again if not 0
        LINEOUT ENDP

        READIN  PROC NEAR
                ----
        READIN  ENDP

        BOTTOM  PROC NEAR       ;Clears bot 2 rows
                mov     dx,1800H ;ready for row 24 col 0
        BOTTOM  ENDP            ;Falls through to CURSOR

;**** BIOS SCREEN HANDLING ROUTINES

        CURSOR  PROC    NEAR    ;Entry: DH = ROW, DL = COL
                push    ax
                push    bx
                sub     bh,bh   ;Screen Display page is 0
                mov     ax,0200H ;set cursor
                int     10H     ;BIOS video display interrupt
                pop     bx
                pop     ax
                ret
        CURSOR  ENDP
        CLEARS  PROC    NEAR    ;Entry DH has row of bot
                push    ax
                push    bx
                push    cx
                sub     cx,cx   ;top row and col, both 0
                mov     dl,79   ;Col of bottom of window
                mov     ax,0600H ;AL = 0 = blank window
                mov     bh,07h  ;Attribute, gray on white
                int     10H     ;BIOS video display interrupt
                pop     cx
                pop     bx
                pop     ax
                ret
        CLEARS  ENDP
;**** DOS DISK FILE HANDLING ROUTINES

        OPENFL  PROC NEAR
                ----
        OPENFL  ENDP

        FSIZE   PROC NEAR
                ----
        FSIZE   ENDP

        CLOSEFL PROC    NEAR
                ----
        CLOSEFL ENDP
```

```
READFL  PROC NEAR
        ----
READFL  ENDP


;**** DOS CHARACTER HANDLING ROUTINES ****

WRITEM  PROC NEAR
        ----
WRITEM  ENDP

DIROUT  PROC NEAR
        ----
DIROUT  ENDP

STRINGO PROC NEAR
        ----
STRINGO ENDP

WRITE PROC NEAR
;Entry Address string in DS:DX, Length in CX
        push    ax
        push    bx
        mov     bx,0001 ; 1 handle for strd output
        mov     ax,4000H ;write to file or device
        int     21H     ; in this case the screen
        pop     bx
        pop     ax
        RET
WRITE ENDP
;Data for the program
PUBLIC TITL,FNAME,NOFILE,NOTFND,FILESZ,BIGFILE
PUBLIC READMS,READER,BUFFR,MES1

titl    DB
MES1    DB      ' Any key = forward  '
        DB      '<ESC> = reverse  ^C = quit'
fname   DB
nofile  DB
notfnd  DB
filesz  DW
bigfile DB
readms  DB
reader  DB
buffr   DB      ?       ;End of our data and
                        ; beginning of file

CODE    ENDS
        END     MAIN
```

CHAPTER 8

Displaying the File

By the end of this chapter tipe.com will be finished. The complete additions are in Fig. 8-8 at the end of this chapter. First, MAIN must be finished. There are only a few more instructions to be added to it:

```
        mov     ax,OFFSET BUFFER - 1   ;1 less
        mov     MEMP,ax        ;because we INC to start
        mov     al,0           ;Dummy we'll go forward
        call    SHOW__IT       ;Show a screenful
DONE:   call    BOTTOM         ;cursor at bot of screen
        int     20H            ;Quit
;End of MAIN
```

Replace the NOP before DONE with the first four instructions. Here is an outline of what the program does: It calls SHOW__IT to display a page (23 lines) of text. SHOW__IT then pauses and waits for user's command—go forward, reverse, or quit. If forward is chosen, the next page is shown, if it is not at the end of file. If reverse is chosen, the previous page is shown, if it is not at the beginning of the file. If quit is chosen, SHOW__IT returns to MAIN, which puts the cursor back at the bottom of the screen and then exits.

KEYBOARD INPUT

You need a way for the user to communicate with the program. The way is using keyboard input, and you shall write a routine to obtain it. You also need to decide what code to use to denote forward, reverse, and quit. I have chosen a simple, but arbitrary code. It is displayed in MES1, which you have already placed in the program. If the ESCape key is pressed, reverse has been chosen. If CTRL-C is pressed, quit has been selected. If any other key is pressed, forward has been selected.

Although you will not be using the keyboard input procedure for a while, let's look at the procedure now, because it helps you understand the beginning of the code to display the text. Here is one version of KEYIN:

```
KEYIN  PROC   NEAR
       sub    ah,ah                              ;asks to read a key
       int    16h                                ;BIOS keyboard interrupt
       ret           ;ASCII code in AL, scan code in AH
KEYIN  ENDP
```

This is not the version that you will put in the program because it violates the rule that if DOS can do the job, then let it do it. I have chosen to show you this version, using a BIOS interrupt in order to more easily teach you about scan codes.

Most of the time when you are dealing with keyboard input, you are interested in the ASCII code for the key pressed. Some keys, however, have no ASCII code. If you want to write programs in which you want to know if the HOME key has been pressed, for instance, or a function key, or ALT-P, or a number of other special keystrokes or combinations, you need to know the key's scan code. Thus, KEYIN is written as a general procedure for any key code. KEYIN uses INT 16H, BIOS's keyboard input/output service. You put zero in AH for the service that returns the ASCII code (if any) in AL and the scan code in AH.

The key codes that you receive from INT 16 in AX consist of a scan code (returned in AH) and an ASCII code (returned in AL). These codes are determined by another interrupt, 9, which is activated when a key is pressed or released. In the simplest and most frequent case, one key is pressed. Each key has a particular scan code associated with it. As an example, if you press the key with the letter A on it, it will always return the scan code in AH of 31 or 1FH. (You can find tables of scan codes in other references.) If the Caps Lock is on or if you are also pressing a shift key, the scan code in AH will still be 31, but the ASCII code in AL will be 41H, capital A. When the Shift key is not pressed, the ASCII code is 61H. When you press CTRL and the A key, the ASCII code is 1, which is CTRL-A. The result in each case is the same scan code, but different ASCII codes.

The keyboard has a number of keys that do not return character codes. The function keys and arrow keys are some of these. For these keys, AL will be zero, but AH will have the particular scan code associated with the key. For these keys, the difference in shift state (e.g., SHIFT-RIGHT ARROW or CTRL-HOME) is reflected by different scan codes, but AL is still zero. Because any of these special keys or key combinations have a character code of zero in AL, it is simple to test to see if the key pressed returns an ASCII code or not by using CMP AL,0. If AL is not zero, you can jump to a routine that treats ASCII entries. If it is zero, you can jump to a routine that looks for special key entries.

Exercise 8-1: Examining the Key Codes

This time you use Debug to look at the codes returned in AX by INT 16H. You can use the A (assemble command) to create a tiny program to do this, like you did when you were exploring windows. Essentially, you enter the code for KEYIN by hand. You set it in an endless loop so you can run through it as many times as you wish.

At the hyphen prompt enter A100, to start the assembly at 100H. You could start the assembly anywhere, but by starting at 100H, you can save the code as a .com program. Here is the code with the offsets that Debug provides:

```
100    SUB    AH,AH (ask to read a key)
102    INT    16
104    JMP    100
106
```

Once you have the program assembled, go to 104. BIOS awaits your keyboard input. When you have made it, observe the AX register, which has the scan code in AH and the ASCII code in AL. Trace back to 100; then go to 104 again.

Try uppercase, lowercase, numbers, and function keys; try any key you want. Look at the difference between a, A, CTRL-A, and ALT-

A. How about function 3 and CTRL-function 3? Again, reference tables help you find the scan codes you want for your programs. You could save this little program by doing the following before you exit Debug. Use N, the name command, to give the program a name, such as scancode.com. At the asterisk, enter Nscancode.com. Then you need to tell Debug how long the program is in bytes. It goes from 100 to 106, 106 being the next address after JMP 100, so it is six bytes long. Put six in the CX register with the R command. Make sure BX is still zero, because Debug uses BX:CX for the size of the file; BX contains the most significant word, and CX the least significant word.

Now a name has been entered and CX is set. Just enter W for write, and the file is saved to your disk. Whenever you need to know a particular scan code, instead of getting out the books, you can enter Debug with scancode.com and find it immediately.

Scanning Codes Using DOS Functions

Now that you have some understanding of scan codes, you can rewrite KEYIN to use a DOS function. The DOS functions 1, 6, 7, or 8 could all serve your purposes. Each returns the ASCII code for the key in AL, function 1 with an echo (display) to the screen, and functions 6, 7, and 8 without an echo. Function 7 is my choice, because the character is not echoed to the screen, and DOS does not check to see if CTRL-BREAK or CTRL-C is pressed. Function 1 and 8 make that check, and if either has been pressed, DOS aborts the program.

Because I have chosen CTRL-C as the key combination to end the program, you might wonder why I chose a function that does not check for it. The answer is that my choice of CTRL-C to end the program is arbitrary. You, for instance, might choose a simple Q for quit. By using function 7, you can be assured that the program quits only when you want it to, not by a mistaken key press. Suppose, for instance, that your program was a word processor, and after typing in a couple of pages, you accidentally pressed CTRL-C. If you were using function 1 or 8 to receive keyboard input, DOS would take over and quit—good-bye text.

Although all of these DOS functions return just one byte, the one in AL, they can be used to check for keys like HOME or the function keys. If such a key is pressed, AL will return a zero. You can check to see if AL is zero. If it is not, it is an ASCII code. If it is, you call the function a second time. This time AL will hold the scan code. Figure 8-1 has the working version of KEYIN.

The checking of the code returned in AL is necessary, as I learned

```
KEYIN   PROC NEAR
        mov     ah,7            ;Keybrd input without echo
        int     21h             ; and CTRL-BREAK check
        cmp     al,0            ;ASCII code?
        jz      KEYIN           ;No, scan code
        ret                     ;character code in AL
KEYIN   ENDP
```

Fig. 8-1. Procedure to obtain keyboard input.

in developing the program, because without the check, the screen would sometimes scroll two pages, not just one, even though I pressed just one key. This is because when you press a key that returns a zero in AL, such as an arrow key, the scan code is left in a special keyboard buffer waiting to be retrieved. Upon the next call to this DOS function, because a character is waiting (in a special buffer for key codes), the character is returned, just as if a key had been pressed—which is why the screen scrolled twice with just one key press.

KEYIN is the last of the input/output procedures for the program. Type it in with the other DOS character-handling routines. The two special keys you will be looking for are CTRL-C and ESC. They are represented by the ASCII codes to be returned in AL of 3 and 1BH, respectively. Although you refer to each only once in the program, you add the following to the EQUs at the top of the program:

```
BACKKEY    EQU        1BH          ;Escape
ENDKEY     EQU        3            ;CTRL-C
```

There are two reasons for using labels for constants. Labels are usually easier to remember than numbers, especially if they are to be used more than once in a program, as I have discussed before. Also, if you want to change the value of a constant in a program, it is easier to change the value of a label once, rather than to find and edit each statement that used the constant.

Suppose that these labels were used several times and that you would rather have reverse indicated by the letter R and quit by Q. You could change each and every instance of BACKKEY and ENDKEY in a program by changing the value of the labels like this:

```
BACKKEY    EQU        'R'
ENDKEY     EQU        'Q'
```

Except for also changing MES1 to reflect the new keys, all other changes will be made by the assembler when it encounters these labels.

SHOWING A PAGE

Now, let's get to SHOW__IT, the reason all the rest of the code was written in the first place. Here again is the setup in MAIN before the call to SHOW__IT:

```
        mov     ax,OFFSET BUFFR - 1    ;1 less
        mov     MEMP,ax                ;because we INC to start
        mov     al,0                   ;Dummy we'll go forward
```

A short preview of SHOW__IT explains this setup. There is one run through SHOW__IT to display the first screenful. At the end, KEYIN is used to obtain the user's choice. If CTRL-C is pressed, the procedure returns. If not, it loops back to the start. SHOW__IT continues forever until CTRL-C is pressed, or until you turn off the computer. In brief, SHOW__IT does this:

    Check if BACKKEY was pressed:
       if so, CALL REVERSE to get the start of last page
       if not, start with last character shown (MEMP)
    Show each line in sequence until end of file or 23 lines
    CALL KEYIN
    Check if ENDKEY was pressed
       if not, jump to the top
       if so, RET

First you need to define a variable to be used to keep track of where you are in the text file. I've chosen MEMP, for MEMory Pointer. It points to an address in BUFFR, moving up as you send out characters, moving back as you look for the start last screen. Place MEMP with the data:

```
MEMP    DW      ?
```

SHOW__IT is designed to be looped through again and again, until the user quits. The loop always begins with MEMP set to the offset of the last character displayed. When SHOW__IT is called from MAIN, no characters have yet been displayed, so MEMP is set to the offset of the first character minus one. In going forward, SHOW__IT increases the content of the pointer by one to get to the next character. When that happens, it is right where you want it, pointing to the start of BUFFR. Thus, these two instructions are used:

    mov   ax,OFFSET BUFFR-1
    mov   MEMP,ax

Now I'll explain why AL gets a zero in the next instruction, MOV AL,0. The first pass through the routine obviously has to be in a forward direction. After that, however, the display could be forward or backward. Note that the first thing SHOW__IT does is to determine whether or not KEYIN has returned BACKKEY in AL. By putting a zero in AL, even if you change BACKKEY, it will not be a zero, so the first pass is guaranteed to go forward.

SHOW__IT is more complex than other procedures you have written. Rather than trying to write it completely from the first instruction to the last, I will start with its heart, displaying a line of text to the screen. If it can display one line, it can display 23. By using this strategy, you can compile and test the procedure piece by piece.

In writing procedures like SHOW__IT, it is good practice to start with the most central function, test it, and then continue building the procedure outward. Figure 8-2 shows you how to start SHOW__IT.

```
SHOW_IT PROC NEAR
        nop
FORW:   mov     bx,MEMP     ;holds last char shown
        nop
        mov     dh,22       ;Clear thru to row 22
        call    CLEARS
        nop
        sub     cx,cx       ;Character count
        mov     dl,EOF      ;Put numbers in DL
        mov     dh,LF       ; and DH for our tests
LINELP: inc     bx          ;Increase the offset
        inc     cx          ;  And the count
        mov     al,[BX]     ;And get the next char
        cmp     al,dl       ;Is it an EOF
        jz      SHOWLN      ;Yes - show the line
        cmp     al,dh       ;Is it a LF
        jnz     LINELP      ;No, get the next one
SHOWLN: nop
SHOMORE:nop
        ret
SHOW_IT ENDP
```

Fig. 8-2. Skeleton of SHOW__IT, the procedure to display the text.

The NOPs are unnecessary, but make it easier for me to refer to places to put further code. First, the content of MEMP is moved into BX. BX is used to hold the offset in this procedure because you can use that register to indirectly access its contents in memory, in this case DS:[BX]. The screen is then cleared through the 23rd row. Even though the screen is originally clear, you will want to clear it each time a new screenful of text is shown.

The next step is to search through the line to find its end. You cannot see it in this version of SHOW__IT, but you use WRITE to display the line, so you want CX to contain the number of characters in the line. CX is initialized to zero. ASCII files typically end their lines with a carriage return (0DH) and then a line feed (0AH), so when BX reaches an offset that contains an 0AH, it has reached the end of the line. When you enter this loop to display the line, BX starts at the end of a line and is pointing to an 0AH.

There is another ASCII code you need to watch for, 1AH, which signifies the end of the file. You also want to test for that character to know when the end is reached. You already have defined LF. Add the following to the equates:

```
EOF        EQU        1AH          ;End of file marker
```

You continue the preparations by moving EOF into DL and LF into DH for the upcoming comparisons. It is not necessary to move these numbers into registers, for you could say CMP AL,EOF and CMP AL,LF. However, comparing a register with a register is faster for the 8088 to accomplish than comparing a register with a number. In this program the difference between the two methods is negligible, but in programs requiring long involved comparisons, the difference is noticeable.

The loop is begun by increasing both CX and BX. BX now has the offset of the first character, and CX has one. The character is placed in AL, which is tested in turn to see if it is an EOF or an LF. The loop is continued until one or the other is found, at which time BX will contain the offset of that character, AL holds that character, and CX has the count. Now you are ready to write the line to the screen using WRITE. Remember that WRITE asks for the offset of the beginning of the string in DX. MEMP still holds the offset of that address minus one. Replace the NOP at SHOWLN with this:

```
SHOWLN:    mov        dx,MEMP      ;Offset of last shown
           inc        dx           ; in DX for the write
                                   ;and increase it
           call       WRITE        ;Show the line
```

```
SHOW_IT  PROC  NEAR
         nop
FORW:    mov    bx,MEMP       ;holds last char shown
         nop
         mov    dh,22         ;Clear thru to row 22
         call   CLEARS
         nop
         sub    cx,cx         ;Character count
         mov    dl,EOF        ;Put numbers in DL
         mov    dh,LF         ; and DH for our tests
LINELP:  inc    bx            ;Increase the offset
         inc    cx            ;  And the count
         mov    al,[BX]       ;And get the next char
         cmp    al,dl         ;Is it an EOF
         jz     SHOWLN        ;Yes - show the line
         cmp    al,dh         ;Is it a LF
         jnz    LINELP        ;No, get the next one
SHOWLN:  mov    dx,MEMP       ;Offset of last shown
         inc    dx            ; in DX for the write
                              ;and increase it
         call   WRITE         ;Show the line
SHOMORE: nop
         ret
SHOW_IT  ENDP
```

Fig. 8-3. Version of SHOW_IT displaying one line to the screen.

Add SHOW_IT as written to this point right after MAIN. Figure 8-3 gives SHOW_IT as it looks now.

Now test SHOW_IT to see if it can print the first line of a text file. You probably have to look quickly to see your line, especially when you run the program to the screen. Because of the call to BOTTOM at the end of the program, the cursor goes to the bottom of the screen; then DOS's prompt pops up, scrolling the screen upward. Here are two little tricks you can use to get rid of the call to BOTTOM and avoid having your line scrolling off the top of the screen: First, in tipe.asm, put a semicolon before the statement CALL BOTTOM. Because of the semicolon, the assembler treats the statement as a comment and thus ignores it. Many times in developing a program you might want to "comment out" code you have already written and want to keep, but not use for a current test. The only thing to remember is to delete the semicolons in subsequent versions of your program. The second method is to use Debug to alter your program. The next exercise shows you how.

Exercise 8-2: Changing Your Program with Debug

In Exercise 8-1, you created a program with Debug, using its A (Assemble) command to develop instructions, the N (Name) command to give a name to the file, and the W (Write) command to write it to disk. Here, you learn how to take an existing file, in this case tipe.com, change it with Debug, and write it back to the disk. The procedure is similar, except now you enter Debug with an existing program. In this case enter debug tipe.com. (You could include a text file name after tipe.com so you can continue the test after altering tipe.com.)

For this exercise, you want to get rid of CALL BOTTOM at DONE so the line shown to the screen does not flit off the screen. You follow a similar procedure as in Exercise 8-1, except you do not need to enter a name. The Name command is necessary only if you have entered Debug with no file name following or if you want to change the name, so it is not necessary for present purposes. You use A and then W to change tipe.com.

To rid CALL BOTTOM at DONE, you first need to find its offset with U and then use the Assemble (A) command to delete the call. Now you really cannot delete the call as with a word processor. The call to BOTTOM takes three bytes of memory, and the rest of the program is structured to follow it. To get rid of the three bytes, you just need to fill them in with instructions that do nothing. Remember NOP that I have been using as a filler? Find the offset of CALL BOTTOM. Use that offset with A (if it were 150, enter A150). Then enter NOP three times. Press NOP and then ENTER, three times. Assemble should then be showing you the offset of INT 20, the next instruction, so just press ENTER to finish the assembly. Now, enter W and press ENTER; the NOPed version of tipe.com will be written back to its disk.

When Debug sets up a program for debugging, it puts the size of program file in BX:CX. Because you have not changed these registers, the name is right, the size is right, and W will write back the changes you have made to disk. Now CALL BOTTOM is gone, not only for Debug, but in tipe.com. Even though you have changed the actual program file by following this procedure, it is best to continue with the actual debugging, just in case there is something else wrong with the code.

Whether you continue with the debugging or not, you will find it useful to know that you can make changes in the program code directly from Debug and save them back to the disk, without having to go back and reassemble and recompile the source code. You will eventually want to do that, but you do not have to do so when you are doing intermediate steps.

Using a Loop to Display the Page

It takes just a little more to show the page of 23 lines. Because you know exactly how many lines you want, this is a perfect place to use LOOP. Figure 8-4 has the expanded SHOW_IT.

As this procedure is built, I put the code already written in lowercase, or skip it as I have done with LINELP. This helps clarify what has been added. In this case, you set up a loop encompassing the line loop already written. It is not uncommon in any type of programming to have loops within loops within loops. You see that the loop to display the page is simple.

Put 23 in CX for the count. Start PAGELP with a push—it should be clear why you do so—and end it with a pop. Note that after you WRITE a line to the screen, you store the address that is in BX into

```
        SHOW_IT PROC NEAR
                nop
FORW:           mov     bx,memp         ;holds last char shown
                nop
                mov     dh,22           ;Clear thru to row 22
                call    CLEARS
                MOV     CX,23           ;Line count
PAGELP:         PUSH    CX              ;Save it for LINELP
                SUB     CX,CX           ;Character count
                mov     dl,EOF          ;Put numbers in DL
                mov     dh,LF           ; and DH for our tests
LINELP:         ;The code you have written is here
SHOWLN:         MOV     DX,MEMP         ;Offset of last shown
                INC     DX              ; in DX for the write
                                        ;and increase it
                CALL    WRITE           ;Show the line
                MOV     MEMP,BX         ;Reset for next loop
                POP     CX              ;Get the line count
                LOOP    PAGELP          ;loop again
shomore:        nop
                ret
        SHOW_IT ENDP
```

Fig. 8-4. Version of SHOW_IT with a page loop.

110 IBM Assembly Language Simplified

MEMP so that when SHOWLN is reached again, you are set to put it into DX. (Thanks to the fact you pushed and popped BX in WRITE, it has not been changed.) When you reach the end of the page, MEMP will also be pointing to the last character displayed, ready for the next one. That is almost all there is to it. Pause for a moment to think what this loop will do. Can you think of a potential problem?

There is one. The loop is set to display 23 lines to the screen. What if, as the end of the file nears, there are less than 23 lines to be displayed? You might see some strange characters displayed, or perhaps you might never return from LINELP because there may be no more LFs or EOFs stored in memory. There is an easy solution. Like the jump instructions, LOOP can be conditional or unconditional. Like JMP, LOOP is unconditional. The 8088 provides two conditional loop instructions: LOOPZ (or LOOPE, loop equal) and LOOPNZ (or LOOPNE, loop not equal). Either of these instructions test the condition of the zero flag. The loop continues only if the flag is in the appropriate condition. In this case, you can use LOOPNZ after testing to determine whether or not AL holds EOF.

Change the last instructions you typed in to look like this:

```
mov     MEMP,bx         ;Reset for next loop
cmp     al,EOF          ;Last char an EOF?
pop     cx              ;Get the line count
loopnz  PAGELP          ;If not, loop again
```

AX has been saved by WRITE, so AL still has the character contained in [BX], either a LF or EOF. The loop will continue until either CX is zero or the zero flag is set. Note that EOF was used in this comparison, not DH as before. Here's another question for you: Why not use DL? Don't peek. The answer is that it is highly unlikely that its value is 1AH. You moved MEMP into DX for the WRITE.

Figure 8-5 shows just the current version of SHOW__IT. Test the program to make sure it is working to this point. You should be able to display the first 23 lines of a text file. Also try it with a text file that has less than 23 lines. The display should stop at the end of the file.

The user is told that pressing any key (except for CTRL-C or ESC) will continue the display. Let's enable that capability and finish SHOW__IT. You see that the new additions make SHOW__IT one grand loop, which contains a page loop, which in turn contains a line loop.

Figure 8-6 shows the completed procedure. Also type in the procedure REVERSE like this:

```
REVERSE PROC NEAR
         ret
REVERSE ENDP
```

This is done so that when you make your next test of SHOW_IT, the assembler will not complain that REVERSE does not exist. It does exist—it just doesn't do much.

REVERSE also needs the variable TOPADD, so add it to the data:

```
TOPADD    DW        ?
```

I will start the explanation with SHOMORE. Actually, little explanation

```
         SHOW_IT PROC NEAR
                 nop
FORW:            mov     bx,MEMP         ;holds last char shown
                 nop
                 mov     dh,22           ;Clear thru to row 22
                 call    CLEARS
                 mov     cx,23           ;Line count
PAGELP:          push    cx              ;Save it for LINELP
                 sub     cx,cx           ;Character count
                 mov     dl,EOF          ;Put numbers in DL
                 mov     dh,LF           ; and DH for our tests
LINELP:          inc     bx              ;Increase the offset
                 inc     cx              ;  And the count
                 mov     al,[BX]         ;And get the next char
                 cmp     al,dl           ;Is it an EOF
                 jz      SHOWLN          ;Yes - show the line
                 cmp     al,dh           ;Is it a LF
                 jnz     LINELP          ;No, get the next one
SHOWLN:          mov     dx,MEMP         ;Offset of last shown
                 inc     dx              ;  in DX for the write
                                         ;and increase it
                 call    WRITE           ;Show the line
                 mov     MEMP,bx         ;Reset for next loop
                 cmp     al,EOF          ;Last char an EOF?
                 pop     cx              ;Get the line count
                 loopnz  PAGELP          ;If not, loop again
shomore:         nop
                 ret
         SHOW_IT ENDP
```

Fig. 8-5. Version of SHOW_IT to display a page.

```
SHOW_IT  PROC NEAR
         CMP      AL,BACKKEY      ;Key is pressed. ESC?
         JNZ      FORW            ;No, go forward
         CALL     REVERSE         ;Sets up last screen
         JZ       SHOBEL          ;No last screen
FORW:    mov      bx,memp         ;holds last char shown
         MOV      AL,[BX]         ;Put it in AL
         CMP      AL,EOF          ;Is it the end of file
         JNZ      SHOWOK          ;No, show next screen
SHOBEL:  MOV      AL,7            ;Can't move
         CALL     DIROUT          ; So ring the bell
         JMP      SHORT SHOMORE   ; and try again
SHOWOK:  MOV      TOPADD,BX       ;Maybe rev. next time
         mov      dh,22           ;Clear thru to row 22
         call     clears
         mov      cx,23           ;Line count
PAGELP:  push     cx              ;Save it for LINELP
         ;the rest of the code
         pop      cx              ;Get the line count
         loopnz   PAGELP          ;If not, loop again
SHOMORE: SUB      DX,DX           ;Cursor to the top
         CALL     CURSOR          ; ready for next page
         CALL     KEYIN           ;Ask for choice
         CMP      AL,ENDKEY       ;Want to quit?
         JNZ      SHOW_IT         ;No, start again
         ret
SHOW_IT  ENDP
```

Fig. 8-6. Additions to complete SHOW__IT.

is necessary because it should be clear to you what the program is doing: setting the cursor to the top of the screen, getting the user's input with KEYIN, and then checking whether to continue or not. If a CTRL-C is entered, the procedure returns to MAIN, which puts the cursor at the bottom of the screen and quits. Any other key takes you back to the top of SHOW__IT, which now checks to see if the key was an ESC. If so, REVERSE is called. REVERSE goes back and finds the offset of the top of the previous screen displayed. If the current display is the beginning of the file, REVERSE returns with the zero flag set. When this happens, a jump is taken to SHOBEL, where ASCII code 7 (the bell) is sent to the console. Then the actual display routines are skipped with a jump to SHOMORE.

The next step is to check to see if you have just displayed the last page—the one with the EOF. If you have, you will ring the bell to indicate the end of the file and skip to SHOMORE, because there is nothing new to see. You know MEMP has the address of the last character of the last line shown. If you are not at the EOF, you save the current MEMP in TOPADD (top address) for REVERSE. When that procedure is called, MEMP will be holding the offset of the bottom of the screen, and TOPADD the address of the top of the screen.

SHOW_IT is now complete. You can check your code against that in Fig. 8-8, which is near the end of this chapter. Once you test it and find you can go forward in the display to the end of file, you are ready to activate the ESC key to reverse the display.

REVERSING THE DISPLAY

The logic of REVERSE is this: First, check to see if the current display is the first page. If it is, return. If not, find the top of the last page by counting back 23 lines. Put that address in MEMP for the rest of SHOW_IT.

Figure 8-7 shows REVERSE in its entirety. The SI register is used here because you can use the handy LODSB instruction to put its contents in AL for the test, while decreasing SI for the next test. I did not use LODSB in SHOW_IT because I wanted to increase the address before the test in LINELP and otherwise did not want it increased at all.

Starting at the top, you move TOPADD into SI. Remember that TOPADD holds the offset of the top of the page being displayed (minus one). If TOPADD is the same as the offset of BUFFR-1, the beginning

```
        REVERSE PROC NEAR   ;ESC pressed, show last screen
                mov     si,TOPADD       ;top of screen minus 1
                mov     di,OFFSET BUFFR - 1
                cmp     si,di           ;Start of the file?
                jz      REV_EX          ;Yes, ret zero flag set
                mov     cx,24           ;Line counter go back 24
                mov     dl,LF           ;for the comparison
                std                     ;Set to go in reverse direction
        REV1:   lodsb                   ;Char into AL and dec SI
                cmp     al,dl           ;Is it an LF?
                jnz     REV1            ;No, try again
                loop    REV1            ;Yes, dec CX, go again
                inc     si              ;Increase it to the LF
                mov     MEMP,si         ;Set now for SHOW_IT
                cld                     ;Set direction forward
        REV_EX: ret
        REVERSE ENDP
```

Fig. 8-7. Procedure to reverse the display.

of the file is presently being displayed. You can't go back. Therefore, if the zero flag is set, a jump is taken to the exit. Otherwise, if you count back to the beginning of the 23rd line, you now have the address of the top of the previous display. Keep in mind that you have used TOPADD to hold the address right before the top of the display, so you have to find one extra LF. Thus, CX is initialized at 24 for the loop, not 23.

To illustrate, suppose you wanted to go back to the beginning of the fourth, rather than 23rd, line. Here is a representation of the text in memory:

```
Stop-    LF ...................... CR,LF
         ...................... CR,LF
         ...................... CR,LF
         ...................... CR,LF      Start
```

To move the offset back to the address right before the beginning of the fourth line, you need to count five LFs.

Next put LF into DL for the comparison. (Again, you could have used the direct CMP AL,LF.) The direction flag is set to down or reverse with STD because you want SI to be decreased after each load. After the loop, the direction flag is cleared with CLD. This is not necessary because the only instruction that requires the direction flag from this point forward in the program is the LODSB in this procedure. This is a quirk of mine. I always want the direction flag to be pointing forward because that is usually the way I use it, so whenever I change it, I put it back.

You now come to the loop, which once again contains a loop. The inner loop is as follows:

```
REV1:       lodsb                ;Char  into AL and dec SI
            cmp     al,dl        ;is it an LF?
            jnz     REV1         ;No, try again
```

Add the instruction LOOP REV1, and you have the outer loop. After the discussion on LOOPNZ, this might be confusing at first. When I looked at this set of code, which I had written some time ago, right after writing the discussion of conditional loops, I asked myself, Why not just get rid of JNZ REV1 and change LOOP REV1 to LOOPNZ REV1? That was because I forgot that REV1 was the return label for two loops, not just one. Look what would happen if you write it as one loop:

```
REV1:   LODSB
        CMP     AL,DL   ;Is it an LF?
        LOOPNZ  REV1    ;No, try again
```

The effect would be to check the first 24 characters, stopping the loop before that if an LF was found. That would hardly get us back to the beginning of the last screen. The correct way reaches the LOOP statement, and thus decreases CX only when an LF is found.

In the inner loop you could also have added the following instructions:

```
        MOV     BX,OFFSET BUFFER-1
        CMP     SI,BX
        JZ      (put a label at INC SI)
```

You can save these three instructions if you know there is an LF at BUFFR-1, and you can know that if you put one there. Put one in so that the end of the data section looks like this:

```
        DB      LF
BUFFR   DB      0
```

Once the outer loop is finished, the direction flag is cleared, and then SI is increased. It is necessary to increase SI because, thanks to LODSB, SI is one offset less than the one holding the LF. The offset is then stored in MEMP ready for the display upon return to SHOW__IT. You know that the zero flag is clear because the last instruction that would affect it was INC SI, and you know for sure that SI is not zero.

Tipe.asm is now finished. This time, when you test tipe.com, it will be the finished program. Figure 8-8 shows the code added in this chapter, and the listing of the completed tipe.asm is in Appendix A. Your program may not look exactly like it. The ordering of the procedures is arbitrary except for BOTTOM and CURSOR. The ordering of the equates is also arbitrary, as is the ordering of the data—with three exceptions. BUFFR must be last, and it must be preceded by the LF. FNAME must follow MES1 (or you need to replace FNAME in the statement MOV CX,FNAME-MES1 with the label for the variable that you have following MES1).

You now have a working program that you might keep on your disks for those times when you want to display an ASCII file and want

```
;TIPE.ASM - PROGRAM TO DISPLAY ASCII FILES
;        ALLOWING THE DISPLAY TO BE REVERSED
CR      EQU     0DH     ;Carriage return character
LF      EQU     0AH     ;Line feed character
BACKKEY EQU     1BH     ;Escape
ENDKEY  EQU     3       ;CTRL-C
EOF     EQU     1AH     ;End of file marker

PUBLIC WRITEM,GET_FILE,DIROUT,STRINGO,OPENFL,FSIZE
PUBLID CLOSEFL,READIN,READFL,CLEARS,LINEOUT,BOTTOM
PUBLIC WRITE,CURSOR,KEYIN,SHOW_IT,REVERSE
CODE    SEGMENT
        ASSUME CS:CODE,DS:CODE
        ORG     100H
MAIN:   ----
        ----
MAIN1:  ----
MAIN2:  ----
        ----
MAINBG: ----
        ----
MAIN3:  ----
        ----;CALL CURSOR was last instruction here
        mov     bx,OFFSET BUFFR - 1    ;1 less
        mov     MEMP,bx  ;because we INC to start
        mov     al,0     ;Dummy we'll go forward
        call    SHOW_IT  ;Show a screenful
DONE:   call    BOTTOM   ;cursor at bot of screen
        int     20H      ;Quit
;End of MAIN

SHOW_IT PROC NEAR
        cmp     al,BACKKEY ;Key is pressed. ESC?
        jnz     FORW       ;No, go forward
        call    REVERSE    ;Sets up last screen
        jz      SHOBEL     ;No last screen
FORW:   mov     bx,MEMP    ;holds last char shown
        mov     al,[bx]    ;Put it in AL
        cmp     al,EOF     ;Is it the end of file
        jnz     SHOWOK     ;No, show next screen
SHOBEL: mov     al,7       ;Can't move
        call    DIROUT     ; So ring the bell
        jmp     SHORT SHOMORE  ; and try again
SHOWOK: mov     TOPADD,bx  ;Maybe rev. next time
        mov     dh,22      ;Clear thru to row 22
        call    CLEARS
        mov     cx,23      ;Line count
PAGELP: push    cx         ;Save it for LINELP
        sub     cx,cx      ;Character count
```

Fig. 8-8. Additions to complete Tipe.com.

Displaying the File

```
            mov     dl,EOF          ;Put numbers in DL
            mov     dh,LF           ; and DH for our tests
    LINELP: inc     bx              ;Increase the offset
            inc     cx              ;   And the count
            mov     al,[BX]         ;And get the next char
            cmp     al,dl           ;Is it an EOF
            jz      SHOWLN          ;Yes - show the line
            cmp     al,dh           ;Is it a LF
            jnz     LINELP          ;No, get the next one
    SHOWLN: mov     dx,MEMP         ;Offset of last shown
            inc     dx              ; in DX for the write
                                    ;and increase it
            call    WRITE           ;Show the line
            mov     MEMP,bx         ;Reset for next loop
            cmp     al,EOF          ;Last char an EOF?
            pop     cx              ;Get the line count
            loopnz  PAGELP          ;If not, loop again
    SHOMORE:sub     dx,dx           ;Cursor to the top
            call    CURSOR          ; ready for next page
            call    KEYIN           ;Ask for choice
            cmp     al,ENDKEY       ;Want to quit?
            jnz     SHOW_IT         ;No, start again
            ret
    SHOW_IT ENDP


    REVERSE PROC NEAR   ;ESC pressed, show last screen
            mov     si,TOPADD       ;top of screen minus 1
            mov     di,OFFSET BUFFR - 1
            cmp     si,di           ;Start of the file?
            jz      REV_EX          ;Yes, ret zero flag set
            mov     cx,24           ;Line counter go back 24
            mov     dl,LF           ;for the comparison
            std                     ;Set to go in reverse direction
    REV1:   lodsb                   ;Char into AL and dec SI
            cmp     al,dl                   ;Is it an LF?
            jnz     REV1                    ;No, try again
            loop    REV1            ;Yes, dec CX, go again
            inc     si              ;Increase it to the LF
            mov     MEMP,si         ;Set now for SHOW_IT
            cld                     ;Set direction forward
    REV_EX: ret
    REVERSE ENDP


    KEYIN   PROC NEAR
            mov     ah,7            ;Keybrd input without echo
            int     21H             ; and CTRL-BREAK check
            cmp     al,0            ;ASCII code?
            jz      KEYIN           ;No, scan code
            ret                     ;character code in AL
    KEYIN   ENDP
    ;Here are all the other procedures.
```

118 IBM Assembly Language Simplified

```
            ;Data for the program
            PUBLIC TITL,FNAME,NOFILE,NOTFND,FILESZ,BIGFILE
            PUBLIC READMS,READER,BUFFRMES1,MEMP,TOPADD

            titl    DB
            mes1    DB
            fname   DB
            nofile  DB
            notfnd  DB
            filesz  DW
            bigfile DB
            readms  DB
            reader  DB
            MEMP    DW      ?
            TOPADD  DW      ?
                    DB      LF
            buffr   DB      ?       ;End of our data and
                                    ; beginning of file

            CODE    ENDS
                    END     MAIN
```

to have the reverse capability. Even if you do not use tipe.com, you have learned quite a bit about 8088 assembly programming. There is still much to learn, and you will learn a bit more in this book in the next chapters.

First, you will convert tipe.asm to produce a working .exe file. Then, you will add some enhancements to tipe.com and look at some variations in it. The enhancements are some changes you really should add to the program to make it generally useful. I skipped them in the development of the program because I thought they would make more sense once you had gotten to this point. The variations are simply a means to expand on tipe.com to learn a few more programming instructions and techniques.

CHAPTER 9

Creating .Exe Files

You have created many .exe files while you were developing tipe.com. In this chapter, you learn how to create one that works. The .exe structure is more flexible than the .com structure in that you can take advantage of the memory capabilities of the IBM computer by defining any number of segments of up to 64K apiece to be used by your programs. You are required to define at least two segments: a code segment and a stack segment. This is why you have been getting the no-stack-segment warning in linking tipe.obj. A code segment was defined, but not a stack segment. If you had defined a stack segment, the linker would not complain, but EXE2BIN would because it is a requirement of .com files that they not have a defined stack segment.

You will define three segments for tipe.exe, a code, a data, and a stack segment. MASM assembles the segments in the order given in the .asm file unless told otherwise. Once again, the data is placed last so that the text file can be written starting at BUFFR. An alternative would be to specifically define an extra segment just to hold the file. The order of the code segment and stack segment is optional. The stack segment is traditionally placed first, and I shall follow that tradition.

THE STRUCTURE OF .EXE FILES

You will create two versions of tipe.exe. The structure is exactly the same in both. Before you make any changes in tipe.asm, copy it to a file named tipe1.asm, so you will have saved the code for the .com file. Before reading the explanation of the specific changes, take a look at Fig. 9-1 and note the differences between tipe.asm as structured for an .exe file and tipe.asm as structured a .com file. You see the three different segments. In tipe.asm delete the following statements:

```
;TIPE.ASM - .EXE VERSION 1
;equates here are the same as for tipe.com

MYSTACK SEGMENT PARA STACK ;Define a stack segment
        DB      100H DUP (0)
MYSTACK ENDS

MYCODE  SEGMENT PARA PUBLIC
        ASSUME  CS:MYCODE,DS:MYDATA

MAIN    PROC    FAR        ;MAIN becomes a procedure
        push    ds         ;Push PSP segment
        mov     ax,0       ; and an offset of zero
        push    ax         ; in preparation for RET
        mov     ax,MYDATA  ;ES to be the data seg
        mov     es,ax      ; for MOVSB
        push    ax         ;Has MYDATA
        call    GET_FILE   ;Do before showing title
        pop     ax
        mov     ds,ax      ;Put data seg in DS
        mov     dx,OFFSET TITL
        call    WRITEM     ;Show title of program
        ----
        ----               ;The rest of MAIN is same
        ----
        ----
        ret                ;Replace INT 20H with RET
MAIN    ENDP

;Put rest of procedures here. Same as for tipe.com

MYCODE  ENDS ;End the segment before the data seg.

MYDATA  SEGMENT PARA PUBLIC
;Put the same data as in tipe.com here
MYDATA  ENDS

        END     MAIN
```

Fig. 9-1. Tipe.asm structured as an .exe file—Version 1.

```
CODE       SEGMENT
           ASSUME CS:CODE,DS:CODE
           ORG     100H

CODE       ENDS
```

Where CODE SEGMENT was, enter the following:

```
MYSTACK    SEGMENT PARA STACK
           DB      100H DUP (0)
MYSTACK    ENDS
```

With the label, MYSTACK, and with the SEGMENT and ENDS directives, you have directed MASM to define a segment. After the segment directive is the term PARA for paragraph. This tells MASM you want the segment to start at the beginning of a paragraph. This is its *alignment*. For other purposes, particularly when you are linking several files using the same segments, you might want a segment in a subsequent file to start elsewhere, like at the first available byte, because that segment is really a continuation of an already defined segment. Because this is your first (and only) definition of MYSTACK, like all segments, you want it to start at a paragraph. If the alignment statement is absent, MASM assumes it to be PARA. Thus for your purposes, it is optional, and you will remember that you did not use an alignment statement in the definition of CODE for tipe.com.

Next comes STACK. This particular term is necessary in an .exe file. After a segment directive and the optional alignment statement, the next term (also optional) tells the assembler to tell LINK how to combine segments. One *combine type* is STACK, and the lack of this is what makes LINK say, "Warning. No stack segment." MASM also allows you to add further information to the definition line; this is useful when you are linking several modules to be combined into a program file. For your purposes, that will be enough.

Move down to the data. You will now define it as a segment. Right before the data add this statement:

```
MYDATA     SEGMENT    PARA    PUBLIC
```

and right after BUFFR DB ? add this:

```
MYDATA     ENDS
```

Now you have the data segment. The difference between its definition and that of MYSTACK is that you have used the combine type PUBLIC. This PUBLIC is different from the same term used to define labels as public. If you had other files that you were to link with tipe.asm, all segments with the name MYDATA and the combine type PUBLIC would be loaded together in memory.

Last is the code segment. To be consistent, name it MYCODE. Put this statement right before the beginning of the code, before MAIN:

MYCODE   SEGMENT   PARA   PUBLIC

With both MYCODE and MYDATA the PARA PUBLIC part is optional for a single source file program. Now go to the end of the code, right before the data segment definition and enter this:

MYCODE   ENDS

Before considering the other changes to be made, here, briefly is what happens to the segment registers when DOS sets up an .exe program: Just as with a .com file, DOS finds the first available paragraph of free memory and puts in the 100H byte PSP. The DS and ES registers are then given that segment address. The segments defined with the SEGMENT directive are then placed into memory, starting 100H beyond the beginning of the PSP, in the order given by the assembler (in this case in the order they appear in the source code). The segment address of the stack segment is put in SS, and the SP is set to the top of that segment. As you have put the stack segment first in tipe.exe, it will begin immediately following the PSP.

Finally, as with a .com file, CS is given the initial code segment, and the IP is given the offset of the first executable instruction—but now your program helps compute these addresses. Recall from Chapter 2 that the offset of the first executable instruction can be defined with the END directive. END MAIN defines the start of the program instructions to be at MAIN. Because MAIN is at the beginning of its segment, its offset is zero, and zero will be placed in the IP. The CS is the segment in which MAIN resides. If you chose, for instance, to start your program with the instructions at MAIN1 (END MAIN1), CS would be the same, but the IP would start with the offset of MAIN1. ORG 100H is no longer necessary to help the assembler compute offsets because the PSP is no longer within the code segment, and the first instruction will start at offset zero.

Contrast this setup with the beginning of the .com file, where all segment registers have the segment address of the beginning of the PSP and the IP is given 100H.

To make tipe.asm appropriate for an .exe file, some changes are necessary at the beginning of the code segment and at the beginning and end of MAIN. I will show you two versions of tipe.exe. Figure 9-1 holds the first version, and Fig. 9-2 holds the final version. In both versions, the difference between them and the .com version is in the initial instructions and the end instructions in MAIN. The second version is the simpler, making use of a DOS function introduced with Version 2.0. Because there are some useful lessons to be learned from the old way, and in case you want to write programs that can run under all DOS versions I will start with the first version.

THE OLD VERSION

Notice in Fig. 9-1 that the first directive in MYCODE is **ASSUME CS:MYCODE,DS:MYDATA**. The reason for this change should be obvious to you. The assembler needs to know where to find your code and your data variables, and they now are in two different segments.

Next you see that the label, MAIN:, has been deleted and that MAIN is defined as the name of a procedure, one with a FAR attribute. That definition of MAIN, in conjunction with the following instructions, will allow for the proper termination of the program.

```
MAIN PROC FAR
        PUSH    DS
        MOV     AX,0
        PUSH    AX
        . . . .
        . . . .
        RET
MAIN    ENDP
```

I must say that it took me quite a bit of researching to find out why this sequence was necessary. The implication (sometimes explicitly stated) in most of my references was that command.com of DOS called the initial procedure, and this was a way to return from a FAR procedure, a procedure in a different segment. Indeed, it is a way to return from a FAR procedure, but the purpose is not to return directly to DOS, but sneakily to issue an INT 20H to terminate the program, just as you did with tipe.com. To follow that logic, it is first necessary to understand what happens when a FAR procedure is called.

Remember that procedures can have the attributes NEAR or FAR.

You have used NEAR procedures up to this point. Conceptually, the difference is whether you are calling procedures in the same segment of not. Technically, the difference is what happens to the stack when a CALL and then a RET is made. If the procedure called has the attribute NEAR, the offset of the next instruction is pushed onto the stack and is popped back off to the IP by the RET. You learned this in Chapter 6.

On the other hand, if you make the call across segments, not only must IP be loaded with the offset of the first instruction called, but also the segment must be loaded into CS. Upon the return, both the original CS and the next instruction for the IP must be retrieved. Thus the difference between making a call to a NEAR procedure and making a call to a FAR procedure is that in the latter case, not only the IP but the CS must be saved. When the call is made, first the number in CS and then the offset of the next instruction are pushed onto the stack. Upon encountering a RET from a FAR procedure, a number is popped off the stack and placed in the IP; then a number is popped and placed in CS.

You may also jump to FAR procedures. When a jump is made, CS:IP is given the appropriate address. You may also either call or jump to a far label. Now, the assembler knows that a procedure is FAR or NEAR by its definition. How does it know the distance attribute of a label? To the assembler a label is NEAR if it is followed by a colon and FAR if the colon is absent. MAIN1 is NEAR because it is followed by a colon, as are all instruction labels in tipe.asm.

By giving the procedure MAIN the attribute FAR, whether it is called by DOS or not (and it is not, thanks to the END MAIN directive), the effect of the RET is to pop one number into the IP and then the next number into CS. Why not just say INT 20H? Because, and I quote from the 2.10 *DOS Technical Reference*, "Important. Every program must ensure that the CS register contains the segment address of its Program Segment Prefix control block prior to issuing interrupt hex 20."

When tipe.exe is ready to terminate, CS will have the segment address of MYCODE, not of the PSP. Thus by defining the initial procedure as FAR, and by first pushing DS (which begins as the segment of the PSP) and then pushing AX with a value of zero, when the RET is executed, you are assured of the following: First, that a zero will be popped into the IP, and second, that the next value popped by the return into CS will be the segment address of the PSP. Finally, recall once again that in the PSP there are two bytes stored at offset zero: 20 CD, backwards for CD 20—INT 20H. That instruction will now be executed. The purpose of these instructions is not to RET to DOS, but to issue a proper INT 20H—rather clever, really.

Recall that you can also exit with a RET in a .com program, because in setting up the program for execution, DOS places the number (offset) zero as the very first value on the stack. DOS does nothing of this sort with .exe programs, so the program has to do the task itself.

The instructions listed above which allow for this exit via INT 20H are not needed in the final version.

Another change that must be made to the program is the reversal of the order of GET_FILE and the instructions to show TITL. In the .com file you did not have to concern yourself with the segment registers. Now you do. Because getting the file is more important than showing the title, and because the segment of the PSP that holds the file name at 82H is in the DS register when the program begins, a good time to retrieve the name is before you change the DS to hold the data segment. Another option would be to save the present DS and restore it later for the move. Making the move at the outset seems the simplest.

Except for the way the program is set up to prepare for the RET to PSP:0, the major difference between this file and the .com file is that the ES and DS registers have to be *manually* loaded with the data segment, MYDATA. You set up for the call to GET_FILE by moving the data segment address into the ES register. Remember that MOVSB requires that the segment for DI be in ES. DS is properly set to the PSP for the SI register (82H). In MAIN, the segment of MYDATA is moved into ES indirectly, through another register. The assembler does not allow segment registers to be loaded directly. Almost any register can be used except another segment register. So you **MOV AX,MYDATA** and then move AX into ES. Because you want to put MYDATA in DS after the call to GET_FILE (which changes AX), AX is saved on the stack with **PUSH AX**.

At this point, take a look at the procedure GET_FILE. You do not need to change it in any way, but some of you might wonder how it works now that the DS register does not yet hold the data segment. Specifically, you ask to put OFFSET FNAME into DI. How does the CPU know what that offset is? It is computed by the assembler properly thanks to the **ASSUME DS:MYDATA** directive. Even though the DS register does not hold the data segment, the assembler can calculate the offset from any segment you give it in an ASSUME directive. The difference to keep in mind, which was hard for me at first, is the difference between assembler directives, which in this case helps the assembler do its math, and assembly-language instructions, which are used by the CPU to carry out an operation.

Upon return from GET_FILE, MYDATA is popped back into AX and is loaded into the DS register. An alternative to pushing and popping AX would be to move MYDATA once again into AX then into DS. You now show the title, then check the zero flag, which was not affected in WRITEM, and continue as before.

Now that you have changed tipe.asm to look like Fig. 9-1, go ahead and create tipe.exe. (Do not use lk.bat if you have been doing so, because you do not want a .com file.) It is instructive to trace tipe.exe through GET_FILE to the call to WRITEM to show the title, keeping a particular eye on the segment registers. Also go to the RET at the end of MAIN and trace to the INT 20H, noting what happens to CS and IP.

THE MODERN VERSION

I said there were two versions of tipe.exe. A brief skeleton is enough to show the difference between the old version and the modern (DOS 2.0 and up) version. In this version you do not need MAIN defined as a FAR procedure; in fact it need not be defined as a procedure at all, as with a .com file. Delete the PROC and ENDP directives. The label, MAIN:, once again is necessary because the END statement indicates that is where the code starts.

Because of the difference in terminating the program, you do not have to do the pushing required by the FAR return, so delete the first three instructions in MAIN:

```
PUSH    DS
MOV     AX,0
PUSH    AX
```

Replace the RET with these two instructions:

```
MOV     AX,4C00h
INT     21H
```

Figure 9-2 shows MAIN as it now looks. Everything else is the same as in Fig. 9-1.

The developers of DOS found a sensible way to terminate a program that is even better for computers with the IBM's capabilities than INT 20H. The advantage of the function 4CH of INT 21H (called *terminate a process*) is that not only does it close the program properly as does INT 20H, but also 1) CS can have any number in it, not

```
     MAIN:    mov      ax,MYDATA  ;ES to be the data seg
              mov      es,ax      ; for MOVSB
              push     ax         ;Has MYDATA
              call     GET_FILE   ;Do before showing title
              pop      ax
              mov      ds,ax      ;Put data seg in DS
              mov      dx,OFFSET TITL
              -call    WRITEM     ;Show title of program
              ----                ;The rest of MAIN is same
              ----
              ----
     DONE:    call     BOTTOM
              mov      ax,4C00H   ;DOS's terminate a process
              int      21H
     ;end of MAIN
```

Fig. 9-2. Changes in MAIN for Tipe.exe—Version 2.

just the PSP segment, 2) it returns to whatever invoked it in the first place, allowing for chaining of programs, and 3) it will return an error code that is placed in AL. This last is particularly handy for batch files, if you know that indeed a program returns error codes.

Tipe.exe, as written, does not return different error codes, so I simply put zero in AL—any number would do. Although tipe.exe would probably not be the kind of program you would include in a batch file, you could rewrite the code so that if the file were not entered, AL would have one value; if it were not found, AL could have another; if it were too big, AL could have yet another; if there was an error in reading, a fourth, and if there was a successful execution, a fifth. Just tell the user what all the values mean.

All files, .com or .exe, may use function 4CH to terminate. Keep this in mind when you write more .com files, for there certainly might be some in which you would like to be able to return an error code, especially in programs that might be executed by other programs to which they will return. On the other hand, remember that INT 20H will work under all versions of DOS, while function 4CH will work only with DOS versions of 2.0 or higher.

Your program will not work under all versions of DOS. Here is the reason it will not: DOS 1.0 retained strong similarities to its ancestor, the BDOS (Basic Disk Operating System) of 8080 and Z80 computers. These used a rather cumbersome (by DOS 2.0 standards) method of handling files. It is a method I will not describe, except to say as a programmer that it was a bit tedious. The DOS 2.0 system of using handles makes both the redirection of input and output and file handling simple. As DOS developed these capacities, they were added to the interrupts already available under DOS 1.0. DOS is now into the threes in its version and has added many new interrupts to accomplish a variety of tasks.

The handle-using method of file handling that I have shown you which opens, checks the file size, and reads a file into memory does not work unless the computer is running under a version of DOS that is 2.0 or above. (My version, by the way is 2.10.) Therefore, simply ending a program with INT 20H will not ensure that it will run under all versions of DOS. (It will only end, if it gets there, under all versions of DOS, but you might not get that far.)

If you want to write programs that work under all versions of DOS, you need to replace the handle-using functions with the old fashioned ones. These I will not teach you, for the simple reason that I believe that now, and certainly in the future, very few people will be using versions of DOS older than 2.0. But, keep in mind that those functions are there, particularly if you are concerned with the compatibility of 8080 programs with 8088 programs.

Here is a simple chart showing which DOS functions work under which version of DOS. Keep in mind that the higher versions can use all of the functions for the lower versions:

Version 1.0 +   functions to 2EH
Version 2.0 +   functions to 57H
Version 3.0 +   functions up to 0FFH (many of which do not exist yet)

If you have saved generic.asm as suggested in Chapter 2, I suggest you change INT 20H to MOV AH,4CH and INT 21H. Then you will have an up-to-date ending, allowing your programs to be called by others and to return an error code. I chose to end tipe.com with INT 20H simply because it was easier to explain from the outset.

Because the changes in this version of tipe.exe are minor, you might be satisfied with the first version and not create the second version. Either version of tipe.exe will produce exactly the same results as tipe.com, but the .exe version will be longer than the .com version. If you use DOS's DIR command with tipe.exe and tipe.com, you will see the difference. Tipe.exe has a few extra instructions, but most of the difference is due to a *header* in the file, which gives DOS the information needed to set it up for execution. The .com files are mirror images of what will be put in memory starting at 100H of the program segment, so DOS needs no special instructions. This means .com files load faster than .exe files. With a program of 1K length, the difference is negligible. If the program were 60K, it would make a bit of a difference.

After testing tipe.exe, use RENAME to give tipe.asm a different name, such as tipex.asm, if you want to save it. From now on, when I refer to tipe.asm, it will be code for a .com file. Copy tipe1.asm back to tipe.asm. You should now have three .asm files: tipe1.asm, the first .com version; tipex.asm, the .exe version; and tipe.asm, the working version. You are now going to give tipe.com some enhancements, which means you also want to rename tipe.exe and tipe.com if you want to save them. How about using tipex.exe and tipe1.com?

CHAPTER 10

Enhancements to Tipe.com

Even though tipe.com is a good working program, you can add some enhancements to it that allow the addition of some color (so you can learn more about color) and the utilization of a full 64K for the text file. Before continuing this chapter, you might want to review the discussion of character attributes in Appendix B.

If you do not have color capabilities, you can still add the color enhancements, but you will need to use more ingenuity in testing the program with Debug and ultimately will need to find a friend with a color monitor.

DETERMINING AND SAVING THE DISPLAY CHARACTERISTICS

If you want to use color, then the first thing you need to know is if you can do so. You cannot do so if a monochrome monitor is being used. Therefore, the first enhancement of tipe.asm is to add a procedure that saves the current screen characteristics and then checks to see whether a monochrome monitor is being used. If a monochrome monitor is not being used, the procedure sets the display to the 80 x 25 color mode and sets the active display page to zero.

When you display to the screen, you can then use color if you have color capabilities and black and white if you don't. You will also know the active display page is zero and will not have to assume that it is zero. Because you might have tampered with display characteristics by changing the mode, the active page, and the character attributes, as a courteous programmer you will write another procedure to put them back when the program finishes. Personally, I dislike programs that leave my screen in living color that I do not want.

The characteristics are saved in these variables:

```
OLDMODE    DB        0         ;Current mode
OLDATT     DB        0         ;         attribute
OLDPAGE    DB        0         ;         active page
```

Two different attributes are used: one for the first 23 lines where the text is displayed and the other for the bottom two lines. Because these attributes are no longer constants, but depend upon the availability of color, they are defined as variables—ATTRIB and BOTATT. Their initial values are set for color monitors.

Here are my choices: ATTRIB, the variable to hold the attribute for the main screen, is given the initial value of 70H, black on gray:

```
ATTRIB     DB        70H       ;Attrib for main screen
```

Why? Because I like to look at text in reverse video on my color monitor; it is easy on my eyes. Your choice may be different. Refer again to Appendix B and make your choice. For BOTATT, the attribute to be used on the two bottom lines, I chose 03, cyan on black—an arbitrary choice.

```
BOTATT     DB        3         ;Attribute for last 2 rows
```

Whenever you put value in the variables when you define them in the data section (rather than the generic question mark), they keep those values until changed. In this case, they will be changed if you find that the program is running on a computer with a monochrome monitor.

Exercise 10-1: Changing the Screen Attributes

If you have color capabilities, here is a little program you can write with Debug to help you experiment with screen attributes. With A100, assemble this program:

```
100    MOV    AX,3           (be sure mode is 3, 80 x 25 color)
```

```
103   INT   10           (set it, rest is the CLEARS procedure)
105   MOV   BX,0400      (BH = 4, red on black, BL = 0)
108   MOV   CX,0         (    The value of BL actually does not)
10B   MOV   DX,184F      (          matter to INT 10)
10E   MOV   AX,600
111   INT   10
113   INT   20
115
```

Then, enter Ncolor.com, to give a name to the file. Use RCX to put 15 in CX and W to write the file.

You can change the attribute in BH at any time by entering Debug with color.com and assembling just line 105. When you enter Debug with a .com file and change one or more instructions with A without changing the program's length, you can write the changes to the file with a simple W, as you did in the last chapter, because Debug initially sets up the registers with the program length in BX:CX. Actually, I keep a version of this program on my working disks with BH holding the value 70H, reverse video, so that I can change the screen to reverse video (my preference) whenever a program leaves the screen with some other attribute.

A faster way to experiment with color attributes is to enter Debug with color.com, using, for example, G113. After you have viewed the results, instead of quitting with INT 20, go back to the beginning by changing the Instruction Pointer (IP), which is now pointing to 113, this way: Type RIP. You can change the value in any register including the IP with R, the register command. The value 113 will be displayed. Type in 100. Then enter just R to see that you are at 100, and enter G113. Because you know the mode is 3, you also could skip the setting of the mode and the moving of the attribute into BX by setting the IP to 108.

This time set the IP to 108 and then change BX with RBX, putting the attribute you want to see in BH by entering the attribute in Hex followed by two zeros for BL (or you could actually put anything in BL, because BL is ignored here by BIOS). Now you have a quick way to view any attribute you wish. Just use G113, RIP to set the IP to 108, change BX with RBX, and use G113 again.

Be careful not to enter the same foreground and background characteristic for the attribute, as in 22H, unless you are prepared to work with a blank screen. You can guess the results—same foreground and background colors, in this case green characters on a green background. If you are adventuresome, you might try it, but be prepared to reboot the computer in case you cannot change the screen.

If you are not adventuresome, the lesson is over. If you are, do this. First, make sure the IP is at 108. Use RBX to enter 22. Then enter G113. Note that not only is the screen in green and blank, but there is no cursor showing. Actually, it is there flashing away at you—in green. Also Debug's hyphen prompt is there awaiting your entry. So enter RIP, then 108, then RBX, then 70, then G113. Do not forget to press ENTER after each.

If you were successful, the screen is now in reverse video with the prompt and cursor visible. If not, no harm is done—just reboot. The lesson here is be careful in choosing foreground and background colors (or when allowing the user to do so), because the only alternative might be to reboot.

The SETSCREEN Procedure

Figure 10-1 shows SETSCREEN, the procedure that sets up the

```
        SETSCREEN PROC NEAR
            mov     ah,8      ;Gets char and attribute at
            int     10H       ;current cursor position.
            mov     OLDATT,ah ;Attribute in AH.
            mov     ah,15     ;mode and active disp. page
            int     10H       ;AL has mode, BH disp. page
            mov     OLDMODE,al       ;Save them
            mov     OLDPAGE,bh
            cmp     al,7      ;If 7, is monochrome
            jnz     SETSC1    ;Anything else is color
            mov     al,07H    ;For monochrome
            mov     ATTRIB,al ;Screen to be gray
            mov     al,070H   ;         on black
            mov     BOTATT,al ;Bot lines rev. video
            jmp     SHORT SETSCX
SETSC1:     cmp     al,3      ;Is mode already 3
            jz      SETSCX
            mov     ax,0003H  ;No, 3 = 80 X 25 color
            int     10H              ;change it
SETSCX:     cmp     bh,0      ;Still has active page
            jz      SETSX     ;It's 0, so ok
            mov     ax,0500H  ;Set active page to 0
            int     10H
SETSX:      ret
        SETSCREEN ENDP
```

Fig. 10-1. Procedure to set up the screen.

screen. SETSCREEN gets and saves important display characteristics and sets the program's display characteristics to fit the monitor.

In brief, SETSCREEN uses the video services of BIOS INT 10H several times. First, it uses service 8, which returns the character in AL and the attribute in AH at the current cursor position. I am presuming that the whole screen is using that attribute. The value in AH, then, is the current attribute that you will save in OLDATT to be restored later.

Next, service 15 returns the current mode in AL and the active display page in BH. These, too, you save. Now test the current mode. If the mode is 7, it has to be a monochrome monitor. Why? Because 7 means a monochrome monitor and that mode is not used otherwise.

The next section of code sets up the attributes for monochrome monitors that replace those you have set for color. After setting the attributes a jump is taken to the exit, which assures that the active page is zero, color or not. If the mode was anything but 7, a jump is made to SETSC1, where the first step is to test the mode again. You are going to want it to be mode 3, 80 x 25 color. If it is not 3, you can use service 0, which sets the mode to the one called for in the AL register.

You need a call to SETSCREEN in tipe.asm. You can put it almost anywhere in MAIN before the first CLEARS. Probably the best spot for it is right before the setup and call to CLEARS in MAIN, before the statement MOV DX,184FH. By putting it there, you do not have to change the screen characteristics, save them, and put them back if the program terminates early, as it might if no file name were entered, or no files were found.

ADDING COLOR

To make use of your work in SETSCREEN, you need to change the statement in CLEARS that says MOV BH,07H. It sets the attribute to clear the screen using gray on black. Instead, you will use the variable and change it to MOV BH,ATTRIB. Before you make any more changes, assemble and create tipe.com with the added variables, the new SETSCREEN procedure, and the change in CLEARS. The program should run as before, but now the main screen will appear in the attribute of your choice.

Next you need a way to set the attributes of the bottom two lines. First you must write a general procedure to clear or blank any columns in a row starting from the cursor position. Video service 9 does that for you. Starting at the cursor position, it writes the ASCII character in AL, having the attribute in BL, to the page in BH the number of

```
CLRLN PROC NEAR         ;Clears from cursor position
;Entry attribute in BL, Number to clear in CX
        push    ax
        push    bx          ;Writes char in AL with
        mov     ax,920H     ;with attribute in BL
        mov     bh,0        ; AL is 20H, a blank
        int     10H         ; BH - active page
        pop     bx
        pop     ax
        ret
CLRLN ENDP
```

Fig. 10-2. Procedure to clear characters on the screen.

times in CX. Add CLRLN, shown in Fig. 10-2, to the BIOS screen handling routines.

Because the character in AL is a blank, this procedure clears any number of columns in a particular row depending upon the entry value in CX. You use it to clear the row from the cursor forward. If you start the cursor at column zero, and CX has 80, CLRLN not only clears the row, but effectively sets the attribute for the entire row. CLRLINE uses CLRLN to do just that. It is in Fig. 10-3.

CLRLINE is written as a general procedure that clears a row forward from the cursor position given it in DX. It assumes an 80-column display. Enter CLRLINE into the program. With two more changes, you will be ready to test it. First, in LINEOUT, replace the statement CALL CURSOR with CALL CLRLINE. Precede this statement with MOV AL,BOTATT. LINEOUT now clears the line, sets BOTATT, and then

```
CLRLINE PROC    NEAR
;Entry row in DH, col in DL, attribute in AL
        push    bx
        push    cx
        mov     cx,80       ;80 columns per row
        sub     cl,dl       ;Clear 80 minus entry col
        call    CURSOR      ;set the cursor
        mov     bl,al       ;move in attribute
        call    CLRLN       ;clear it
        pop     cx
        pop     bx
        ret
CLRLINE ENDP
```

Fig. 10-3. Procedure to clear a line from the cursor forward.

sends out the dashes. Second, rewrite bottom so it looks like this:

```
BOTTOM  PROC    NEAR
        mov     al,BOTATT
        mov     dx,1800H    ;Beginning of 24th row
        call    CLRLINE
        ret                 ;no more fall through to cursor
BOTTOM  ENDP
```

You call BOTTOM only once for now, right before MES1 is displayed. Delete the last CALL BOTTOM at DONE. DONE now has just the INT 20.

All set up? You might want to check Fig. 10-5, which shows the changes made in MAIN and the new or changed procedures needed for the display enhancement. The new procedures are shown in their entirety. Other changes are shown in uppercase and highlighted with arrows. There is one more procedure to develop, RESCREEN, but before you insert that procedure and the call to it, you should test the changes made so far.

When you quit tipe.com, the cursor is at the top of the screen, and the DOS prompt appears there. The screen remains in the attribute that was in ATTRIB. This state of affairs will now be corrected.

All that remains to be done to incorporate the screen enhancement changes is to write the procedure RESCREEN, which restores to their original states any changes made to the display by the program. Put the call to the procedure right after SHOW_IT and before DONE so that the end of MAIN looks like this:

```
        call    SHOW_IT
        call    RESCREEN
DONE:   int     20H
MAIN    ENDP
```

If you have a monochrome monitor there is only one possible page, page zero. If you have color capability you have four pages to work with in an 80-column mode and eight pages in a 40-column mode. You know that any one of them can be the active one. An exercise in switching the active page follows.

Exercise 10-2: Switching the Active Page

Again, you need color capability to carry out this exercise. Here

Debug is used to illustrate switching the active display page. Use the Assemble command to enter these instructions. First enter A100 and type this:

```
100    MOV    AX,501      (service 5 changes active page to number in AL)
103    INT    10
105    MOV    AX,500      (put it back to 0)
108    INT    10
10A    NOP
```

This exercise assumes that your active display page is zero, which is usually the case, because it is set at that when you turn on or reboot the computer. (You could check it with service 15.)

Go to 105 and see what happens. Quick, eh? Press ENTER several times to put some asterisks on the display (page 1). Now go to 10A. Everything is as you left it, including the position of the cursor. This is a handy way to redisplay the original screen to the user, and you will use it if tipe.com has changed the active display page.

Set the IP to 100, and run through the exercise once more. Go to 105. You will see that page 1 now has your asterisks, and the cursor is where you left it. If you quit Debug at this point, the display is now using page 1 (a perfectly good page) until changed by you or some program.

RESTORING THE SCREEN

Because you have saved three characteristics of the display, RESCREEN, shown in Fig. 10-4, does quite a bit of checking.

First, OLDPAGE is checked to see if it is zero. If it is not, you simply restore the page using video service 5, knowing that the proper page number is in AL, and you are done. The result is as you saw in the last exercise. If OLDPAGE was zero, OLDATT is put into the variables ATTRIB and BOTATT in preparation for possible calls to BOTTOM or CLEARS. Then you check the mode. If it is 7, it was a monochrome monitor. The mode was not changed, so you jump directly to the instructions at the end of the procedure to place the cursor at the bottom and restore the attribute. You can no longer check to see if OLDATT and BOTATT are the same because they have been made the same earlier in this procedure. Therefore you just call BOTTOM, which will assure that the last line (the line on which the DOS prompt will start) has the proper attribute.

Go back to the top. If the OLDMODE was not 7, you next want

```
            RESCREEN PROC NEAR
                    mov     al,OLDPAGE
                    cmp     al,0            ;was it 0?
                    jz      RESC1
                    mov     ah,5            ;No, AL has old page number
                    int     10H             ;Completely restored
                    jmp     SHORT RESX      ; So quit
            RESC1:  mov     al,OLDATT
                    mov     ATTRIB,al       ;Set these for CLEARS
                    mov     BOTATT,al       ; or BOTTOM
                    mov     al,OLDMODE
                    cmp     al,7            ;Was it monochrome?
                    jz      RESC2           ;Yes cursor to bottom
                    cmp     al,3            ;Was it 80X25 color?
                    jz      RESC2
                    mov     ah,0            ;No, put it back
                    int     10H             ;   and make sure
                    call    CLEARS          ;proper attr is back
                    jmp     SHORT RESEX
            RESC2:  call    BOTTOM          ;Page and mode same
            RESEX:  ret                     ;assure attribute is same
            RESCREEN ENDP
```

Fig. 10-4. Procedure to restore the screen characteristics.

to know if it was 3, the one you used. If it is, you simply jump to the instruction CALL BOTTOM with the same rationale as above. If the OLDMODE is not 3, you must change the mode. AL has the OLDMODE, so all you need to do is put 0 in AH (for set the mode) and call the interrupt. The effect of changing the display mode is to clear and set all display pages to that mode and set the attribute to be 0FH, white on black. Although the screen will then be blank (white on black), CLEARS is called to blank it once again just in case the original attribute was not white on black.

Another way of returning the screen to its state before the program was run is to simply restore the mode, page, and attribute with no checking. The result is a clear screen. You might choose that solution. I chose the one I illustrated with RESCREEN because after I quit a program, I often like to see what is on the screen at the moment I quit. Assuming the page was the same, because RESCREEN just cleared the bottom line, the rest of the text will remain on the screen.

Figure 10-5 shows all of the changes made for the display enhancements.

```
MAIN:       ----
            ----
MAIN3:      ----
            call    readin
            jc      done        ;A read error was given
--->        CALL    SETSCREEN
            ----
            ----
            call    show_it
--->        CALL    RESCREEN
DONE:--->int         20H         ;Rid call bottom

SETSCREEN PROC NEAR
            mov     ah,8        ;Gets char and attribute at
            int     10H         ;current cursor position.
            mov     OLDATT,ah   ;Attribute in AH.
            mov     ah,15       ;mode and active disp. page
            int     10H         ;AL has mode, BH disp. page
            mov     OLDMODE,al          ;Save them
            mov     OLDPAGE,bh
            cmp     al,7        ;If 7, is monochrome
            jnz     SETSC1      ;Anything else is color
            mov     al,07H      ;For monochrome
            mov     ATTRIB,al   ;Screen to be gray
            mov     al,070H     ;          on black
            mov     BOTATT,al   ;Bot lines rev. video
            jmp     SHORT SETSCX
SETSC1:     cmp     al,3        ;Is mode already 3
            jz      SETSCX
            mov     ax,0003H    ;No, 3 = 80 X 25 color
            int     10H         ;change it
SETSCX:     cmp     bh,0        ;Still has active page
            jz      SETSX       ;It's 0, so ok
            mov     ax,0500H    ;Set active page to 0
            int     10H
SETSX:      ret
SETSCREEN ENDP

RESCREEN PROC NEAR
            mov     al,OLDPAGE
            cmp     al,0        ;was it 0?
            jz      RESC1
            mov     ah,5        ;No, AL has old page number
            int     10H         ;Completely restored
            jmp     SHORT RESEX ;  So quit
RESC1:      mov     al,OLDATT
            mov     ATTRIB,al   ;Set these for CLEARS
            mov     BOTATT,al   ;  or BOTTOM
            mov     al,OLDMODE
```

Fig. 10-5. Changes and additions for the display enhancement.

```
                cmp     al,7            ;Was it monochrome?
                jz      RESC2           ;Yes cursor to bottom
                cmp     al,3            ;Was it 80X25 color?
                jz      RESC2
                mov     ah,0            ;No, put it back
                int     10H             ;  and make sure
                call    CLEARS          ;proper attr is back
                jmp     SHORT RESEX
RESC2:  call    BOTTOM          ;Page and mode same
RESEX:  ret                     ;assure attribute is same
RESCREEN ENDP

LINEOUT PROC NEAR
                mov     dh,23           ;Row 23
                sub     dl,dl           ;Column 0
--->    MOV     AL,BOTATT
--->    CALL    CLRLINE
                mov     cx,80           ;Set count to 80
                ---
                ---
LINEOUT ENDP

BOTTOM PROC NEAR
--->    MOV     AL,BOTATT
                mov     dx,1800H        ;Beginning of 24th row
--->    CALL    CLRLINE
--->    RET             ;no more fall through to cursor
BOTTOM ENDP

CLEARS  PROC    NEAR    ;Entry DH has row of bot
                ----
                ----
--->    MOV     BH,ATTRIB ;Attribute now variable
                int     10H
                ----
                ----
CLEARS  ENDP

CLRLN PROC NEAR         ;Clears from cursor position
;Entry attribute in BL, Number to clear in CX
                push    ax
                push    bx      ;Writes char in Al with
                mov     ax,920H ;with attribute in BL
                mov     bh,0    ; AL is 20H, a blank
                int     10H     ; BH - active page
                pop     bx
                pop     ax
                ret
CLRLN ENDP

CLRLINE PROC    NEAR
```

```
                ;Entry row in DH, col in DL, attribute in AL
                push    bx
                push    cx
                mov     cx,80       ;80 columns per row
                sub     cl,dl       ;Clear 80 minus entry col
                call    CURSOR      ;set the cursor
                mov     bl,al       ;move in attribute
                call    CLRLN       ;clear it
                pop     cx
                pop     bx
                ret
        CLRLINE ENDP

        ;Add these to the data:

        OLDMODE DB      0           ;Current mode
        OLDATT  DB      0           ;       attribute
        OLDPAGE DB      0           ;       active page
        ATTRIB  DB      70H         ;Attribute for main screen
        BOTATT  DB      3           ;Attribute for last 2 rows
```

ADDING AN EXTRA SEGMENT

I should imagine that you have the impression that .com files are limited in size to 64K for both the program and the data. You probably have that impression because I have said nothing to dissuade you of that fact. Now I will. The limitation of 64K, determined by the code segment, applies only to the code and data actually written into the program. You can place the stack and any data read into the program anywhere in RAM you wish.

The logical and safest place for new data is after the end of any code or data in the code segment. I have one .com program that given enough RAM, will accept up to four 64K files. If you were limited to the 64K code segment, and let's say, the code and data used 40K of the segment, that would leave only 24K (minus stack space) in that segment for the file. Here is how to get around that limitation in order to use one "extra segment." what you are going to do is to define a 64K segment starting at the very end of the program code and data.

A segment, by definition, starts at a paragraph and includes 64K of memory. What can be done is to determine the first segment address following the data. Simply stated, if the last data address is known, the next address ending with a zero begins the next segment. Find that address, drop the zero, and put it in ES. When you have done so, you have access to your code in CS and data in DS, and access to 64K worth of extra memory in ES. A procedure that does the computations and sets ES to hold the new segment follows. It requires the AX register to have the offset of the last byte or word in the program upon entry. In this case, BUFFR is this byte.

SET_SEG, which is shown in Fig. 10-6, is designed to compute the paragraph address following the last variable in the segment in ES. The program begins with ES being the same as DS, and BUFFR being the last variable. Let's say that DS (and thus ES) is 1423H, and the offset of BUFFR is 279H. The segment that would begin right after BUFFR would have this absolute address: 14230H + 279H + number needed to begin on a paragraph. Here is the math (use Debug's H command to do this):

```
  14230H
+   279H
  ──────
  144A9H
```

The next paragraph starts at 144B0H, so the segment address you want for ES is 144BH.

Because the registers only hold four, not five, bytes, this is another way to do the math using the segment address 1423H without its following zero. Likewise, you can drop the last four bits of the offset (in this case the 9), to get 27H. Increasing this result by one (28H) gives the number of paragraphs to add to the segment address to reach the segment just beyond the offset. Now add the two:

```
  1423H
+   28H
  ─────
  144BH
```

ES will get 144BH, just as above. This is easy to accomplish if you

```
SET_SEG PROC NEAR
;Entry: ax offset of last data in ES
        mov     cl,4        ;Bytes to shift right
        shr     ax,cl       ;Low 4 bits (0 to A) gone
        inc     ax          ;Number of paragr. to add
        mov     cx,es       ;ES same as DS right now
        add     ax,cx       ;Add present segment
        mov     es,ax       ;Exit new segment in ES
        ret
SET_SEG ENDP
```

Fig. 10-6. Procedure to compute an extra segment.

can get rid of the last four bits of BUFFR's offset. The 8088 provides a number of bit-manipulation instructions. The one you will use is SHR, SHift Right. Its format is SHR register, 1, (shift it one time) or SHR register,CL (shift it CL times).

For each shift, the bits are literally shifted right, with a zero placed in the most significant bit. The value of the bit shifted out goes into the carry flag. Given the value in AX of 279H and the instruction SHR AX,1, here is the result in binary:

```
0279H    = 0 0 0 0   0 0 1 0   0 1 1 1   1 0 0 1
 SHR
 AX,1    = 0 0 0 0   0 0 0 1   0 0 1 1   1 1 0 0   = 013CH
                                            EN
```

Given the same value in AX and the instruction SHR AX,CL when CL has 4, here is the result in binary:

```
0279H    = 0 0 0 0   0 0 1 0   0 1 1 1   1 0 0 1
 SHR
 AX,CL   = 0 0 0 0   0 0 0 0   0 0 1 0   0 1 1 1   = 0027H
```

If you have followed the math to this point, the procedure SET_SEG should be clear to you. AX has the offset of BUFFR. You shift the word in AX to the right 4 times, deleting the least significant four bits. Increasing the result by one gives the number of paragraphs to add to DS to start a fresh segment. ES and DS are the same at this point. ES is moved into CX so you can add the segment address to the number of paragraphs in AX. The result in AX, the new segment address, is placed in EX, and the procedure returns.

Reading the text file into a segment referenced by the new value in ES rather than DS requires several changes in the program. This is the price you pay for more memory usage—it will give you some practice in monitoring the segment registers. To fully utilize this new segment, you are going to need to move the stack pointer and to change any procedures that have reference to the location of the file. These procedures are READIN, SHOW_IT, and REVERSE. You can also eliminate the file-size check at MAIN3 because any file 64K or less will fit in the segment in ES and be quite acceptable. Figure 10-7 shows the changes to be made.

Starting with the changes in MAIN, once you know there is text entered at 82H and it has been moved to FNAME, there is no further use for the PSP in the program. Therefore, at MAIN1, you move the stack pointer to 100H, the beginning of the program, so that the stack

```
MAIN:      ----
           ----
MAIN1:-->MOV    AX,OFFSET BUFFR ;Last data entry
  --->    CALL   SET_SEG    ;Put seg for file in ES
          mov    dx,offset fname
          mov    si,dx
          call   openfl
          ----
MAIN2:    mov    bx,ax
          call   fsize      ;NZ means over 64k in size
          jz     main3
MAINBG:   ----
          ----
MAIN3:    call   readin     ;No further checks needed
          jc     done
          ----
          call   cursor
  --->    MOV    BX,-1      ;1 less than start of ES:0
  --->    MOV    MEMP,BX    ;because we INC to start
          mov    al,0       ;Dummy we'll go forward
          call   show_it
          call   rescreen
DONE:     int    20H
;End of MAIN

SET_SEG PROC NEAR
;Entry: ax offset last data in ES
          mov    cl,4       ;Bytes to shift right
          shr    ax,cl      ;Low 4 bits (0 to A) gone
          inc    ax         ;Number of paragr. to add
          mov    cx,es      ;ES same as DS right now
          add    ax,cx      ;Add present segment
          mov    es,ax      ;Exit new segment in ES
          ret
SET_SEG ENDP

SHOW_IT PROC NEAR
          ----
FORW:     mov    bx,memp
  --->    MOV    AL,ES:[BX]    ;Put it in AL
          cmp    al,eof
          ----
PAGELP:   ----
LINELP:   ----
  --->    MOV    AL,ES:[BX]  ;And get the next char
          cmp    al,dl
          jz     showln
          ----
```

Fig. 10-7. Changes and additions for the memory enhancement.

```
SHOWLN:  mov      dx,memp
         inc      dx
--->     PUSH     DS
--->     PUSH     ES
--->     POP      DS
         call     write
--->     POP      DS
         ----
SHOMORE: ----
         ret
SHOW_IT ENDP

REVERSE PROC NEAR
         mov      si,topadd
--->     MOV      DI,-1        ;top of screen minus 1
         ----
         mov      cx,24        ;Line counter go back 24
         mov      dl,LF        ;for the comparison
--->     PUSH     DS           ;Save it
--->     MOV      BX,ES        ;Put es
--->     MOV      DS,BX        ;into ds for lodsb
         std
REV1:    lodsb
--->     CMP      SI,DI        ;if -1 skip to pop
--->     JZ       REV2
         cmp      al,dl
         jnz      rev1
         loop     rev1
         inc      si
--->REV2: POP     DS           ;Back to normal
         mov      memp,si
--->     INC      AL           ;in case zero flag
         cld                   ;set with cmp si,di
REV_EX: ret
REVERSE ENDP

READIN PROC NEAR
;Entry, SI offset of file name, BX has file handle
;   ES has segment to place file
         ----
         mov      cx,filesz    ;# of bytes to read
--->     SUB      DX,DX        ;Start of ES segment
--->     PUSH     DS           ;Save DS
--->     PUSH     ES           ;Put ES
--->     POP      DS           ;   in DS
         call     readfl
--->     POP      DS           ;Back to normal
         jnc      reda
         ----
REDA:    ----
REDX:    ret
READIN ENDP
```

now will grow downward in the PSP. If the SP were not changed, think what might happen if you had a long program AND read in a large file. Once ES is changed you have two overlapping segments as illustrated in Fig. 10-8. There are other solutions, but usually the 256 bytes of the PSP provides plenty of room for the stack.

As soon as the SP is changed, SET_SEG is called. SET_SEG changes the ES register, which is all right, because you have finished using the ES register in GET_FILE to move the file name into the data area and are preparing to open the file. READIN must be changed because function 3FH needs the segment of the data address in DS. The segment of the data address for the text file is now in ES, not in DS, so you have to see that the segment in ES gets into DS before the call to READFL. You can do that in several ways. However you do it, you must save the value in DS so that it can be retrieved.

READIN uses the usual and simple way of pushing it onto the stack and popping it back when READFL is finished. READIN also uses a simple method of moving the value in ES to DS. Remember that you cannot use MOV to move the value in one segment register directly into another. In developing tipe.exe, the method used was to move the value in a segment register into a data register, and then move it from the data register into the second segment register. In this case the alternative is to use the stack to make the move by using; PUSH ES immediately followed by POP DS.

READIN, as now written, has three entry requirements. SI holds the offset of the file name, BX has the handle, and ES has the segment of the place in memory to hold the text file. A second change is to

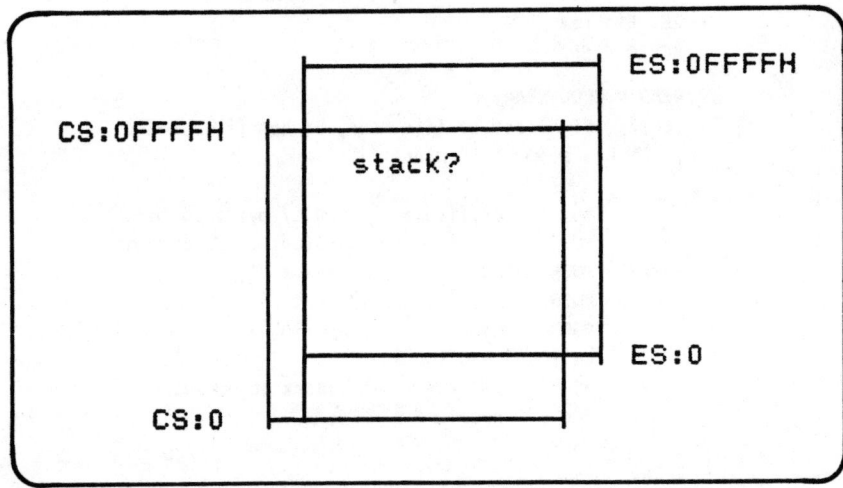

Fig. 10-8. Two overlapping segments.

prepare for the read by placing zero in DX, the offset of the beginning of the file. No longer will that offset be BUFFR.

Next, consider the changes in SHOW_IT. It illustrates a simple technique provided by the assembler to get around the 8088 requirements about use of segment registers. Remember that you used BX in SHOW_IT to point to offsets in the text file. The segment register for BX is DS, but now the file is in ES. The assembler allows *segment overrides*, so that when you want a segment register that is different from the one required to be the base for a pointer, you specify that segment register in the instruction.

The two instructions changed in SHOW_IT are the same: MOV AL,[BX]. Without an override, the CPU will follow the instruction and move the content of BX in DS into AL. However, MOV AL,ES:[BX] has it move the content of BX in ES into AL, which is what you want. Thus, SHOW_IT is changed by the insertion of the segment override, ES:, in these two instructions.

A second change in SHOW_IT is necessary because WRITE, like READFL, expects the address of the data in DS:DX. I have used the same push-pop technique used in READIN to accomplish the task.

Finally, several changes are needed in REVERSE. First, −1 is put into DI for the comparison—more about this in a minute. Next, you cannot resort to a segment override unless you want to rewrite the procedure at REV1 without using LODSB, which requires the segment for SI to be DS. Once again DS is saved, ES is moved into DS (for variety's sake through BX), and then DS is restored immediately after the loop.

Another change is required in the inner loop of REV1, which checks for a LF. Remember that earlier you had put a LF in the data right before BUFFR to make the checking easy. Now, you do not know what is before ES:0, the start of the file in memory. When you place −1 in a register, as you have in DI, it looks the same as 65535, or 0FFFFH. If SI holds zero, and thus is pointing to the beginning of the file, when the register is decreased, it will hold 0FFFFH. You test to see if SI has gone beyond the beginning of the file by comparing it with DI. If it has, the jump is taken to the POP so that INC SI is skipped because you want SI to be one less than the beginning of the file. Finally you add the instruction INC AL just to be sure the zero flag is clear because there are now two paths to finding the top of the screen.

Make the changes shown in Fig. 10-7 and test the program. Tipe.com is now written to accommodate any monitor and to read and display any ASCII file up to 64K. More important than that, it contains a number of procedures that you can insert in your other programs that accomplish basic functions that are common to most computer programs.

With any assembly language program, there are many alternative paths to the same solution. The next chapter shows you some alternatives that could be used with tipe.com.

CHAPTER 11

Variations in Tipe.com

In this chapter you will look at two kinds of variations. First, some variations in the program instructions and organization—other ways to accomplish the same task—are presented. You may have made enough changes in tipe.asm to satisfy you for a while. I present these variations not for you to put in tipe.com (unless you want to), but to show you more about the flexibility of assembly language and to have you think about alternative ways to do some of the tasks accomplished in tipe.com.

Second, I describe some different ways to put the program together for the assembler. This is in preparation for the final chapter—writing to the disk.

PLACEMENT OF THE DATA AND THE STACK

Back in Chapter 3, I said that some programmers prefer to place their data at the start of the program, not at the end as I do. Their main reason is, I believe, that if the assembler encounters the data first and a variable is referenced, the assembler knows how many bytes to reserve for that variable: one for a byte, or two for a word. Particularly with the new versions of the IBM and Microsoft MASMs, this is less important. On the first pass, the assembler checks the register to receive the variable. If it is a byte register, a byte is reserved. If it is a word register, a word is reserved. If, on the second pass, it is found that the variable type does not match the register, the error message "Type mismatch" is displayed. Because the assembler takes two passes through the code, the only real result in putting data at the end is that the assembler may reserve two bytes, when it had to reserve only one, resulting in wasted program space. This too can be avoided.

Consider the instructions:

```
MOV      AL,COUNT
INC      AL
MOV      COUNT,AL
```

There is no problem, no matter where the data resides, because AL requires a byte. But consider the valid alternative:

```
INC      COUNT
```

Now, unless COUNT has already been defined, when the assembler reaches this instruction, it reserves two bytes, because COUNT could be a word.

Those of us who like our data last in a program can save this byte with the following:

```
INC      BYTE PTR COUNT
```

This tells the assembler that COUNT is a byte, so it should reserve only one byte for it.

With the directive PTR, you can give information to MASM that it would not otherwise have on the first pass: you can tell it you want a label used as an operand to be considered as a byte or a word, or as near or far. You can also use PTR to make MASM loosen up on its restrictions on type matching. PTR not only helps you help MASM do its math while assembling, but it is akin to the segment override. Even though you have specifically defined an ATTRIB as a byte, for instance, you could put in a specific instruction, WORD PTR ATTRIB, and the assembler would then allow for this variable (and the byte following it in memory) to be used as a word.

Here is how you can put the data at the top of the program if that is your desire: First, remember that the last step in setting up a .com file for execution is to place the offset 100H in the IP. Therefore, whatever is at 100H will be interpreted as an instruction and executed. This is not a problem. Just start with a JMP, and jump around any data you put after the jump. The model is shown here:

```
MAIN:   JMP          START        (or JMP SHORT if START is close enough)
;Data here
START:  MOV          DX,OFFSET TITL
```

You can put the data anywhere in the program you like, as long as it is not in the way of the instruction flow. If it is, jump around it. Wherever there is an unconditional JMP or a RET in your program, you can place data after that instruction.

Keep the above discussion in mind while you consider where else you might place the stack pointer. In developing tipe.com you first had it starting at the top of the code segment, 0FFFEH, and then you moved it to the top of the PSP, 100H. Actually, you have many options.

You first changed the SP at MAIN1: by saying MOV SP,100H. What would be the effect of saying MAIN1:   MOV SP,MAIN1? Nothing, except to move the SP to point to the offset of MAIN1, which would give a larger stack area if you thought you could use it. But let's say you want to ensure that your stack has 200H bytes of space in which to grow. How about using the following?

```
        ORG          100H
MAIN:   JMP          START
        ORG          200H
START:  MOV          SP,START
```

The assembler directive ORG was discussed in Chapter 2 in relation to the use of ORG 100H. ORG tells the assembler that you want the instructions immediately following to start at the specified offset.

In a .com program, because the first instruction is automatically placed at 100H, the effect of ORG 100H is to aid the assembler in doing the math required for finding appropriate addresses of names and labels. Here I have shown a second and more general use of ORG. In the case of ORG 200H, when the assembler is setting up the program, START will actually be placed at offset 200H.

Using ORG with instruction code is like using DUP for data. Recall that if you wanted to reserve 100 bytes of memory for a variable, you could type in 100 question marks, or use 100 DUP (?). You could accomplish the same effect as ORG 200H does by typing in 100H (minus three for the JMP at 100H) NOPs, but ORG 200H is much simpler. In the program code, the assembler will reserve the appropriate bytes in memory between the last instruction and the one preceded by the ORG directive. Keep in mind, once again, the difference between assembler directives and 8088 instructions. ORG say where to place START in memory. JMP START is the instruction needed for the program to get there.

If you want both a large stack and data at the top, consider using the following code:

```
MAIN:     JMP        START
          ORG        200H
START:    MOV        SP,START
          JMP        BEGIN
;Data here
BEGIN:    MOV        DX,OFFSET TITL
```

NEATNESS, SIZE, OR SPEED

As you get into writing assembly language programs, you will be concerned with either the size of the program or its speed—sometimes both, which can be a dilemma—thanks to the flexibility and options you have. A third characteristic is *neatness*, by which I mean the ease of interpreting what the source code is supposed to do.

One way to achieve neatness is to write structured procedures, so that each procedure performs a specific task. A procedure is called, does its task, possibly using other procedures, and returns. A structured procedure also typically has one entrance and one exit. If either size or speed makes no difference—you have plenty of memory for the program and its data, and it performs its task at a satisfactory speed—a good rule is to write the program in a structured manner.

A sloppy (unstructured) program can do its task as well as (sometimes better than) a structured one. However, understanding what the source code is supposed to be doing and debugging it may become close to impossible. As you know by now, understanding what the program should do and finding out what it actually does is the art and science of writing assembly-language programs.

Tipe.com is written with neat procedures. All but the original BOTTOM ends with a RET. This is a matter of style and preference that is, I think, shared by many programmers. Writing structured code helps us think in a more structured way, and makes the assembly instructions (source code) much easier to follow. Remember, however, that the only time you are *required* to define a procedure is when its attribute is to be FAR, so it can return properly.

As mentioned in Chapter 9, if the distance attribute for a procedure is missing, then the assembler assumes NEAR. All labels for the instructions you have been using have the attribute NEAR because each is followed by a colon. Thus, tipe.com could be written with no procedures at all, by changing the procedure names to labels for the first instruction, just as you have written MAIN both as a procedure and as a subroutine beginning with a label.

Whether you define a subroutine as a procedure or not, it is also not necessary to follow the pattern of ending with a RET. I will show the alternatives. Here I ignore neatness and consider size and speed. All 8088 instructions take one or more bytes of memory. All 8088 instructions take time. You can find other books that describe the full 8088 instruction set including each instruction's size and speed. The general rule is that register-to-register operations are short and fast, constant-to-register operations are longer and slower, and register-to-memory (or vice versa) operations are longer and slower yet.

Sometimes you can reduce size and gain speed without sacrificing neatness. For instance, you have used the SUB instruction rather than the MOV instruction to place zero in a register (when you were not concerned with changing the flag register) in tipe.com. SUB CH,CH is faster (register-to-register) than MOV CH,0 (constant-to-register) and takes fewer bytes of opcode. Several times in the program there are instructions like CMP AL,0. Similarly, there is an alternative, OR AL,AL, that does the trick faster and with fewer bytes. I will leave ANDing and ORing (comparing bits) for your next book in assembly-language programming, but for our purposes I will tell you that the zero flag is set with such an instruction if and only if the value in the register is zero.

Another way to reduce size without sacrificing neatness is to make use of MASM's location counter, which is a dollar sign. During assembly it represents the current location within the current segment. In the original version of tipe.com, BUFFR is defined in this way:

```
BUFFR      DB          ?
```

An alternative that would save that byte would be as follows:

```
BUFFR      EQU         $
```

Now BUFFR is a constant that is given the value of the offset of its location in the program, and one byte is saved. You would not need to change the instructions in the program that refer to BUFFR because MASM will accept either BUFFR or OFFSET BUFFR in instructions.

By expanding this definition of BUFFR and using some of MASM's arithmetic operators, you could eliminate several instructions in SET__SEG in the enhanced version of tipe.com. Here is the expanded definition:

BUFFR   EQU   ($ − MAIN + 110H) / 10H

MASM evaluates this expression by first subtracting the offset of MAIN from the current offset indicated by the dollar sign. To that value, 110H is added, to add back the offset of MAIN, which you know is 100H plus 10H. That sum is divided by 10H, resulting in the number of paragraphs to be added to ES to start a new segment.

I tried this without subtracting MAIN and adding only 10H, but MASM complained. It will add numbers to offsets like $, and subtract numbers from them, but it will not do some other things like divide. By subtracting MAIN from $, the result is a difference, not an offset, and MASM is happy to divide. If BUFFR were defined in this way, then the following instructions could be eliminated in SET_SEG because the assembler would have already done this math:

```
        mov     cl,4        ;Bytes to shift right
        shr     ax,cl       ;Low 4 bits (0 to A) gone
        inc     ax          ;Number of paragr. to add
```

I show you this example to illustrate that the assembler can do much more for you than compute segments and offsets for your programs. Actually I prefer SET_SEG as it is, because keeping the math in the program, rather than doing it at assembly time, allows a variable entry in AX. For instance, you can compute an extra segment starting at the end of your data, read a file into memory, find the end of that file, put that offset in AX, and define another extra segment for use by another file.

All of my other suggestions sacrifice neatness—the source code is much harder to follow. First, you can eliminate the unnecessary RETs in the program. RETurns take up a byte of memory and the process of returning takes time. If the last instruction before the RET in the procedure is a CALL, you can skip the RET and change the CALL to a JMP. This is very similar to BOTTOM-falling through to CURSOR, where there is a RET. If there is a JMP to a subroutine with a RET (or to a subroutine that jumps to one with a RET, and so on), this will be as effective a way to return to the calling routine as using the call, coming back to the instruction following the call, and then returning.

Assuming a proper RET somewhere in DO_IT, these are the choices:

```
        CALL        DO__IT
        RET
```
or
```
        JMP         DO__IT
```

When you can use JMP instead of CALL/RET, your program is ahead in two ways. One, it saves a byte of machine language (the RET), and two, it is faster. So JMP, rather than CALL, serves both the purpose of speed and size, but it is not neat—it is much harder to follow the source code when you are reading and debugging it.

If you decide to replace CALLs with JMPs, be careful to be sure that you do not need the RET that would follow the call. For instance, the procedure READIN ends this way:

```
REDA:   CALL        CLOSEFL
REDX:   RET
```

You can change CALL CLOSEFL to JMP CLOSEFL for a faster execution, but you cannot (or better not) remove REDX: RET because that is needed for an exit if there was a read error.

Another way to speed program execution is to avoid PUSHing and POPping, which also take significant time (in computer speed). It is much faster to move a value in a register to another register than it is to move it to and from the stack. As an example, one of the ways the value in ES was moved into DS was to PUSH ES and then POP DS. A second way was to move ES into a data register, for example, by using MOV BX,ES and then moving the value into DS. The second way takes more bytes of machine language to accomplish the task, but it is much faster. In both cases, you still saved and retrieved the original DS.

With a .com program, you can eliminate pushing and popping DS and speed up your program by using your knowledge of the structure of .com programs. You know the code segment and data segment are identical. Here is how you can eliminate pushing and popping DS:

```
        MOV         BX,ES
        MOV         DS,BX       ;Old DS now gone
        . . . .
        MOV         BX,CS       ;Because CS = old DS
        MOV         DS,BX       ;  it's put back
```

Don't try this with an .exe program unless you know for sure that CS and DS are the same—which is probably not the case.

Here is another example of using register-to-register moves rather than pushing and popping. If you are concerned with speed and not with size, you could change the shell of PAGELP in SHOW_IT from:

```
PAGELP:    PUSH      CX
           . . . .
           POP       CX
           LOOP      PAGELP
```

to:

```
PAGELP:    MOV       BP,CX
           . . . .
           MOV       CX,BP
           LOOP      PAGELP
```

BP has been sitting around and doing nothing, so you could put it to work here. If a register is available, you might choose to use it rather than using PUSH and POP. Because the registers are so few, there is often none available, so be very careful to check that the one you choose is not sitting in the wings with some important value you do not want to lose.

My preference is to write the initial program in the structured manner I have shown you in this book. Then, if I want more speed or want to use less space, after everything is working properly, I go back into the source code and change CALLs that come immediately before RETs to JMPs, or replace PUSHes and POPs with register moves. Then I check very carefully (sometimes not carefully enough) to be sure that I did no damage to the working program.

My best advice is to make only a few changes at one time and then run the program with your debugger to make sure it is accurate. I have made the mistake of making wholesale changes and then spending hours tracking down the bugs. My next best advice is to be sure to save a backup copy of the original working .asm program. This advice is given for two reasons. First, you might really botch up the changed version. Second, because your original program was written in a structured, straightforward manner, it is easier to read and follow it if you later want to review what the source code should be doing.

Finally, to demonstrate how you can gain significant speed in your programs by avoiding unnecessary calls, returns, pushes, and pops,

Variations in Tip.com

I will show you a different version of the code that displays a page of text to the screen in SHOW__IT. This new version does not stop at the end of one line, but continues to count the total number of characters on 23 lines (or to the end of file) before calling WRITE. Thus, a whole screenful of characters is counted and then displayed, rather than just one line at a time. In my unofficial timing (counting seconds), it speeds up the screen display about 25%.

Although the code shown is more compact than that in tipe.com, the reason I did not write the code in this way originally is that if I did, I could not teach you as much about loops, especially LOOPNZ. If you want a faster screen display replace the code in SHOW__IT right after CALL CLEARS and before SHOMORE with the following:

```
        mov     cx,23         ;Line count
        sub     dx,dx         ;Character count
PAGELP: inc     bx            ;Increase the offset
        inc     dx            ;  And the count
        mov     al,[BX]       ;And get the next char
        cmp     al,EOF        ;Is it an EOF
        jz      SHOWPG        ;Yes - show the page
        cmp     al,LF         ;Is it a LF
        jnz     PAGELP        ;No, get the next one
        loop    PAGELP        ;Got a LF
SHOWPG: mov     cx,dx         ;DX now has count
        mov     dx,MEMP       ;Offset of last shown
        inc     dx            ;  in DX for the write
                              ;and increase it
        call    WRITE         ;Show the page
        mov     MEMP,bx       ;At last char on page
```

There are several reasons why this code is faster. First, in the code itself, there is no longer a line loop with 23 pushes and 23 pops and 22 calls to and returns from WRITE (one is finally needed). Even though the difference in speed might be negligible, remember what WRITE does. First it pushes (and subsequently pops) AX and BX. Then it calls INT 21H. Therefore, this version also eliminates 22 calls to and returns from INT 21H.

You also know that interrupts preserve the values in our registers. To do so, INT 21H pushes then pops nine of the 14 registers. To carry out its task, it also does some calling and jumping, which I will ignore. Thus, each time WRITE is called there are at least 11 pushes (two by WRITE and nine by DOS) and 11 pops, a total of 22 pushes and pops. 22 times 22 calls to WRITE is 484 pushes and pops—you can see that the savings in time can begin to add up.

In this illustration of one grand page loop, rather than 23 line loops within a page loop, neatness is not sacrificed for speed. In fact the code is neater and more compact. The main lesson is that if you want to speed up your programs, one good way to do so is to check the loops in the program, particularly if they contain calls to other procedures such as WRITE. Then ask yourself, what is the overhead of such a simple-looking call? If it is great, as with WRITE, put some thought in doing the task differently. Sometimes you will come up with an even simpler solution than the one you started with.

INCLUDE FILES

This section describes a different way to organize your source code for the assembler. As you have developed tipe.com, I have pointed out that many of the procedures can be *generic*, that is, useful for other programs.

There are several ways you can include tried-and-true procedures in new programs. First, you can use your word processor to move the routines into a new file. Second, MASM provides for library routines that you can include in the LINK process. A third way is to develop *INCLUDE files*, files of assembly language code that you want to include or add to the file you are assembling. The directive **INCLUDE file name** is all that is needed in the main file to tell the assembler that there are files of code you want included when you assemble. When it assembles the main file and encounters the INCLUDE directive, it reads in the code in the named file, and proceeds as if the instructions and data were in the original file. The file name, by the way, can be anything you wish; the extension .asm is not necessary.

Look through tipe.asm. Any procedures that seem of general use are the candidates for an include file. I have chosen to make four include files. You can probably guess three: one for disk management, one for screen management, and one for character display. The fourth is one I call PREPARE; it includes the work done, starting at MAIN1, to set up the ES segment and read in the file, or return an error message if it is not successful. Whenever you want to read a file with a name at FNAME, you would probably want to follow the same sequence of instructions; therefore it is advantageous to save them as an include file.

Here are the four include files for you to create. Their names are char.fun, screen.fun, display.fun, disk.fun, and prepare.fun. All are shown in their entirety in Appendix A. The *.fun* stands for *functions*.

To describe the first three, I will just show the beginning of each file. These beginnings have some comments and show what is included and what is required for each file. Here is the beginning of char.fun:

```
;CHAR.FUN - CHARACTER HANDLING PROCEDURES
PUBLIC  KEYIN,DIROUT,WRITEM,WRITE,STRINGO
```

This one is simple. The beginning describes what is in the file and lists the procedures with the PUBLIC instruction. The rest of char.fun contains the procedures listed. The beginning of screen.fun is this:

```
;SCREEN.FUN - SCREEN HANDLING PROCEDURES
PUBLIC CURSOR, CLEARS, CLRLN, CLRLINE,
;*****REQUIRED IN MAIN PROGRAM FILE:
;ATTRIB  DB      ?         ;Variable holding attribute
                           ;for clearing screen in CLEARS
```

Screen.fun contains the four procedures listed. I have also included a reminder that the variable ATTRIB needs to be defined in the main program file. Alternatively, ATTRIB could be defined in this include file. It really makes little difference, but because you may want to use different codes for ATTRIB depending on the program, it may be best to define it in the main program file.

I have not put SETSCREEN, RESCREEN, and BOTTOM in this include file because they are somewhat specific to tipe.com. Although you might want to use similar procedures in future programs, they probably have to be tailored to the specific program.

For handling files, create disk.fun using the following beginning:

```
;DISK.FUN - DISK HANDLING PROCEDURES
PUBLIC  OPENFL,FSIZE,READFL,CLOSEFL
;Uses this variable:
;FILESZ  DW      ?          to hold file size in FSIZE
```

Again, where you define FILESZ is arbitrary, because it is used both in the include file and in the main program file.

At this point, let's create these three files. This is in anticipation of the next chapter, in which you create a .com file that not only reads but also writes a file. Copy tipe.asm to upcase.asm.

For each .fun file, enter the headings shown and copy the procedures indicated. Your word processor should do much of the work for you. Delete the procedures you copied from upcase.asm.

Delete, as well, all the PUBLIC declarations of the procedures, if you had made them. Right before the data put these directives:

```
INCLUDE SCREEN.FUN
INCLUDE DISK.FUN
INCLUDE CHAR.FUN
```

When upcase.asm is assembled, following the same procedure you have been using, the code from these files are entered at the point at which they are INCLUDEd.

Here is the beginning of prepare.fun:

```
;PREPARE.FUN - PROCEDURES TO SETUP BUFFER IN ES TO
;RECEIVE, THEN ORCHESTRATE THE READING OF THE FILE
;TO THE BUFFER

PUBLIC PREPARE,SET_SEG,READIN         ;PROCEDURES
PUBLIC READMS,READER,NOTFND,BIGFILE   ;DATA

;****REQUIRES IN THE MAIN PROGRAM FILE:
;FNAME   DB    '???';Zero terminated string
                    ; holding the file name
;BUFFR   DB    ?    ;offset to compute es segment
;****USES THESE PROCEDURES:
;FROM CHAR.FUN:  WRITEM, STRINGO
;FROM DISK.FUN:  OPENFL, FSIZE, CLOSEFL, READFL

;USES THESE VARIABLES:
READMS   DB    CR,LF,'Reading $'
READER   DB    ' File read error$'
NOTFND   DB    ' not found$'
BIGFILE  DB    ' is too large$'
```

The header lists three procedures included in the file, the variables defined in the file, and those needed in the main file. It also states which procedures it calls—these procedures thus need to be included when prepare.fun is used.

At this point you can create prepare.fun by creating the file with the header and the procedures SET__SEG and READIN. Delete them from upcase.asm and delete the four variables as well. Now take the instructions starting right after MOV SP,100H and going to right before CALL SETSCREEN and make them into the procedure PREPARE. These instructions start with the following:

```
          mov         ax,OFFSET BUFFR
          call        SET_SEG
          . . . .
          . . . .
```
and end with:
```
MAIN3:    CALL        READIN
```

Change the last instruction, JC DONE, to DONE1: RET. Change each JMP SHORT DONE to JMP SHORT DONE1, and add STC before each of these instructions. The result will be the following:

```
PREPARE PROC NEAR
          mov         ax,OFFSET BUFFR
          call        SET_SEG
          mov         dx,OFFSET FNAME
          mov         si,dx
          call        OPENFL
          jnc         MAIN2
          call        STRINGO
          mov         dx,OFFSET NOTFND
          call        WRITEM
          stc
          jmp         SHORT DONE1
MAIN2:    mov         bx,ax
          call        FSIZE
          jz          MAIN3
MAINBG:   call        CLOSEFL
          call        STRINGO
          mov         dx,OFFSET BIGFILE
          call        WRITEM
          stc
          jmp         SHORT DONE1
MAIN3:    call        READIN
DONE1:    ret
PREPARE ENDP
```

PREPARE returns with a carry if any of the following errors occur: file not found, file too big, or read error.

You might want to change the labels used in PREPARE, although you can keep them as they are. Add PREPARE to the file prepare.fun and delete its instructions from MAIN, so that MAIN1 now reads:

```
MAIN1:    mov         sp,100H
          call        PREPARE
          jc          DONE
          call        SETSCREEN
```

Place INCLUDE PREPARE with the other INCLUDE directives. Prepare.fun and the three other include files are shown in Fig. A-3 in Appendix A. Disk.fun and char.fun as shown in that listing include procedures that you shall add in the next chapter.

Now create upcase.com. It, of course, should do exactly what tipe.com does, but it gives you a chance to make sure that you have made no errors during the editing and reorganization. Once upcase.com works properly, you can rewrite it so that it does what its name says: read in an ASCII file, put all letters in uppercase, and then write the new file to disk.

CHAPTER 12

Writing a File to Disk

File management is an important part of almost any assembly-language program. In developing tipe.com, I have given you lessons in reading the contents of disk files into memory. Because you are also going to want to write the contents of memory to disk files, I thought it fitting to conclude this book with a small program that writes the contents of memory back to a file—upcase.com. The program also illustrates how you can use the include files that you created in the last chapter to make program development an easier task than it would have been if you were starting from scratch.

Upcase.com does a simple task. After reading a file into memory, it searches for lowercase letters and convert each one into uppercase. Then it writes the result to a file specified by the user either on the command line or in response to a program prompt. Although you might never use upcase.com in any practical way, it enables you to gain the experience of writing files.

The complete upcase.asm is in Fig. A-2 in Appendix A. Note that screen.fun is not included, because you need none of its procedures for this program. Because you are including disk.fun, char.fun, and prepare.fun, the program itself is rather short. I suggest you delete your present upcase.asm and start with a clean slate by copying generic.asm to upcase.asm. Here is the new MAIN:

```
MAIN:    mov      dx,OFFSET TITL
         call     WRITEM      ;Show title of program
         call     GET_TWO     ;Gets 2 file names
MAIN1:   mov      sp,100H     ;Finished with PSP
         call     PREPARE     ;Sets up ES, gets file
         jc       DONE        ;An error
         call     UPCASEFL    ;Does the job
         call     WRITEIT
DONE:    mov      ax,4C00H    ;Terminate a process
         int      21H
;End of MAIN
```

MAIN sends out the title, calls GET_TWO to get the two file names, sets up, with PREPARE, and then calls the procedure to do the job of converting the letters to uppercase and writing the file.

You need to write only seven new procedures to do the job: GET_TWO, INFILE, UPCASEFL, and WRITEIT in your main file, CREATFL and WRITEFL to go into disk.fun, and READLN to go into char.fun. (Note: For upcase.com, KEYIN in char.fun will not be used. You can either leave it there, because space is not a problem with this program, or delete it, being sure you have a backup copy of the original char.fun.)

RETRIEVING TWO FILE NAMES FROM THE COMMAND LINE

Just as with tipe.asm, the first task is to get the file names. GET_TWO is more complicated but more flexible than the GET_FILE you have used. It allows the user to enter two, one, or no file names on the command line. If one or no file name is found on the command line, the required names can be obtained as responses to prompt. This is similar to MASM, which allows for entry of the name on the command line, as you probably have been doing or in response to its prompts. My main purpose in writing GET_TWO in this way is to show you a DOS function that you will be using quite a bit, one that accepts not just one character, but a whole string of characters as input.

The way GET_TWO works is first to find out if any string has been entered on the command line. If no string was entered, it prompts the user for two file names. If a string was entered, it then checks to see if the string represents one or two file names. If only one was entered, it prompts the user for the second file name. The complete GET_TWO is shown in Fig. 12-1.

GET_TWO is a variation on GET_FILE. In this case you are

```
            GET_TWO  PROC NEAR
                 mov     si,80H
                 mov     cl,[si]       ;Number of characters
                 or      cl,cl         ; which is moved into CL
                 jz      GETBOTH
                 dec     cl            ;If CL is zero, exit
                 sub     ch,ch         ;Make sure CH is zero
                 inc     si            ;Move to space
                 inc     si            ;Now to first char
                 mov     di,OFFSET FNAME ;Place for name
                 push    cx
                 push    di
                 rep     movsb         ;Whole string into FNAME
                 mov     al,0
                 stosb                 ;And end with a zero
                 pop     di
                 pop     cx
                 mov     al,20H        ;Space
                 repne   scasb         ;Scan for the space
                 jnz     GETONE        ;Zero means space is found
                 sub     al,al         ;DI on offset after string
                 mov     OUTFILE,di    ;Store in pointer
                 dec     di            ;Back to space
                 stosb                 ;0 there too, for 1st file
                 ret
            GETBOTH:mov  dx,OFFSET SFILEM
                 call    INFILE        ;SI start of string CX len
                 mov     di,OFFSET FNAME
                 rep     movsb         ;Move it in and stow zero
                 sub     ax,ax
                 stosb
            GETONE: mov  dx,OFFSET OFILEM
                 call    INFILE        ;SI start of string CX len
                 mov     OUTFILE,si
                 add     si,cx         ;Place to put zero
                 mov     di,si
                 sub     ax,ax
                 stosb                 ;Put it in
                 ret
            GET_TWO ENDP
```

Fig. 12-1. Procedure to get two file names.

expecting two file names to follow the program name. There are, as usual, a number of ways you can accomplish the task of obtaining from the command line the offset of two zero-terminated strings, one for each file name. The solution I have chosen is first to move the complete string at 82H (if any) to FNAME. (Be sure to increase the size of FNAME so there is plenty of room for both file names. I have increased it to 82 bytes, 40 for each name and one for each terminating zero.) Because there should be a space (20H) between the names, the next step is to find the space and replace it with a zero. Then save the offset of the next character, which is the first character of the second file, in a variable called OUTFILE, which shall be used as a pointer to the offset of that file.

Look through GET_TWO in Fig. 12-1 as far as the label GETBOTH. Just as in GET_FILE, the number stored at 80H is examined. If it is not zero, the string is moved into FNAME exactly as you have done before. If it is zero, a jump is taken to GETBOTH, where you use the second method of obtaining the file names. Notice that this procedure no longer has an error return, because you get the file names one way or another. Also notice that before moving the string to FNAME, both CX and DI were saved on the stack. You need both of them to search for the space between file names.

Once the string has been found and moved to FNAME, you accomplish the remaining tasks with these instructions:

```
        pop     di
        pop     cx
        mov     al,20H          ;Space
        repnz   scasb           ;Scan for the space
        jnz     GETONE  ;Zero means space is found
        sub     al,al   :DI on offset after string
        mov     OUTFILE,di      ;Store in pointer
        dec     di              ;Back to space
        stosb                   ;0 there too, for 1st file
        ret
GETBOTH: - - -
```

First you *scan* the string to find the space. This is done using the string instruction SCASB (which has the relative SCASW). SCASB scans the string with its beginning offset in DI for the presence of the byte value in AL. As with the other string instructions, the segment register for DI is ES, and the direction of the scan is determined by the state of the direction flag. In this case the direction is forward.

You use a conditional variation of REP. Remember the similarity between REP and LOOP. In each case, the instruction or instructions are carried out until CX is zero. Just as you can use the conditional instructions LOOPZ or LOOPNZ, you can use REPZ or REPNZ. By placing 20H in AL and using the instruction REPNZ SCASB, you are saying to check the character at DI, then increase DI, and decrease

CX. If the character is not 20H, continue the scan. If the character is found, the zero flag is set and the scan stops. If it is not found, the scan continues until CX is zero and returns with the zero flag clear.

When SCASB is finished, you can check the result of the scan with a conditional jump. If the zero flag is not set, a 20H has not been found, so JNZ GETONE is used to jump to GETONE, where you obtain the second file name. If a 20H has been found DI will be on the offset of the character following the space, which should be the start of the second file name.

Because you have already ensured that there is a zero at the end of the second file name, you simply save its starting position by moving the offset held in DI into the pointer OUTFILE. Because there must also be a zero at the end of the first file name (which starts at offset FNAME), AL is set to zero, DI is decreased so it points to the space, STOSB replaces the space with the zero, and the procedure returns. Both file names have been found on the command line. The first one starts at OFFSET FNAME, and the second one starts at the offset pointed to by the variable OUTFILE.

BUFFERED KEYBOARD INPUT

If no string was entered on the command line, you reach GET_BOTH and get ready to prompt the user to input the first file name. First, you need some messages to send to the screen as prompts, so insert these with your data:

```
SFILEM    DB        CR,LF,'Source$'
OFILEM    DB        CR,LF,'Output$'
REST      DB        ' file name: $'
```

Here is GET_BOTH:

```
GETBOTH: mov      dx,OFFSET SFILEM
         call     INFILE   ;SI start of string CX len
         mov      di,OFFSET FNAME
         rep      movsb    ;Move it in and stow zero
         sub      ax,ax
         stosb
GETONE: - - - - -
```

INFILE, which you will soon examine, displays the prompt, obtains the string entry, and returns with SI holding the start of the entered string and CX holding the length of that string. GETBOTH then moves that string so that it starts at offset FNAME and terminates it with a zero.

Before examining how INFILE obtains the string, let's finish this procedure by looking at GETONE:

```
GETONE:   mov     dx,OFFSET OFILEM
          call    INFILE   ;SI start of string CX len
          mov     OUTFILE,si
          add     si,cx             ;Place to put zero
          mov     di,si
          sub     ax,ax
          stosb                     ;Put it in
          ret
```

You get to this point in one of two ways: either by falling through from GETBOTH or by jumping from GET_TWO if a space was not found in the string at 82H. GETONE differs from GETBOTH only in one respect.

Unlike FNAME, which is a label for the offset of the beginning of a string, OUTFILE is a variable, a pointer to an offset somewhere in memory. You know the second file name begins at the offset in SI, only if you obtained it with a prompt. Because the program has two possible locations in memory for the location of the second file name—either at the offset obtained here in SI or somewhere after the first file name in FNAME—you simply use OUTFILE to point to one or another of these locations. In GETONE, you first store the offset held by SI in OUTFILE and then easily find the spot to place the final zero by adding the count in CX to SI. SI now points to the next byte after the end of the string. Finally, you put that offset into DI to store the zero.

INFILE can be used to obtain both file names and is shown in Fig. 12-2. It requires that the beginning of the prompt message (either "Source" or "Output") be in DX. DX is pushed in case the message has to be repeated. The whole prompt is sent out with the two WRITEMs; then the new procedure READLN is called to receive the input.

It is READLN that actually returns SI with the offset of the start of the string and CX with its length. If CX is zero, no string was entered; the user simply pressed ENTER. This is not allowed here (although you could allow it, and have the program quit), so if CX is zero, the prompt is repeated; if it is not zero, INFILE returns.

```
INFILE PROC NEAR   ;Entry DX offset file message
        push    dx
        call    WRITEM
        mov     dx,OFFSET REST ;Rest of prompt
        call    WRITEM
        call    READLN  ;Get the name from user
        pop     dx      ;Retrieve message start
        jcxz    INFILE  ;CX has length of string
        ret             ; if zero repeat
INFILE ENDP
```

Fig. 12-2. Procedure to get a file name using a prompt.

Now you get to the meat of the matter, READLN. First add this variable to the data section in the main program:

```
INBUF       DB          81,82 DUP (0)           ;Buffer for 80 chars
```

Then add the header and the READLN procedure shown in Fig. 12-3 to the beginning of char.fun.

Function 0AH is called *buffered keyboard input.* Because function 0AH is what DOS itself uses to receive input on the command line, you are familiar with using it. You enter the characters you want; you can delete using BACKSPACE and finish your entry with ENTER. (It

```
;*****REQUIRED IN MAIN PROGRAM FILE:
;INBUF  DB      ???     ;Input buffer used by READLN

READLN PROC NEAR
        push    ax              ;Reads a string to INBUF
        push    dx
        mov     dx,OFFSET INBUF
        mov     ah,0AH
        int     21H
        mov     si,OFFSET INBUF+1 ;number of chars
        lodsb                   ;Put in AL
        cbw                     ;Make it a word - 0 AH
        mov     cx,ax           ;Return it in CX
        pop     dx              ;SI at start of string
        pop     ax
        ret
READLN  ENDP
```

Fig. 12-3. Procedure to read a string from the keyboard.

also responds to CTRL-C, so the user could abort the program at this point.)

You need to provide the function with a *buffer*, a place to put the characters, and move its offset into DS:DX. In defining the buffer, the *DOS Technical Manual* says "The first byte must not be zero and specifies the number of characters the buffer can hold." Because it is a byte, it can be any number from one to 255. The second byte is reserved to hold the number of characters actually entered. Thus you always need to reserve an extra byte in the buffer for the one that will hold the count. The string itself starts at the third byte (offset INBUF plus 2). The last character put in the buffer is 0DH, the carriage return.

Thus INBUF as I defined it, allows for up to 80 characters to be entered. The first byte has 81, calling for 80 characters plus an 0DH. If you try to enter more than 80 characters, DOS rings its bell and ignores all characters but the carriage return. Because the 0DH is always put in the buffer, if you put 80 in the first byte, there would be room for only 79 characters.

By defining the size of the input buffer, you can ensure that strings entered are no longer than your specified length. Because 82 bytes have been reserved at FNAME (two for the zeros at the end of the strings), moving more than 81 bytes (and the terminating zero) to FNAME would overwrite the subsequent data and likely cause grief. Following this same logic, you might want to put a check at the beginning of GET_TWO (and similarly in GET_FILE) to ensure that the string entered on the command line is not more than 80 characters long. To write *bug-free* progams, all possible candidates for a crash need to be caught and provided for.

When you define an input buffer, take the maximum number of characters you will allow and add one byte for the 0DH and one byte for the count byte; then make the buffer length placed in the very first byte one less. For instance, if you wanted a buffer to obtain only one character (like Y for yes and N for no), the specification would look like this:

```
MYBUF      DB           2,3 DUP (0)
```

Let's see what INBUF will look like in memory given the entry of the string "filename." I use the letters rather than ASCII codes for simplicity.

```
   Bytes: 0 1 2 3 4 5 6 7 8 9 A B C D .......
INBUF:  51 08 f i l e n a m e 0D 0 0 0 .......
```

Note the similarity (skipping the size at zero) to what you have been seeing at 80H of the PSP.

You have defined the input buffer, placed 0AH in AH, and called the function with INT 21H. You could leave READLN at that, but for your purposes and for practically all purposes in using the procedure, you would eventually need to access the start of the string and know its length. Given the structure of the buffer, you know the length is located at the buffer's offset plus one. To obtain the length and place it in CX so it can be used as a counter, I chose the following instructions:

```
        mov     si,OFFSET INBUF + 1    ;number of chars
        lodsb                          ;Put in AL
        cbw                            ;Make it a word - 0 AH
        mov     cx,ax                  ;Return it in CX
```

Of the several ways this could be done, this is probably the most efficient and leaves SI holding the offset of INBUF + 2, where the string starts.

CBW (Change Byte to Word) is a handy little instruction that converts the value in AL to a word in AX. Thus, if AL has 04, AX will have 0004. (Don't try it if AX might have a value of 80H or more, because the way it works is to reproduce the value in bit 7 throughout AH. If bit 7 holds 0, AH will hold 0. If bit 7 holds 1, AH will hold 1111 1111 binary, 0FFH.) With these four instructions, you ensure that READLN will return with SI holding the offset of the string and CX holding its length.

When READLN returns to INFILE, if CX is not zero, INFILE returns to the calling routine. If CX is zero, no characters were entered, and INFILE reloops until something is entered (or CTRL-C is pressed and the program returns to DOS).

One way or another, you have obtained the two file names. Upon the return to MAIN, PREPARE is called, and assuming no error, the first file has been read into the buffer referenced in ES. UPCASFL then carries out the simple task of checking the contents of the file for lowercase characters and changing them to uppercase.

UPCASFL is shown in Fig. 12-4. UPCASEFL is a file-sized loop. CX is given FILESZ for the count. SI is used to point to the characters in the file, so it is initialized to zero, the beginning of the ES segment. A lowercase character is any ASCII code that is greater than 61H and less than 7BH. You could try to remember these numbers, look them up in the ASCII table, or let the assembler do the conversion as I have done. The assemser will convert *a* to its ASCII code of 61H and will convert *z + 1* to the ASCII code of 7AH and add one to it.

```
        UPCASEFL PROC NEAR
                 mov      dx,OFFSET CONVERT
                 call     WRITEM       ;Say what is happening
                 mov      cx,FILESZ    ;For the big loop
                 sub      si,si        ;Starting at zero
                 mov      dl,'a'
                 mov      dh,'z'+1
        UPLOOP:  mov      al,es:[si]   ;Get the char
                 cmp      al,dl
                 jc       UPCAS1       ;Less than 'a'
                 cmp      al,dh
                 jnc      UPCAS1       ;Greater than 'z'
                 sub      al,20H       ;Make upper case
                 mov      ES:[si],al   ; and put it back
        UPCAS1:  inc      si           ;Ready for next
                 loop     UPLOOP
                 ret
        UPCASEFL ENDP
```

Fig. 12-4. Procedure to uppercase letters in a text file.

The loop is started by moving the character contained in ES:[SI] into AL. LODSB could be used, but first ES would have to be moved into DS. Primarily, I did not use LODSB because it would increase SI, something I did not want done until after the lowercase check. If the byte in AL is found to represent a lowercase letter, in the range of 61H to 7AH, 20H is subtracted, effectively making it an uppercase letter, and it is put into ES:[SI]. Then SI is increased, and the loop continues until the end of the file is reached. All that remains is to save the file.

WRITING A FILE TO DISK

WRITEIT carries out the task of saving the file. It requires two procedures, CREATFL and WRITEFL. They both are shown in Fig. 12-5. Add them to disk.fun.

Remember that OPENFL is used to open files that exist and to prepare them for reading or writing. DOS function 3CH creates a new file for the directory, or if the file exists, it effectively erases it and then creates a new one. You might have programs that when you ask to save a file that exists on the disk, ask something like "File exists? Erase it?" That is because an OPEN was first attempted before the CREATE and the OPEN returned no carry, indicating an existing file. The programmer wants you to think about the fact that whatever file exists

```
            CREATFL  PROC    NEAR
        ;Entry, DS:DX address of zero terminated string
                    mov     ah,3CH
                    mov     cx,0      ;Normal file attribute
                    int     21H
                    ret
            CREATFL  ENDP

            WRITEFL PROC NEAR
            ;Entry BX handle, CX number, DS:DX address of data
                    mov     ah,40h
                    int     21H
                    ret
            WRITEFL ENDP
```

Fig. 12-5. Procedures to create and write a file.

with the file name, will be completely replaced with whatever is to be written to it. Some other programs create backup files of the original before writing the new one.

For the purpose of learning to write a file to disk, I will keep it simple. I will not check to see if the file exists, nor do some other checking that might be wise, such as seeing if there is sufficient disk space to hold the new file—a very good thing to know before erasing an existing file.

Like function 3DH, Open File, function 3CH requires the offset of a zero-terminated string representing the file name in DS:DX. It further requires the file attribute in CX. A file can have one of several attributes. For instance, it can be *hidden*, meaning it does not appear in the directory listing, it can be *read only*, meaning it can be read but not written to, or it can have other kinds of attributes.

Normal files have the attributes of zero, which is what is put into CX in CREATFL. CREATFL returns with a carry if there was an error; otherwise the handle is in AX. There are not too many possible errors in creating brand new files. The most usual errors are "no more directory space" or "too many open handles."

WRITEFL, with the exception of the function number, is exactly like READFL with exactly the same requirements: the handle in BX, the address of the data in DS:DX, and the count in CX. You, of course, have already used the write function 40H in the procedure, WRITE.

Make sure that these two procedures have been added to disk.fun; then turn your attention to the WRITEIT procedure in Fig. 12-6. Also add these two variables to the data:

```
        WRITEIT PROC NEAR
                mov     dx,OFFSET SVING  ;Show 'saving'
                call    WRITEM
                mov     si,OUTFILE
                mov     dx,si            ;In DX for CREATFL
                call    STRINGO          ;Show the name
                call    CREATFL          ;Set up new file
                jc      DERR             ;Something is wrong
                mov     bx,ax            ;Handle
                mov     cx,FILESZ        ;Length
                push    ds               ;Save DS
                mov     dx,es            ;  Our file is in ES
                mov     ds,dx
                sub     dx,dx            ;Start at zero
                call    WRITEFL
                pop     ds               ;Get this back
                jc      DERR             ;A write error
                call    CLOSEFL
                ret
        DERR:   mov     dx,OFFSET DISKER
                jmp     WRITEM           ;WRITEM won't
        WRITEIT ENDP                     ;  affect the flags
```

Fig. 12-6. Procedure to orchestrate the writing of a file.

| SVING | DB | CR,LF,'Saving $' |
| DISKER | DB | 'Write error$' |

The first five instructions are familiar to you. They send out the message "Saving <filename>." CREATFL is called. If there is an error, a jump is taken to DERR, the error exit. If there is no error, the setup is exactly the same as that in READIN. BX gets the handle; CX gets the number of bytes to write (FILESZ because that has not changed); DX is zeroed to mark the beginning of the file in memory; DS is pushed and ES placed in it; WRITEFL is called; DS is restored. If there was no error in writing the file, it is properly closed with a call to CLOSEFL. If there was an error, the error exit is taken.

If there was an error, either in the creation or writing of the file, the same message "write error" is given. In future versions of WRITEIT, you might want to be more specific and allow for different types of errors in your messages. There are few errors in writing a properly created file. An error would probably mean some sort of problem with the disk itself. Another kind of error is not writing the number of bytes requested in CX.

Function 40H returns in AX the number of bytes actually written, so as you expand WRITEIT, you probably will want to check that with CMP AX,CX. If they are different, the most likely explanation was that there was not enough room on the disk to write all the bytes in CX. If there is an error in writing to the disk, upcase.com tells the user, then quits. A better solution is to show the error message and give the user the opportunity to try again with a different disk or a disk in a different drive, because the data still sits there in memory.

Although DOS is an invaluable friend, if you do not anticipate errors and provide for them in one way or another, you will find that DOS will take over with its "Abort, Retry, Ignore" message, and often there is nothing to do but abort and lose what is in memory. In upcase.com, error or not, WRITEIT returns to INT 20H, so there is no chance to recoup.

I will not describe my solutions to the problems described above, because my purpose has been to give you a start in assembly-language programming, not to teach you everything I know. As you learn more, your solutions might be different—indeed, better—than mine. Add WRITEIT and its data to upcase.asm. Create the .com file. Although you might seldom or never use upcase.com in a practical way, you now know how to write the contents of memory to a disk. In fact, upcase.asm could serve as a shell for a number of other tasks. One last example is discussed below.

As the end of the book approaches and I face a publication deadline, I am inspired to use the shell of upcase.asm to help me meet that deadline. It seems that the publisher wants no blank lines between paragraphs, while my word processor insists that they be there. Rather than tediously going through each chapter and removing each blank line and then having to do so again upon any revisions, my solution is to replace UPCASEFL with a procedure that eliminates blank lines. Using two file names is handy, because I can keep one file for my word processor and have another for the publisher. Some of you might find the program useful, but primarily it illustrates how the code you have painstakenly developed can be used again and again.

If you want a program to eliminate blank lines from text files, copy upcase.asm to noline.asm. Then, replace the call to UPCASEFL with a call to NOLINE delete UPCASEFL, and insert NOLINE, which is shown in Fig. 12-7. (You will also want to give the program a new TITL definition.)

In this case, I will let the code speak for itself. With a little study, it should be clear what it is doing. My lessons are over. You will find there is much to learn, but you have the foundation to do what you want with assembly-language programming—such as unerasing files (BIOS), creating a spreadsheet that will do your taxes (DOS), or writing your favorite game (BIOS/DOS)—you can do anything that the computer can do, quickly and efficiently.

```
NOLINE  PROC NEAR
        sub     di,di           ;Start of text
NOL1:   mov     al,ES:[di]
        cmp     al,EOF          ;at end?
        jz      NOLX            ;Yes, done
        inc     di              ;Set for next
        cmp     al,LF
        jnz     NOL1            ;Not an LF
        mov     si,di           ;Source for move
NOL2:   mov     al,ES:[si]
        cmp     al,CR           ;Is next a CR?
        jnz     NOL3
        inc     si              ;Yes
        inc     si              ;Go past lf to next
        jmp     NOL2            ;And try again
NOL3:   mov     ax,si
        sub     ax,di           ;Still the same?
        jz      NOL1            ;No change, continue
        mov     cx,FILESZ       ;Ready for the move
        mov     bx,cx
        sub     bx,ax           ;AX has number skipped
        mov     FILESZ,BX       ;Reduce it for next move
        sub     cx,si           ;Number to move
        push    ds
        push    di              ;Save it
        mov     ax,es
        mov     ds,ax
        rep     movsb           ;Do the move
        pop     di              ;Ready for next check
        pop     ds
        jmp     nol1
NOLX:   ret                     ;Done, with new FILESZ
NOLINE  ENDP
```

Fig. 12-7. Procedure to delete blank lines.

APPENDIX A

Complete Program Listings

This appendix includes the following program listings: the complete Tipe.asm for Tipe.com (Fig. A-1), the complete Upcase.asm for Upcase.com (Fig. A-2), and the include files (Fig. A-3).

```
;TIPE.ASM - PROGRAM TO DISPLAY ASCII FILES
;       ALLOWING THE DISPLAY TO BE REVERSED

CR       EQU     0DH     ;Carriage return character
LF       EQU     0AH     ;Line feed character
BACKKEY  EQU     1BH     ;Escape
ENDKEY   EQU     3       ;CTRL-C
EOF      EQU     1AH     ;End of file marker

PUBLIC WRITEM,GET_FILE,DIROUT,STRINGO,OPENFL,FSIZE
PUBLIC CLOSEFL,READIN,READFL,CLEARS,LINEOUT,BOTTOM
PUBLIC WRITE,CURSOR,KEYIN,SHOW_IT,REVERSE

CODE     SEGMENT
         ASSUME CS:CODE,DS:CODE
         ORG    100H

MAIN:    mov    dx,OFFSET TITL
         call   WRITEM       ;Show title of program
         call   GET_FILE     ;string from PSP at 80H
         jnz    MAIN1        ;Zero flag set = no text
         mov    dx,OFFSET NOFILE ;Set up message
         call   WRITEM       ;  Show it
         jmp    SHORT DONE   ;  and exit
MAIN1:   mov    dx,OFFSET FNAME ;Start of the file
         mov    si,dx        ; name Also to SI
                             ; for writing it later
         call   OPENFL       ;Open file for reading
         jnc    MAIN2        ;Carry = error
         call   STRINGO      ;  Show file name
         mov    dx,OFFSET NOTFND ;    and
         call   WRITEM       ;  Say not found
         jmp    SHORT DONE   ;  And exit
MAIN2:   mov    bx,ax        ;FSIZE needs handle in BX
         call   FSIZE        ;Returns AX = size of file
         jz     MAIN3        ;NZ means over 64k in size
MAINBG:  call   CLOSEFL      ;BX still has handle
         call   STRINGO      ;Show file name
         mov    dx,OFFSET BIGFILE ; say that
         call   WRITEM       ;Program can't take it
         jmp    SHORT DONE   ;And exit
MAIN3:   mov    di,OFFSET BUFFR ;Start of file
         mov    cx,0FEFFh    ;Leave 100H for Stack
         sub    cx,di        ;Memory left for our file
         cmp    cx,ax        ;Space minus file size
         jc     MAINBG       ;Carry means too big
         call   READIN       ;Reads the file into buffr
         jc     DONE         ;A read error was given
         mov    dh,24        ;Last row
```

Fig. A-1. The complete Tipe.asm for Tipe.com.

```
            call    CLEARS      ;Clr screen thru row in DH
            call    LINEOUT     ;Dashes across row 23
            call    BOTTOM      ;Cursor at start of row 24
            mov     dx,OFFSET MES1   ;Prompt message
            mov     cx,FNAME-MES1    ;Number of chars
            call    WRITE       ;Write to the screen
            sub     dx,dx       ;Set row and col to 0
            call    CURSOR      ;Put the cursor there
            mov     bx,OFFSET BUFFR - 1    ;1 less
            mov     MEMP,bx     ;because we INC to start
            mov     al,0        ;Dummy we'll go forward
            call    SHOW_IT     ;Show a screenful
DONE:       call    BOTTOM      ;cursor at bot of screen
            int     20H         ;Quit
;End of MAIN
SHOW_IT PROC NEAR
            cmp     al,BACKKEY  ;Key is pressed. ESC?
            jnz     FORW        ;No, go forward
            call    REVERSE     ;Sets up last screen
            jz      SHOBEL      ;No last screen
FORW:       mov     bx,MEMP     ;holds last char shown
            MOV     al,[bx]     ;Put it in AL
            CMP     al,EOF      ;Is it the end of file
            JNZ     SHOWOK      ;No, show next screen
SHOBEL: mov al,7                ;Can't move
            call    DIROUT      ; So ring the bell
            JMP     SHORT SHOMORE   ; and try again
SHOWOK: mov TOPADD,bx           ;Maybe rev. next time
            mov     dh,22       ;Clear thru to row 22
            call    CLEARS
            mov     cx,23       ;Line count
PAGELP: push cx                 ;Save it for LINELP
            sub     cx,cx       ;Character count
            mov     dl,EOF      ;Put numbers in DL
            mov     dh,LF       ; and DH for our tests
LINELP: inc  bx                 ;Increase the offset
        inc  cx                 ; And the count
        mov  al,[BX]            ;And get the next char
        cmp  al,dl              ;Is it an EOF
        jz   SHOWLN             ;Yes - show the line
        cmp  al,dh              ;Is it a LF
        jnz  LINELP             ;No, get the next one
SHOWLN: mov dx,MEMP             ;Offset of last shown
        inc  dx                 ; in DX for the write
                                ;and increase it
            call    WRITE       ;Show the line
            mov     MEMP,bx     ;Reset for next loop
            cmp     al,EOF      ;Last char an EOF?
            pop     cx          ;Get the line count
            loopnz  PAGELP      ;If not, loop again
SHOMORE:sub  dx,dx              ;Cursor to the top
```

```
                call    CURSOR      ; ready for next page
                call    KEYIN       ;Ask for choice
                cmp     al,ENDKEY   ;Want to quit?
                jnz     SHOW_IT     ;No, start again
                ret
SHOW_IT ENDP
REVERSE PROC NEAR   ;ESC pressed, show last screen
                mov     si,TOPADD   ;top of screen minus 1
                mov     di,OFFSET BUFFR - 1
                cmp     si,di       ;Start of the file?
                jz      REV_EX      ;Yes, ret zero flag set
                mov     cx,24       ;Line counter go back 24
                mov     dl,LF       ;for the comparison
                std                 ;Set to go in reverse direction
REV1:           lodsb               ;Char into AL and dec SI
                cmp     al,dl       ;Is it an LF?
                jnz     REV1        ;No, try again
                loop    REV1        ;Yes, dec CX, go again
                inc     si          ;Increase it to the LF
                mov     MEMP,si     ;Set now for SHOW_IT
                cld                 ;Set direction forward
REV_EX: ret
REVERSE ENDP

GET_FILE PROC NEAR
                mov     si,80H      ;Command line chars
                mov     cl,[SI]     ;Number of characters
                cmp     cl,0        ; which is moved into CL
                jz      GT_EX       ;If CL is zero, exit
                dec     cl          ;First char is a space
                sub     ch,ch       ;Make sure CH is zero
                inc     si          ;Move to space
                inc     si          ;Now to first char
                mov     di,OFFSET FNAME ;Place for name
                cld                 ;Go forward
                rep     movsb       ;CX has count for move
                mov     al,0        ;Make it 0 and stow it
                stosb               ; after the last char
GT_EX:  ret                         ;If zero set, not found
GET_FILE ENDP

LINEOUT PROC NEAR
                mov     dh,23       ;Row 23
                sub     dl,dl       ;Column 0
                call    CURSOR
                mov     cx,80       ;Set count to 80
                mov     al,'-'
LLOOP:  call    DIROUT              ;Send out the dash
                loop    LLOOP       ;Decrease CX and
                ret                 ;go again if not 0
LINEOUT ENDP
```

```
READIN   PROC NEAR
;Entry SI address of file name, BX has file handle
         mov     dx,OFFSET READMS  ;Show 'Reading'
         call    WRITEM
         call    STRINGO                     ;File name
         mov     cx,FILESZ         ;# of bytes to read
         mov     dx,OFFSET BUFFR   ;where to put them
         call    READFL
         jnc     REDA
         mov     dx,OFFSET READER  ;Somethg is wrong
         call    WRITEM
         jmp     SHORT REDX
REDA:    call    CLOSEFL           ;BX still has handle
REDX:    ret
READIN   ENDP


BOTTOM   PROC NEAR
         mov     dx,1800H  ;ready for row 24 col 0
BOTTOM   ENDP                      ;Falls through to CURSOR

;**** BIOS SCREEN HANDLING ROUTINES

CURSOR   PROC    NEAR      ;Entry: DH = ROW, DL = COL
         push    ax
         push    bx
         sub     bh,bh     ;Screen Display page is 0
         mov     ax,0200H  ;set cursor
         int     10H       ;BIOS video display interrupt
         pop     bx
         pop     ax
         ret
CURSOR   ENDP

CLEARS   PROC    NEAR      ;Entry DH has row of bot
         push    ax
         push    bx
         push    cx
         sub     cx,cx     ;top row and col, both 0
         mov     dl,79     ;Col of bottom of window
         mov     ax,0600H  ;AL = 0 = blank window
         mov     bh,07h    ;Attribute, gray on black
         int     10H       ;BIOS video display interrupt
         pop     cx
         pop     bx
         pop     ax
         ret
CLEARS   ENDP

;**** DOS DISK FILE HANDLING ROUTINES

OPENFL   PROC NEAR
```

```
        ;Entry DX address of 0 terminated string in DS
        mov     ax,3D02H    ;3D = Open
        int     21H         ; 02 = read OR write
        ret
OPENFL  ENDP

FSIZE PROC NEAR ;Entry BX, handle of opened file
        push    dx
        push    cx
        sub     cx,cx       ;CX:DX offset for
        sub     dx,dx       ; start of move both 0
        mov     ax,4202h    ;Move pointer, 2 = to EOF
        int     21H         ; New pointer in DX:AX
        cmp     dx,0        ;If DX > 0, more than 64K
        jnz     FSZEX       ; exit zero flag clear
        push    ax          ;save on the stack and
        mov     FILESZ,ax   ;in FILESZ for later
        mov     ax,4200H    ;CX and DX still 0
        int     21H         ;AL = 0 go back to start.
        pop     ax          ;Has file size
FSZEX:  pop     cx          ;Retrieve the pushed values
        pop     dx
        ret                 ;Ret zero if 64K or less
FSIZE ENDP                  ; and size in AX

CLOSEFL PROC    NEAR        ;BX has handle
        mov     ax,3E00H
        int     21H
        ret
CLOSEFL ENDP

READFL PROC NEAR
;Handle in BX, address in DS:DX, num in CX
        mov     ax,3F00H
        int     21H         ;Carry set if error
        ret                 ; else AX has bytes read
READFL  ENDP

;**** DOS SCREEN HANDLING ROUTINES ****

WRITEM PROC NEAR
;entry DS:DX address of $ terminated string
        push    ax          ;Save AX
        mov     ah,9        ;print $ terminated string
        int     21H         ;Call the interrupt
        pop     ax          ;Get it back
        ret
WRITEM ENDP

DIROUT PROC NEAR ;send a char in al to the screen
        push    ax
```

```
                push    dx
                mov     dl,al
                mov     ah,6
                int     21H
                pop     dx
                pop     ax
                ret
DIROUT  ENDP

STRINGO PROC NEAR
;Entry SI has offset of 0 terminated string in DS
                lodsb           ;Put content in AL and inc SI
                cmp     al,0    ;Is it 0?
                jz      STREX   ;Yes, exit
                call    DIROUT  ;No, display it
                jmp     STRINGO ;Keep going
STREX:  ret
STRINGO ENDP


WRITE PROC NEAR
;Entry Address string in DS:DX, Length in CX
                push    ax
                push    bx
                mov     bx,0001 ; 1 handle for strd output
                mov     ax,4000H ;write to file or device
                int     21H     ; in this case the screen
                pop     bx
                pop     ax
                RET
WRITE ENDP


KEYIN   PROC NEAR
                mov     ah,7    ;Keybrd input without echo
                int     21H     ;  and CTRL-BREAK check
                cmp     al,0    ;ASCII code?
                jz      KEYIN   ;No, scan code
                ret             ;character code in AL
KEYIN   ENDP

;Data for the program
PUBLIC TITL,FNAME,NOFILE,NOTFND,FILESZ,BIGFILE
PUBLIC READMS,READER,BUFFR,MES1,MEMP,TOPADD


TITL    DB      'Tipe - Displays ASCII files'
        DB      CR,LF,'$'
MES1    DB      ' Any key = forward  '
        DB      '<ESC> = reverse  ^C = quit'
FNAME   DB      50 DUP (0)
NOFILE  DB      'No file entered$'
NOTFND  DB      ' not found$'
FILESZ  DW      ?
```

```
BIGFILE  DB      ' is too large$'
READMS   DB      CR,LF,'Reading $'
READER   DB      ' Disk read error$'
MEMP     DW      ?
TOPADD   DW      ?
         DB      LF         ;Needed FOR REVERSE
BUFFR    DB      ?          ;End of our data and
                            ; beginning of file

CODE     ENDS
         END     MAIN
```

```
;Upcase.asm - Takes text file, makes upper case,
;             writes to output file
PUBLIC GET_TWO,UPCASEFL,WRITEIT,INFILE

CR      EQU     0DH             ;Carriage return
LF      EQU     0AH             ;Line feed
EOF     EQU     1AH             ;End of file marker
CODE    SEGMENT
        ASSUME CS:CODE,DS:CODE
        ORG     100H

MAIN:   mov     dx,OFFSET TITL
        call    WRITEM          ;Show title of program
        call    GET_TWO         ;Gets 2 file names
MAIN1:  mov     sp,100H         ;Finished with PSP
        call    PREPARE         ;Sets up ES, gets file
        jc      DONE            ;An error
        call    UPCASEFL        ;Does the job
        call    WRITEIT
DONE:   mov     ax,4C00H        ;Terminate a process
        int     21H
;End of MAIN

WRITEIT PROC NEAR
        mov     dx,OFFSET SVING ;Show 'saving'
        call    WRITEM
        mov     si,OUTFILE      ;Offset of 2nd file
        mov     dx,si           ;In DX for CREATFL
        call    STRINGO         ;Show the name
        call    CREATFL         ;Set up new file
        jc      DERR            ;Something is wrong
        mov     bx,ax           ;Handle
        mov     cx,FILESZ       ;Length
        push    ds              ;Save DS
        mov     dx,es           ; Our file is in ES
        mov     ds,dx
        sub     dx,dx           ;Start at zero
        call    WRITEFL
        pop     ds              ;Get this back
        jc      DERR            ;A write error
        call    CLOSEFL
        ret
DERR:   mov     dx,OFFSET DISKER
        jmp     WRITEM          ;WRITEM won't
WRITEIT ENDP                    ; affect the flags

UPCASEFL PROC NEAR
        mov     dx,OFFSET CONVERT
        call    WRITEM          ;Say what is happening
```

Fig. A-2. The complete Upcase.asm for Upcase.com.

```
                mov     cx,FILESZ       ;For the big loop
                sub     si,si           ;Starting at zero
                mov     dl,'a'
                mov     dh,'z'+1
        UPLOOP: mov     al,es:[si]      ;Get the char
                cmp     al,dl
                jc      UPCAS1          ;Less than 'a'
                cmp     al,dh
                jnc     UPCAS1          ;Greater than 'z'
                sub     al,20H          ;Make upper case
                mov     ES:[si],al      ; and put it back
        UPCAS1: inc     si              ;Ready for next
                loop    UPLOOP
                ret
        UPCASEFL ENDP

        GET_TWO PROC NEAR
                mov     si,80H
                mov     cl,[si]         ;Number of characters
                or      cl,cl           ; which is moved into CL
                jz      GETBOTH         ;If CL 0 get 2 from user
                dec     cl
                sub     ch,ch           ;Make sure CH is zero
                inc     si              ;Move to space
                inc     si              ;Now to first char
                mov     di,OFFSET FNAME ;Place for name
                push    cx
                push    di
                rep     movsb           ;Whole string into FNAME
                mov     al,0
                stosb                   ;And end with a zero
                pop     di
                pop     cx
                mov     al,20H          ;Space
                repne   scasb           ;Scan for the space
                jnz     GETONE          ;Zero means space is found
                sub     al,al           ;DI on offset after string
                mov     OUTFILE,di      ;Store in pointer
                dec     di              ;Back to space
                stosb                   ;0 there too, for 1st file
                ret
        GETBOTH:mov     dx,OFFSET SFILEM
                call    INFILE   ;SI start of string CX len
                mov     di,OFFSET FNAME
                rep     movsb    ;Move it in and stow zero
                sub     ax,ax
                stosb
        GETONE: mov     dx,OFFSET OFILEM
                call    INFILE   ;SI start of string CX len
                mov     OUTFILE,si
```

```
                add     si,cx           ;Place to put zero
                mov     di,si
                sub     ax,ax
                stosb                   ;Put it in
                ret
        GET_TWO ENDP


        INFILE  PROC NEAR   ;Entry DX offset file message
                push    dx
                call    WRITEM
                mov     dx,OFFSET REST  ;Rest of prompt
                call    WRITEM
                call    READLN  ;Get the name from user
                pop     dx      ;Retrieve message start
                jcxz    INFILE  ;CX has length of string
                ret             ; if zero repeat
        INFILE  ENDP


                INCLUDE CHAR.FUN
                INCLUDE DISK.FUN
                INCLUDE PREPARE.FUN

        PUBLIC  FNAME,BUFFR,TITL,OUTFILE,SVING
        PUBLIC  CONVERT,INBUF,FILESZ,SFILEM,OFILEM,REST
        INBUF   DB      81,82 DUP (0)   ;Buf for 80 chars
        CONVERT DB      CR,LF,'Converting$'
        SFILEM  DB      CR,LF,'Source$'
        OFILEM  DB      CR,LF,'Output$'
        REST    DB      ' file name: $'
        SVING   DB      CR,LF,'Saving $'
        DISKER  DB      'Write error$'
        OUTFILE DW      0       ;Pointer to second file name
        FILESZ  DW      0
        TITL    DB      'UPCASE - CHANGES LOWER CASE'
                DB      ' TO UPPER',CR,LF,'$'
        FNAME   DB      62 DUP (0) ;will hold two names
        BUFFR   DB      0
        CODE    ENDS
                END     MAIN
```

```
;SCREEN.FUN - SCREEN HANDLING PROCEDURES

PUBLIC CURSOR,CLEARS,CLRLN,CLRLINE,

;*****REQUIRED IN MAIN PROGRAM FILE:
;ATTRIB DB       ?       ;Variable holding attribute
                         ;for clearing screen in CLEARS

CURSOR  PROC    NEAR    ;Entry: DH = ROW, DL = COL
        push    ax
        push    bx
        sub     bh,bh   ;Screen Display page is 0
        mov     ax,0200H ;set cursor
        int     10H     ;BIOS video display interrupt
        pop     bx
        pop     ax
        ret
CURSOR  ENDP

CLEARS  PROC    NEAR    ;Entry DH has row of bot
        push    ax
        push    bx
        push    cx
        sub     cx,cx   ;top row and col, both 0
        mov     dl,79   ;Col of bottom of window
        mov     ax,0600H ;AL = 0 = blank window
        mov     bh,Attrib
        int     10H     ;BIOS video display interrupt

        pop     cx
        pop     bx
        pop     ax
        ret
CLEARS  ENDP

CLRLN PROC NEAR         ;Clears from cursor position
;Entry attribute in BL, Number to clear in CX
        push    ax
        push    bx              ;Writes char in Al with
        mov     ax,920H ;with attribute in BL
        mov     bh,0    ; AL is 20H, a blank
        int     10H     ; BH - active page
        pop     bx
        pop     ax
        ret
CLRLN ENDP

CLRLINE PROC    NEAR
```

Fig. A-3. The include files.

```
            ;Entry row in DH, col in DL, attribute in AL
        push    bx
        push    cx
        mov     cx,80       ;80 columns per row
        sub     cl,dl       ;Clear 80 minus entry col
        call    CURSOR      ;set the cursor
        mov     bl,al       ;move in attribute
        call    CLRLN       ;clear it
        pop     cx
        pop     bx
        ret
CLRLINE ENDP

;End of screen.fun
------------
;DISK.FUN - DISK HANDLING PROCEDURES

PUBLIC OPENFL,FSIZE,READFL,CLOSEFL,CREATFL,WRITEFL

;****REQUIRED IN MAIN PROGRAM FILE
;FILESZ DW    ?      to hold file size in FSIZE

OPENFL  PROC NEAR
;Entry DX address of 0 terminated string in DS
        mov     ax,3D02H    ;3D = Open
        int     21H         ; 02 = read OR write
        ret
OPENFL  ENDP

FSIZE PROC NEAR ;Entry BX, handle of opened file
        push    dx
        push    cx
        sub     cx,cx       ;CX:DX offset for
        sub     dx,dx       ; start of move both 0
        mov     ax,4202h    ;Move pointer, 2 = to EOF
        int     21H         ; New pointer in DX:AX
        cmp     dx,0        ;If DX > 0, more than 64K
        jnz     FSZEX       ; exit zero flag clear
        push    ax          ;save on the stack and
        mov     FILESZ,ax   ;in FILESZ for later
        mov     ax,4200H    ;CX and DX still 0
        int     21H         ;AL = 0 go back to start.
        pop     ax          ;Has file size
FSZEX:  pop     cx          ;Retrieve the pushed values
        pop     dx
        ret                 ;Ret zero if 64K or less
FSIZE ENDP                  ; and size in AX

CLOSEFL PROC    NEAR        ;BX has handle
        mov     ax,3E00H
        int     21H
```

```
                ret
CLOSEFL ENDP

READFL   PROC NEAR
;Handle in BX, address in DS:DX, num in CX
         mov     ax,3F00H
         int     21H       ;Carry set if error
         ret               ;  else AX has bytes read
READFL   ENDP

CREATFL PROC    NEAR
;Entry, DS:DX address of zero terminated string
         mov     ah,3CH
         mov     cx,0      ;Normal file attribute
         int     21H
         ret
CREATFL ENDP

WRITEFL PROC NEAR
;Entry BX handle, CX number, DS:DX address of data
         mov     ah,40H
         int     21H
         ret
WRITEFL ENDP
; end of disk.fun
---------

;CHAR.FUN - CHARACTER HANDLING PROCEDURES

PUBLIC KEYIN,DIROUT,WRITEM,WRITE,STRINGO,READLN
;*****REQUIRED IN MAIN PROGRAM FILE:
;INBUF   DB      ???      ;Input buffer used by READLN

READLN PROC NEAR
         push    ax        ;Reads a string to INBUF
         push    dx
         mov     dx,OFFSET INBUF
         mov     ah,0AH
         int     21H
         mov     si,OFFSET INBUF+1 ;number of chars
         lodsb                     ;Put in AL
         cbw                       ;Make it a word - 0 AH
         mov     cx,ax             ;Return it in CX
         pop     dx                ;SI at start of string
         pop     ax
         ret
READLN ENDP

WRITEM PROC NEAR
;entry DS:DX address of $ terminated string
         push    ax        ;Save AX
         mov     ah,9      ;print $ terminated string
```

```
            int      21H        ;Call the interrupt
            pop      ax         ;Get it back
            ret
WRITEM ENDP

DIROUT PROC NEAR    ;send a char in al to the screen
            push     ax
            push     dx
            mov      dl,al
            mov      ah,6
            int      21H
            pop      dx
            pop      ax
            ret
DIROUT ENDP

STRINGO PROC NEAR
;Entry SI has offset of 0 terminated string in DS
            lodsb               ;Put content in AL and inc SI
            cmp      al,0       ;Is it 0?
            jz       STREX      ;Yes, exit
            call     DIROUT     ;No, display it
            jmp      STRINGO    ;Keep going
STREX:      ret
STRINGO ENDP

WRITE PROC NEAR
;Entry Address string in DS:DX, Length in CX
            push     ax
            push     bx
            mov      bx,0001   ; 1 handle for strd output
            mov      ax,4000H  ;write to file or device
            int      21H       ; in this case the screen
            pop      bx
            pop      ax
            RET
WRITE ENDP

KEYIN   PROC NEAR
            mov      ah,7       ;Keybrd input without echo
            int      21H        ; and CTRL-BREAK check
            cmp      al,0       ;ASCII code?
            jz       KEYIN      ;No, scan code
            ret                 ;character code in AL
KEYIN   ENDP

; end of char.fun
------------

;PREPARE.FUN - PROCEDURES TO SETUP BUFFER IN ES TO
;RECEIVE, THEN ORCHESTRATE THE READING OF THE FILE
```

```
            ;TO THE BUFFER

            PUBLIC  PREPARE,SET_SEG,READIN          ;PROCEDURES
            PUBLIC  READMS,READER,NOTFND,BIGFILE    ;DATA

            ;****REQUIRES IN THE MAIN PROGRAM FILE:
            ;FNAME   DB      '???';Zero terminated string
                                    ;   holding the file name
            ;BUFFR   DB      ?       ;offset to compute es segment

            ;****USES THESE PROCEDURES:
            ;FROM CHAR.FUN:  WRITEM, STRINGO
            ;FROM DISK.FUN:  OPENFL, FSIZE, CLOSEFL, READFL

            ;USES THESE VARIABLES:
            READMS   DB     CR,LF,'Reading $'
            READER   DB     ' File read error$'
            NOTFND   DB     ' not found$'
            BIGFILE  DB     ' is too large$'

            PREPARE PROC NEAR
                    mov     ax,OFFSET BUFFR ;Last data entry
                    call    SET_SEG    ;Put seg for file in ES
                    mov     dx,OFFSET FNAME ;Startof the file
                    mov     si,dx      ; name Also to SI
                                       ; for writing it later
                    call    OPENFL     ;Open file for reading
                    jnc     PREP1      ;Carry = error
                    call    STRINGO    ;  Show file name
                    mov     dx,OFFSET NOTFND ; Not found
                    call    WRITEM
                    stc                ;  and exit
                    jmp     SHORT PREEX ;  with carry set
            PREP1:  mov     bx,ax      ;FSIZE needs handle in BX
                    call    FSIZE      ;Returns AX = size of file

                    jz      PREP2      ;NZ means over 64k in size
                    call    CLOSEFL ;BX still has handle
                    call    STRINGO         ;Show file name
                    mov     dx,OFFSET BIGFILE ; say that
                    call.   WRITEM ;Program can't take it
                    stc                ;Set to show wrror
                    jmp     SHORT PREEX ;And exit
            PREP2:  call    READIN ;Reads the file into buffr
            PREEX:  ret             ;  Carry means an error
            PREPARE ENDP

            SET_SEG PROC NEAR
            ;Entry: ax offset last data in ES
                    mov     cl,4       ;Bytes to shift right
                    shr     ax,cl      ;Low 4 bits (0 to A) gone
```

```
                inc     ax              ;Number of paragr. to add
                mov     cx,es           ;ES same as DS right now
                add     ax,cx           ;Add present segment
                mov     es,ax           ;Exit new segment in ES
                ret
SET_SEG ENDP

READIN PROC NEAR
;Entry SI address of file name, BX has file handle
;  ES has segment to place file
                mov     dx,OFFSET READMS ;Show 'Reading'
                call    WRITEM
                call    STRINGO                  ;File name
                mov     cx,FILESZ       ;# of bytes to read
                sub     dx,dx           ;Start of ES seg
                push    ds              ;Save DS
                push    es              ;Put ES
                pop     ds              ;  in DS
                call    READFL
                pop     ds              ;back to normal
                jnc     REDA
                mov     dx,OFFSET READER ;Somethg is wrong
                call    WRITEM
                jmp     SHORT REDX
REDA:           call    CLOSEFL         ;BX still has handle
REDX:           ret
READIN ENDP
; end of prepare.fun
```

APPENDIX B

Character Attributes

It is the specific combination of the eight bits of the character attribute that gives the various screen-display effects that can be achieved. The eight bits encode these variables: color (eight options), background (blinking or solid) and foreground (dark or light). With the eight bits, there are 256 possible combinations; however, the organization of the attribute byte makes it simple to understand:

The Attribute Bit:

	Bits:	7	Background				Foreground		
			6	5	4	3	2	1	0
		B	color			I	color		

Bit 7 controls the blink (B) part of the attribute. If bit 7 is 1, the character will blink or flash. If it is 0, the character will remain solid. Bit 3 controls the intensity (I). If bit 3 is 1, the foreground colors will be light; if it is 0, they will be dark. Therefore, there are eight choices of colors for the background, but 16 choices, dark or light, for the foreground. Tables B-1 and B-2 provide the hex equivalents for the various bit combinations for the high and low four bits of the attribute byte.

Character Attributes

Table B-1. Background Colors—the Four High Bytes.

Background bits 7 6 5 4	Color	Hex equivalents if bit 7 is 0 No Blink	is 1 Blink
? 0 0 0	Black	0	8
? 0 0 1	Blue	1	9
? 0 1 0	Green	2	A
? 0 1 1	Cyan	3	B
? 1 0 0	Red	4	C
? 1 0 1	Magenta	5	D
? 1 1 1	Yellow	6	E
? 1 1 1	White	7	F

Here are some examples in using these tables. Suppose you want to display characters with a blue background and a black foreground. The byte would be 10H. 18H would give a blue background and a dark grey (light black) foreground. 98H would produce blinking characters with a blue background and a dark gray foreground. The best way to become familiar with the actual effect of the various combinations is to try them out. Particularly with the foreground colors, it is probably best to view the results. There are differences among dark black (black), light black (dark gray), dark white (light gray), and light white (white). Dark yellow looks brown, while light yellow looks yellow, and the effect might differ somewhat from monitor to monitor.

Table B-2. Foreground Colors—the Four High Bytes.

Foreground bits 3 2 1 0	Color	Hex equivalents if bit 3 is 0 Dark	is 1 Light
? 0 0 0	Black	0	8
? 0 0 1	Blue	1	9
? 0 1 0	Green	2	A
? 0 1 1	Cyan	3	B
? 1 0 0	Red	4	C
? 1 0 1	Magenta	5	D
? 1 1 1	Yellow	6	E
? 1 1 1	White	7	F

APPENDIX C

ASCII Codes

Table C-1. The ASCII Code.

Printing Character	Hex Value	Decimal Value	Control* Character	Meaning
BLANK NULL	00	0	^@	Null
☺	01	1	^A	
☻	02	2	^B	
♥	03	3	^C	
♦	04	4	^D	
♣	05	5	^E	
♠	06	6	^F	
•	07	7	^G	Bell
◘	08	8	^H	Backspace
○	09	9	^I	Tab
◎	0A	10	^J	Line feed
♂	0B	11	^K	
♀	0C	12	^L	
♪	0D	13	^M	Carriage Return
♫	0E	14	^N	
☼	0F	15	^O	

ASCII Codes

Printing Character	Hex Value	Decimal Value	Control* Character	Meaning
▶	10	16	^P	
◀	11	17	^Q	
↕	12	18	^R	
‼	13	19	^S	
¶	14	20	^T	
§	15	21	^U	
■	16	22	^V	
↨	17	23	^W	
↑	18	24	^X	
↓	19	25	^Y	
→	1A	26	^Z	
←	1B	27	^[	Escape
∟	1C	28	^\	
↔	1D	29	^]	
▲	1E	30	^^	
▼	1F	31	^_	
BLANK (SPACE)	20	32		Space
!	21	33		
"	22	34		
#	23	35		
$	24	36		
%	25	37		
&	26	38		
'	27	39		Apostrophe
(	28	40		
)	29	41		
*	2A	42		
+	2B	43		
,	2C	44		Comma
-	2D	45		Minus
.	2E	46		Period
/	2F	47		
0	30	48		
1	31	49		
2	32	50		
3	33	51		
4	34	52		
5	35	53		
6	36	54		
7	37	55		
8	38	56		

Printing Character	Hex Value	Decimal Value	Control* Character	Meaning
9	39	57		
:	3A	58		
;	3B	59		
<	3C	60		
=	3D	61		
>	3E	62		
?	3F	63		
@	40	64		
A	41	65		
B	42	66		
C	43	67		
D	44	68		
E	45	69		
F	46	70		
G	47	71		
H	48	72		
I	49	73		
J	4A	74		
K	4B	75		
L	4C	76		
M	4D	77		
N	4E	78		
O	4F	79		
P	50	80		
Q	51	81		
R	52	82		
S	53	83		
T	54	84		
U	55	85		
V	56	86		
W	57	87		
X	58	88		
Y	59	89		
Z	5A	90		
[	5B	91		
\	5C	92		
]	5D	93		
^	5E	94		
_	5F	95		Underline
'	60	96		
a	61	97		

Printing Character	Hex Value	Decimal Value	Control* Character	Meaning
b	62	98		
c	63	99		
d	64	100		
e	65	101		
f	66	102		
g	67	103		
h	68	104		
i	69	105		
j	6A	106		
k	6B	107		
l	6C	108		
m	6D	109		
n	6E	110		
o	6F	111		
p	70	112		
q	71	113		
r	72	114		
s	73	115		
t	74	116		
u	75	117		
v	76	118		
w	77	119		
x	78	120		
y	79	121		
z	7A	122		
{	7B	123		
	7C	124		
}	7D	125		
~	7E	126		
	7F	127		

*^Stands for the Ctrl key.

BIBLIOGRAPHY

International Business Machine Corporation. *Technical Reference. Personal Computer - PCjr*. IBM: Boca Raton, FL, 1983.

> [Yes, I am one of those who have a PCjr which I have used and expanded for three years. Much of the material in this manual speaks of hardware and is uninteresting to me. Yet, it is invaluable to an assembly-language programmer because it contains the complete listing (with programmer's comments) of ROM-BIOS routines. I suggest you obtain a similar manual for your computer because not only can you learn what these routines can do for you, but you can also see the exact program listing for the routines and learn much about writing assembly-language programs.]

Microsoft Corporation *Disk Operating System: Technical Reference*. Version 2.10. IBM: Boca Raton, FL, 1983.

> [This is my version of DOS. Although you can buy other books that supply most of the information contained, the technical reference is the "bible."]

Microsoft Corporation *Microsoft Macro Assembler for the MS-DOS Operating System: Reference Manual*. Microsoft Corp.: Bellevue, WA, 1985.

[This is the reference manual for the assembler I use. As such manuals go, it is actually quite clear with good examples.]

Norton, Peter *Programmer's Guide to the IBM PC*. Microsoft Press: Bellevue, WA, 1985.
[This is a very complete reference to all varieties of IBM personal computers, including in depth descriptions of memory usage, DOS and ROM-BIOS functions, and services.]

Scanlon, Leo J. *IBM PC Assembly Language: A Guide for Programmers.* Robert J. Brady Co.: Bowie, MD, 1983.

Willen, David C. & Krantz, Jeffrey I. *8088 Assembler Language Programming:* The IBM PC. Howard W. Sams & Co.,Inc.: Indianapolis, IN, 1983.
[Both of these books are very helpful references to the 8088 language. They describe the instructions in depth and give many useful examples and assembly language routines.]

INDEX

INDEX

8088 machine language, 1
8088 registers and instructions, 25-33

A

A (assemble), 90
absolute addresses, 13
accumulator (AX) data register, 28
active display page, 86, 88
   switching from, 136
addresses, 11, 12, 26
   absolute, 13
   relative, 13
   using Debug to find, 12-15
alignment, 121
arrow keys, 101
ASCII code, 8, 196-199
   files of, 9
   keyboard input and, 100
assembler, 17
   function of, 32
ASSUME directive, 19
ATTRIB, 131, 137
attributes, 86
   changing, 87
   changing screen, 131
   hidden, 173

   read only, 173

B

background attributes, 194
BACKKEY procedure, 103
base (BX) data register, 29
base pointer register, 27
BASIC, 11
BIGFILE message, 73
binary numbers, 2, 3
   decimal and hex equivalents for, 4
BIOS, 14
   display services of, 85
bits, 3
   identification of, 7, 8
   storage of, 30
blank lines, deletion of, 176
BOTATT, 131, 137
BOTTOM procedure, 93, 107
buffered keyboard input, 167, 169
buffers, 70, 71, 84, 170
BUFFR, 70, 71, 84
   reducing program size with, 153
bug-free programs, 170
bytes, 3, 4, 13, 37
   addresses for, 12

   attribute, 86
   storage of, 30

C

CALL command, 43, 44
carriage return, 38, 39
carry flag, 27, 53
   testing of, 53
CBW (change byte to word), 171
central processing unit (CPU), 1
CHAR.FUN, 159
   program listing for, 190-191
character attributes, 194-195
CHECK.COM, 203-205
CLC (clear carry flag), 53
clear, 8, 52
   line, 135
   screen, 89, 135
CLEARS procedure, 89
CLOSEFL procedure, 75
closing files, 75
CLRLINE procedure, 135
CLRLN procedure, 135
CMP (compare), 51, 76
code, 16, 18, 23
   program, 15

205

code segment register, 25
color, 130, 194
    addition of, 134
    changing attributes for, 131, 132, 194
COM extension files, 10, 16
    creation of, 20
    stack management in, 66
combine type, 121
command, 10
command line, finding file name entered on, 59
comments, 17
    deleting temporary, 107
conditional jumps, 53, 54, 57, 58
conditional transfers, 52
constants
    defining of, 39
    labels for, 103
control codes, 38
COUNT, 150
count (CX) data register, 29
crashes, 72
CREATFL procedure, 172, 173
CTRL-C, 101
cursor
    clearing line with, 135
    control of, 87
    movement of, 88, 91
CURSOR procedure, 91, 92

D

D (dump) command, 30, 40, 48
data, 15, 16, 19, 23
    placement of, 149
data (DX) data register, 29
data registers, 28, 29
data segment register, 25
DB (define byte), 37
Debug, 20
    altering programs with, 108-109
    changing memory contents with, 41
    changing screen attributes with, 131
    finding addresses with, 12-15
    key code examination with, 101-102
    looking at stacks with, 65-66
    program testing with, 24, 40
    reading memory contents with, 30
    simulating conditions with, 79
    switching active page with, 136
    viewing program segment prefix with, 47-49
    viewing program with, 22-24

window creation with, 90
debuggers, 20
DEC (decrease), 55, 93
decimal numbers
    binary and hex equivalents for, 4
    conversion to hexadecimal from, 6, 7
defining variables, 68
destination, 28
    position of, 32
destination index (DI), 28, 51
direction flag, 55
directives, 18
DIROUT procedure, 63, 64, 67, 68, 92
DISK.FUN, 159
    program listing for, 189-190
display, 86
    adding color to, 134
    color in, 130
    determining and saving characteristics of, 130
    mode of, 86
    restoring, 137
    reversing of, 113
display services, BIOS, 85
displaying files, 99-118
dollar sign, 36, 39
DOS
    commands understood by, 10, 11
    functions of, 36
    prompt for, 10
    scanning key codes with, 101
doubleword, 37, 74
DUP (duplicate) operator, 49, 151
DW (define word), 37

E

E (enter) command, 41
END, 19
ENDKEY procedure, 103
ENDP, 43
EOF (end of file), 74, 106
EQU, 39
ERASE, 22
error catching, 79
EXE files, 10
    creation of, 119-129
    DOS action in creation of, 122
    structure of, 119
EXE2BIN, 20, 22
    use of, 21
execution speed, 43
exiting files, 69
extra data, 15, 16, 23, 25
    addition of, 141

F

FAR procedure, 43, 124
file control block (FCB), 47, 48
filenames
    retrieval of, 46-60
    retrieving two from command line, 164
files
    closing, 75
    creation and writing of, 173
    display of, 99-118
    exiting, 69
    finding size of, 74
    include, 158
    management of, 163
    normal, 173
    opening and reading of, 61-84
    opening of, 69
    reading to memory of, 79
    retrieving two file names from command line, 164
    updating data section of, 49
    uppercasing letters in text of, 171
    writing to disk, 163-176
flag register, 23, 27
    pushing and popping, 67
flags, 27, 52
    clear and set, 52
FNAME, 46
foreground attributes, 194
FSIZE procedure, 73, 74, 79
function keys, 101
functions, 36, 85

G

G command, 41
GETONE procedure, 168
GET_BOTH procedure, 167
GET_FILE procedure, 49, 50, 146
GET_TWO procedure, 164, 165

H

handles, 62, 128
headers, 128
hexadecimal numbers, 3
    binary and decimal equivalents for, 4
    decimal conversion to, 6, 7
hidden attributes, 173
high-level languages, 11, 39

I

if . . . then . . . else, 52
INBUF procedure, 169, 170
INC (increase), 55
INCLUDE, 158

Index 207

include files, 158
  complete program listings for, 188-193
index registers, 28
INFILE procedure, 167, 169
initializing variables, 71
instruction pointer (IP) register, 23, 26
instructions
  8088 set, 31, 32
  syntax of, 32
insufficient memory, 77
INT instruction, 45
interrupts, 17, 23, 34, 35, 157

J

JCXZ, 54
JMP (jump) command, 44, 52, 58
JNC, 57
JNZ, 53
jumps, 57
  NEAR and FAR procedures and, 124
  types of, 57
JZ, 52, 53, 57, 58

K

key codes, 101-102
  DOS function scanning of, 101
keyboard input, 100
  buffered, 167
KEYIN procedure, 100, 101, 103

L

labels, 37, 103
  constant, 39, 103
least significant bit, 8, 30
line feed, 38, 39
LINEOUT procedure, 91, 92
lines, clearing of, 135
LINK, 20, 22, 121
  use of, 21
LODSB (load string byte), 63, 64
LODSW, 64
long jumps, 57
LOOP, 93, 109, 114, 166
LOOPE, 110
LOOPNE, 110
LOOPNZ, 110, 114, 166
loops, 106, 114, 115, 157
  displaying pages with, 109
LOOPZ, 110, 166
low memory, 15

M

machine language, 1
  mnemonics for, 2

MAIN procedure, 19, 34
  EXE version of, 123
memory, 1
  addressing, 11
  changing contents of, 41
  checking capacity of, 72
  enhancement of, 141
  low, 15
  numbers in, 30
  reading contents of, 30
  reading files to, 79
  registers to access, 51
  segments of, 11
  stacks in, 65
MEMP, 104
Microsoft Macro Assembler (MASM), 17, 20
  use of, 21
mnemonics, 2
mode
  changing, 87
  display, 86
most significant bit, 30
MOV (move), 36, 40, 55
MOVSB, 55
MOVSW, 56, 64
MYSTACK, 121

N

NEAR attribute, 43, 124
NOLINE procedure, 176
NOP, 60
normal files, 173
number conversion, 6, 7
number crunching, 2
numbers, memory storage of, 30
numerical code, 1-9

O

object file, 20
offsets, 11-13, 37, 38, 65
OLDATT, 137
OLDMODE, 137, 138
OLDPAGE, 137
opcode, 32
OPENFL procedure, 61, 62
opening files, 61, 69
operand, 32
ORG, 19, 20, 151
overrides, 50, 147
overwriting, 72

P

PAGELP procedure, 109
pages (see also, active display page), 86

  display of, 104
  using loops to display, 109
  viewing, 87
paragraph, 13
piping, 48
pointer registers, 26, 27
pointers, 23, 65
POP, 43, 45, 65, 66
  program speed and, 155
POPF, 67
PREPARE procedure, 161
PREPARE. FUN, 160
  program listing for, 191-193, 191
PROC, 43
procedures, 34, 43
  naming of, 45
processes, termination of, 127
program listings, 177-195
program segment prefix (PSP)
  accessing of, 47
  viewing of, 47-49
program segments, 15
program structure, 10-24
programs
  altering of, 108-109
  bug-free, 170
  code portion of, 15
  data portion of, 15
  extra data portion of, 15
  neatness, size, or speed of, 152
  overwriting and crashing, 72
  running of, 42
  size of, 153
  speed of, 153
  stack portion of, 15
  testing of, 24, 40
  TIPE.COM: VERSION 1, 16
  useing Debug to view, 22-24
prompt, 10
pseudo-op, 18
PTR, 150
PUSH, 43, 45, 65, 66
  program speed and, 155
PUSHF, 67

Q

Q (quit) command, 41

R

R (register) command, 22, 79
random-access memory (RAM), 1
read only attributes, 173
read-only memory (ROM), 1
READFL procedure, 80, 81
READIN procedure, 80, 143, 146, 147

redirection, 48
registers, 11, 16, 23
　8088, 25, 29
　data, 28, 29
　flag, 27
　index, 28
　memory access, 51
　pointer, 26, 27
relative addresses, 13
relative jumps, 58
REP (repeat), 56, 166
REPNZ, 166
REPZ, 166
RESCREEN procedure, 137, 138
RET (return) command, 43, 45
REVERSE procedure, 110-113, 143
ROM BIOS, 14
routines, 35

S

scan code, 100
scanning, 166
SCASB, 166
SCASW, 166
screen (see display)
SCREEN.FUN, 159
　program listing for, 188-189
scrolling, 89
segment, 11-13, 18
　adding extra, 141
　defining of, 121
　overlapping, 146
　overriding, 50, 147
　program, 15
services, 85
set, 8, 52
SETSCREEN procedure, 133, 134
setting up screen, 85-98
SET_SEG procedure, 142, 143, 146
SHOMORE procedure, 111, 112
SHORT, 58
short jumps, 57, 58
SHOW_IT procedure, 99, 104, 105, 143, 147

completed, 112
　one line to screen display in, 107
　page display in, 111
　page loop in, 109
simulating conditions, 79
source, 28
source code, 18
　organization of, 158
source index (SI) register, 28, 51
stack pointer register, 23, 26, 65
stack segment register, 25, 26
stacks, 15, 16, 23, 121
　looking at, 65-66
　management of COM file, 66
　placement of, 149
　use of, 65
standard output devices, screen as, 95
status flags, 27
STC (set carry flag), 53
STOSB, 56
STOSW, 64
STRINGO procedure, 63
strings, 35
　moving, 54
　on-screen writing of, 35
　scanning of, 166
　writing to standard output device of, 94
SUB, 51, 91
switching active page, 136
SYMDEB symbolic debugger, 20
system, 1

T

T (trace) command, 41
terminating processes, 127
text file, 9
TIPE.COM, 16
　beginning program, 17
　complete program listing for, 178-184
　completed program for, 116-118
　display enhancement changes and additions to, 139

enhancements to, 130-148
EXE file version 1 of, 120
exiting for an error in, 69
exiting for insufficient memory, 77
finding file name on command line for, 59
memory enhancement additions and changes to, 144
preparing screen for display, 96
reading file into memory, 82
title display for (version 1), 40
title display for (version 2), 44
variations in, 149-162
TITL, 37
title line display, Version 1, 35-41
title line display, Version 2, 42-45
tracing, 41
type mismatch error, 38, 150

U

U (unassemble) command, 22, 31, 41
UPCASE.COM, 163
　complete program listing for, 185-187
UPCASFL procedure, 171, 172, 175
uppercase text, 171

V

variables, 19
　defining of, 37, 68
　initializing, 71

W

windows
　creation of, 90
wipe, 48
WRITE procedure, 94, 95, 147
WRITEFL procedure, 172, 173
WRITEIT procedure, 172, 174, 175
WRITEM procedure, 43
writing to the screen, 34-45

Z

zero flags, 27, 53

Other Bestsellers of Related Interest

MS-DOS® UTILITY PROGRAMS: Add-On Software Resources—Ronny Richardson

Combining the most useful features of a product catalog and magazine reviews, this book is the most comprehensive guide available for finding the utility programs you need to optimize your DOS-based computer system. Richardson candidly describes the capabilities and operation of virtually every DOS utility on the market. He clearly explains what each package does, who might benefit from the package, and what specific problems it can solve. 672 pages, Illustrated. Book No. 3278, $19.95 paperback, $28.95 hardcover

MS-DOS BATCH FILE PROGRAMMING . . . Including OS/2—Ronny Richardson

"A thorough and pleasantly written tutorial and reference...highly recommended for both those just getting their feet wet with DOS and those with more experience."—**Booklist**

Tap the programming power that lies within your operating system! Ronny Richardson shows you how to create batch file menus, develop a document archival system, and expand the usage of your batch files. 224 pages, Illustrated. Book No. 3028, $17.95 paperback, $25.95 hardcover

AMIGA™ ASSEMBLY LANGUAGE PROGRAMMING—Jake Commander

Here, machine language specialist and expert program designer Jake Commander provides an in-depth introduction to Commodore's new generation computer, the Amiga, and its sophisticated 68000 microprocessor. He reveals all the assembly language programming techniques you need to make your programming as efficient and effective as possible. If you're a serious programmer, you will welcome this opportunity. 240 pages, 35 illustrations. Book No. 2711, $14.95 paperback, $19.95 hardcover

ADVANCED MS-DOS® BATCH FILE PROGRAMMING—Dan Gookin

Batch file programming is a way of communicating with your computer...a way of transforming DOS into a system that works the way you want it to. In this book, Dan Gookin explains unique methods of using batch files to create a work environment that will improve your efficiency, productivity, and overall relationship with your computer. All the necessary tools, batch file structures, commands, and helpful techniques can be found here. 400 pages, 733 illustrations. Book No. 3197, $24.95 paperback, $34.95 hardcover

UNIVERSAL ASSEMBLY LANGUAGE—Robert M. Fitz and Larry Crockett

Find out how universal assembly language can be made machine independent and how you can use a table driven, complete assembler on any machine from the IBM® PC, Apple®, or Macintosh® to the expert guidance in the writing of all programs—the dos and don'ts, structured programming techniques, documentation, the use of compact code, subroutines, and more! 420 pages, 63 illustrations. Book No. 2730, $18.95 paperback, $27.95 hardcover

Look for These and Other TAB Books at Your Local Bookstore

To Order Call Toll Free 1-800-822-8158
(in PA and AK call 717-794-2191)

or write to TAB BOOKS Inc., Blue Ridge Summit, PA 17294-0840.

Title	Product No.	Quantity	Price

	Subtotal $	
☐ Check or money order made payable to TAB BOOKS Inc.	Postage and Handling ($3.00 in U.S., $5.00 outside U.S.) $	
Charge my ☐ VISA ☐ MasterCard ☐ American Express	In PA, NY, & ME add applicable sales tax $	
Acct. No. _____ Exp. _____	TOTAL $	

Signature: _____

Name: _____

City: _____

State: _____ Zip: _____

TAB BOOKS catalog free with purchase; otherwise send $1.00 in check or money order and receive $1.00 credit on your next purchase.

Orders outside U.S. must pay with international money order in U.S. dollars.

TAB Guarantee: If for any reason you are not satisfied with the book(s) you order, simply return it (them) within 15 days and receive a full refund. **BC**